1/27/12

R
1

D1562813

KINK

Stephanie Clifford-Smith is a food writer who spends her spare time reading about food and cooking. She has a weekly column in the *Sydney Morning Herald*'s *Good Living* supplement, reviews for the *Good Food Guide* and co-edits *Sydney Eats* restaurant guide. She writes about seasonal produce, reviews cookbooks and answers readers' eating-out queries on the Eatstreets website. In an effort to dispel her concern that she is becoming one-dimensional, she also does a bit of salsa dancing. She has two sons and lives in Sydney with her husband.

KINK

A STRAIGHT GIRL'S INVESTIGATION

STEPHANIE
CLIFFORD-SMITH

ALLEN&UNWIN

First published in 2010

Allen & Unwin
83 Alexander Street
Crows Nest NSW 2065
Australia
Phone: (61 2) 8425 0100
Fax: (61 2) 9906 2218
Email: info@allenandunwin.com
Web: www.allenandunwin.com

Cataloguing-in-Publication details are available
from the National Library of Australia
www.librariesaustralia.nla.gov.au

ISBN 978 1 74175 912 9

Set in 11.5/16pt Bembo by Midland Typesetters, Australia
Printed and bound in Australia by Griffin Press

10 9 8 7 6 5 4 3 2 1

INTRODUCTION

Have you ever wondered what happens the first time someone with a sexual fetish shares it with their lover? Say you had a kink, something you knew was really unusual. Would you risk having your lover run screaming from the room by asking if they'll let you lick their eyeballs, or would you find some oblique way of bringing it up, perhaps when they were struggling with a stray lash? Or would you just go behind their back and find a willing partner on the internet?

The topic engaged a girlfriend and me for hours over lunch one day. It wasn't the sexual nuts and bolts of fetishes that kept us talking—our vanilla backgrounds would have made that a pretty short conversation—but the human angle intrigued us. How do kinks affect relationships and how does one person suss another out? How does someone gauge the right moment to broach nappy-wearing as a turn-on? Do marriages fall apart over these desires or do they remain hidden, frustrated?

The questions lingered with me long after lunch and multi-plied as the evening went on. I wanted to know if kinks were timeless or whether there were certain periods when particular tastes became recognised as kinks. Were there things that today we'd see as kinky but weren't viewed as such in the past? And who were history's great kinksters? I'd heard a bit about the Marquis de Sade, rumours about Hitler, but I'd soon learn there was still Percy Grainger, James Joyce and prominent sexologist Havelock Ellis himself to consider.

My curiosity also ran to the mundane side of things, like how you cope with the laundry when you want quantities of messy substances involved in the act? Do kids ask their parents awkward questions when props or accessories are left lying around? And what is it, exactly, that makes a person need that trigger to get them going?

So why should I care? Call it curiosity. I'm a journalist so that characteristic comes with the territory, but I wonder who among us hasn't shared this inquisitiveness, even if only fleetingly. Or maybe there was something else operating here. I studied psy-chology at university and worked for years in medical publishing and while the mathematical part of my brain has only ever really functioned at a rudimentary level, the scientific bit was always reasonably easy to rev up. Here was a subject which was giving that corner of the cortex a charge it hadn't had since I became a food writer a few years ago. Yes, food and sex. They've always been connected so it's probably not surprising I should be curi-ous about them both. I guess I'm specialising in the journalism of primal urges.

My husband, David, was never enthusiastic about my

researching this subject but wouldn't say why; my hunch was that he thought it'd be risky business meeting and interviewing strangers about their sex lives. But rather than come out and say so, he bombarded me with alternatives. Actually it was really only one, in various guises—to write a cookbook. Of course, it made sense. I'm a keen cook, he's an enthusiastic and appreciative eater, what could be better? Perhaps nothing, but by this point I was obsessed with getting answers to my growing list of questions.

I knew I'd be dealing with some pretty confronting stuff, but I felt fairly confident that I was unshockable. I'd recently finished writing a biography of celebrity chef Bernard King, a man who constantly challenged me with bluer and bluer stories, waiting for me to blush. I'd laugh. A lot. But blush? Never. To be so jaded and yet so young! Okay, so I'm kidding myself, but here at least was a way of finding out just how thick my skin was.

I rang the local paper and placed my ad. The girl who took my call was enthralled by the idea and we debated where best to run it. She advised against the personal columns because she thought I might get calls from weirdos; I told her I didn't want to rule that out. She asked her boss for advice and I ended up running it in public notices.

I started small, no bolding, in just one paper at a cost of $14.10.

```
Turned on by something unusual? Interview
subjects  required  for  ultra-confidential
research into fetishes. Call Sandra.
```

I thought the name Sandra would be easy to remember and sounded ordinary and approachable.

For S. and my boys, with love

1

IT PAYS TO ADVERTISE

The advertisement appeared on a Thursday and I got my first response the next day. Bruce called as I was rushing out the door.

'Sorry, Bruce, I can't really talk now. But just tell me, briefly, what are your fetishes?'

'Um, body decoration, specifically piercings, and women of the fuller figure,' he said.

'Okay, fine. Now would you like to meet for a chat or would you prefer to do it over the phone?'

'I think we'd better do it on the phone. I don't think my wife would like it very much if I met you.'

I only want to talk *to you, Bruce,* I thought, but we agreed I'd call him at 10 am on Monday.

An electrician, Bruce was at work when I rang his mobile and spoke quite openly, though he said he preferred the term 'interest' to 'fetish'. He didn't elaborate on his reasons but as I didn't want to alienate him, I stuck with his terminology. Happy to give me his surname and its correct spelling, he was totally upfront. In fact he made it all sound a bit pedestrian.

He'd become interested in body piercing after reading an article on it as a teenager, but in the late sixties it wasn't exactly mainstream. 'But the fuller-figured woman was, and I tended to seek them out rather than the skinny beach-bunny type. We're not talking grossly full, three or four hundred kilos or anything. We're talking a hundred to a hundred and fifty kilos.'

Light- to middle-weight women just didn't interest him, he said. 'But when I got a woman that was what everyone would describe as too fat, I found that they were more interesting women and a lot nicer to be around.'

Does 'interesting' mean more sexually attractive?

'To me they are. Every woman I've met, no matter how skinny or how full they were, was always too fat as far as she was concerned. Even the ones who were *Playboy* centrefold material would say, "I'm too fat. Look, I've got a bit of fat here", and you'd really have to look hard to find it. Unfortunately the world is obsessed with big tits and skinny women.'

In the seventies, when Bruce decided to try getting pierced, he had to go underground to find someone to do it for him. 'And that was just the nipple piercings, not the genitalia. I did have a navel piercing, but because I wear pants with a belt it was uncomfortable so I let it grow out.'

He thinks facial piercings 'look a bit gross' but quite likes navel, nipple, penis and labial ones. But his first wife thought he was a freak.

'She didn't mind my nipple piercings, she could put up with those, but the penis piercing she didn't like. I've got one through the eye of the penis and it comes down underneath and the other one's across the shaft underneath.'

The piercings were one of many things that led to the end of the relationship.

'She went around and mean-mouthed me to all my supposed friends, and in the seventies everyone thought I was a real bad deviant. So I got a divorce and I met the second lady and she said, Yeah, so what?'

His current wife is big and she pierced her ears, nipples and labia after she met Bruce.

'It was her decision to have them done but she found that the nipple and labial ones were uncomfortable as she got bigger. She said she was taking them out and that was the end of the story.'

Now when he tells people about the piercings they say, 'Oh, is *that* all you've got?' Today it's a bit of an anticlimax.

That doesn't worry him because he didn't have them done to impress anyone.

'It's just that some people like gardening, some people like fishing and I happen to like this. I just think it looks nice. You might say it's disgusting but it's the same with art. I go to the art gallery and everybody's raving about a painting and to me it just looks like somebody threw up on a canvas.

'I did it because it was going to look good when it was finished. It wasn't done because I liked the pain.'

He keeps the rings in all the time to keep the holes open; nipples, he's discovered, start closing after a day.

'I had to take the one through the eye of the penis out when I had my heart operation because I had to have a catheter in there. It was out for about a month and it didn't close up.'

They're decorative sometimes and sensual at other times, particularly when fondled during foreplay, he says. But seeing pierced bodies at the beach isn't necessarily a turn-on.

'It's not arousal, it's just interest. It's like a woman wearing a pearl necklace or a nice pair of earrings. It dresses the part up.'

The interview lasted about half an hour and, although he told me some pretty intimate stuff, I had the sense he was holding something back. He seemed reluctant to link the piercings and dimpled flesh to sexual arousal and I guessed his aversion to the adjective 'fat' was because he didn't like its derogatory overtones.

Although Bruce liked the aesthetics of piercing, many people are attracted by the pain involved. There's a body modification website (www.bmezine.com) where people post stories of their experiences. One guy writes that a voyeuristic interest in tattooing was replaced by piercing when he saw an image of a woman who'd had her nipples done. This was a turn-on he was prepared to try himself rather than simply view. He wrote that he will only ever do the piercing himself, not so he can be sure that everything will be thoroughly sterilised, but because he likes to extend the experience, and the professionals tend to work too quickly.

Piercing had many advantages over tattoos. You can do play piercings. And a piercing will disappear if you take it out.

So I fell in love with sewing needles. I used to sterilise them with a flame, then when they were cool pierce my scrotum over and over. Delicious!

While this guy's devotion to the needle might still be unusual, facial piercing and other body modifications such as pubic coiffure and tatts have become so mainstream in the last decade they rarely raise an eyebrow. When the geometric Polynesian tribal band around the bicep became a fashion statement favoured by private school boys holidaying in Thailand, tattoos immediately lost any of the tough-guy connotations that the bikers' snakes and dagger designs of earlier decades once had. Obviously it's harder to tell by visiting the nearest beach if genital tattoos are gaining popularity but, given the skin's sensitivity and the pain involved in the process, they're unlikely to ever be as popular as those on the upper arm. Sometimes a submissive will have their genitals tattooed to declare, albeit privately, ownership by a particular dominant. And there are cases of the penis being flagrantly, colourfully decorated as a sexual lure. The briefest internet search shows up all kinds of variations. Some genital tatts are designed to be funny, like the one of a man pushing a lawn mower through a dense crop of pubic hair, which requires shaving a strip of hair behind the mower for maximum effect. Or there's the elephant's head tattooed on the groin with the penis itself modelling the trunk. But I wonder what the appeal is of a tiny pair of cherries tattooed on shaved labia; presumably, by the time a woman is in the position to display this miniature work of art, her partner has other things than stone fruit in mind.

In some cultures, scarification often accompanied tattooing, and was practised instead of tattooing by some dark-skinned people on whom tattoos were hard to see. While it is traditionally undertaken as a means of tribal and social identification, as part of initiation rites and for simple aesthetic adornment, in parts of Africa it also has sexual or erotic connotations. It can mark significant stages of development among women, such as puberty and marriage, and is said to make it easier for a woman to find a mate because it advertises her ability to withstand pain and, by logical extension, the pain of childbirth. A Nigerian tribe, the Tiv people, believe that a scarified woman is more sexually appealing and therefore more likely to bear children, and the raised scars are thought to create erotic sensations in both partners when touched or stroked.

Tamer and less permanent, but a body modification nonetheless, is pubic hair styling. The pendulum on the pudenda has swung right back to baldness, or to obsessive trimming at least, but the issue seems to be as much about fashion as any sort of fetish. In fact today, wanting a sexual partner who *has* pubes is seen as a fetish and it's listed on sex websites in the same way as an interest in fisting, latex or spanking. So it's the reverse that seems to have taken off in the mainstream. Of course classical and Renaissance nudes of both sexes were always hairless down there until Michelangelo gave his statue of David a neat stylised crop. Ancient Egyptians sometimes portrayed the hair as a tidy black triangle and Sanskrit manuscripts show Indian women with shaved front bottoms. So why are pubes so out of favour today? Surely it's not that we're prudish or trying to adhere to classical artistic stereotypes, so, although I'm speculating, I can't help thinking it's porn's fault. Yes, there's always been porn and when the bush was big in the seventies, it was big in porn too; actress Pam Grier was as well known for her pubic afro as the one on her head. But with the growth of the internet in the early nineties, explicit porn spread at record speeds and became a multi-billion-dollar industry. I don't think it's co-incidence that it was around this time that porn stars went bald downstairs. Why? Because if you're a porn maker aiming for close-ups, you don't want the money-shot obscured by any-thing. Following this trend were ordinary women taking up pubic waxing because porn viewers develop their tastes based on what they're watching, and being hairless became the sexual ideal. It wasn't long before pubes all over the western world were being ripped out by the roots.

But John Cleland, author of *Memoirs of a Woman of Pleasure* (1748–9), a work also known as *Fanny Hill*, believed pubic hair had erotic purpose as this passage about a young lady's maid being taught about lovemaking by another girl shows:

> My breasts … amus'd her hands a-while, till, slipping down lower, over a smooth track, she could just feel the soft silky down that had but a few months before put forth and garnish'd the mount-pleasant of those parts, and promised to spread a grateful shelter over the seat of the most exquisite sensation, and which had been, till that instant, the seat of the most insensible innocence. Her fingers play'd and strove to twine in the young tendrils of that moss, which nature has contrived at once for use and ornament.

2

FROM MILD TO WILD

After my interview with Bruce I'd slightly reworded the ad, replacing 'fetishes' with 'sexual interests'; if Bruce didn't like the 'f' word there were bound to be others who didn't either. I also asked the classifieds department to move it to the adult services column, as I'd only had one reply when it was in public notices. However, a glitch meant the ad didn't go in the next week. I was glad for the reprieve, though—on further consideration I worried that adult services cast me in a bit of a dodgy light. So when I rang to find out what happened to the ad, I asked them to run it in public notices again. This time it read:

> Turned on by something unusual? Writer seeks
> interview subjects for ultra-confidential
> research into sexual interests.

I thought it was important to state that I was a writer to avoid confusion.

Shane, thirty-three, rang the Wednesday night before the paper came out, having read the ad on the internet. This guy was keen.

'So, Shane, what are you into?'

'Hh, hh, quite a bit actually.'

'Yes, like what?'

'Women. Definitely women.'

'Any particular *kind* of woman, Shane?' I asked, resisting the urge to lead him with suggestions.

'Oh, I like them to be fit. And to have a good personality. That's really important.'

This was like an interview on *Perfect Match*.

'And would you say there was anything *unusual* about your particular sexual interests? I mean, I'd have thought most men would have shared those interests.'

'Oh, I dunno, I can't speak for other guys. That's just what *I'm* into.'

'Right. What I'm actually looking for is people who have *very unusual* sexual interests. It sounds like you're a straight bloke who's into fit women, which is not—'

'Oh I like them to be confident, and take pride in their appearance ...'

The day the ad came out the phone rang hot on into the night. My mobile ringtone has a creepy submarine kind of sound to it, and by 9 pm I was dreading hearing it. All the callers were men, most of whom were turned on by lots of things rather than being obsessed with just one. A caller in his early thirties, Robert, turned out to be a pest. He got his jollies talking about sex and he also asked way too many questions about me.

He said he was into 'older women' (in their forties with good bodies, he said) and wanted to know how old I was. I refused to say and told him I wasn't prepared to discuss anything about myself. He also seemed to think I was doing this because I wanted to indulge in a series of dirty phone calls, and rang and texted several times. When I suggested that what he was into wasn't really all that weird, he was prepared to change his story to stay involved.

I got a total of fifteen calls from that ad. It wasn't until I looked at the ad myself the next day, Friday, that I realised why there were so many: they'd placed the ad in the 'adult work opportunities' column. I promptly rang back everyone who I'd made appointments with to stress there was no money in this. They all still wanted to talk.

Next morning Martin rang. He was into plenty: 'Pissing, enemas, B&D, waxing ...'

Martin, who was now fifty, told me he was about eighteen when he first experienced a golden shower.

'I was at a barbecue, outside, and most of us were pretty drunk and this woman was pissing. I said, "Well, why don't you piss on me?" and she did, she was okay with that. I found that very erotic and stimulating. It was a bigger turn-on than I thought it would be.'

She also liked Martin pissing on her and they ended up finding more people into 'water sports' by placing ads. That introduced them to anal sex, dildos and role-playing. Things were going well between them so they decided to marry.

'Then we started going to parties. We weren't swinging but

we were certainly having public sex and that was a turn-on as well. As the years went on, one of the things she wanted to try was me shaving her pussy, which I did, and then she did the same for me, and then about three years later we moved into waxing. Now that's very, very stimulating to both of us. It's a very special experience as well as cosmetic. We also do that to other couples.'

He says the pain of waxing is worth it for the effect, but is not really part of the attraction.

'I think a bigger part is more the public vulnerability and just exposing yourself to somebody and knowing that you're at their mercy.'

He's still with his wife, who is, he says, a good sexual partner, though her libido is lower than his and she's lost interest in some of their more unusual practices.

'To be honest I play around with other women as well. I'm probably more adventurous with them. One of the things I really enjoy is having sex in semi-public places like women's change rooms at department stores. I organise those times beforehand, mostly on the internet. It's a lot easier to find like-minded souls that way.'

The internet's also useful for another of Martin's interests.

'I like to dress up in women's underwear and be spanked, but Maria just doesn't get that at all. Also wearing her knickers to work, that sort of stuff, she's just not into that at all. Doesn't understand it.'

But it's the pissing he misses most with Maria, even though he finds it elsewhere. When she first said no to that, it tested the marriage.

'I guess age gets the better of all of us and sex has slowed down a bit for her. She just said pissing doesn't interest her any more. Maybe it's because we're all getting on a bit. In winter it's too cold or summer it's too hot, I don't know . . .'

I wondered whether sodden mattresses were a problem with golden showers but he assured me they weren't; at home he would spread a large rubber sheet on the floor and cover it with towels, avoiding the bed altogether.

Martin was brought up in a strict Catholic household and thinks this might have something to do with his sexual tastes. 'As I came into puberty I had to experiment somehow and found that the more surreptitious it was, the more forbidden the fruit, the tastier it was. Conventional sex doesn't really do it for me. I mean I could *do* it but it wouldn't be fulfilling. I could get a hard-on, and go through the motions and it would depend how horny I felt, but my preference would certainly be for kinky rather than conventional.'

There's a theory that urolagnia, watching someone urinate or having them urinate on you, is a turn-on because it involves the genitals and is all the more titillating because it's usually a private act, which might fit with Martin's first experience of it. Perhaps a longer bow to draw is that the practice is rooted in primitive biochemistry, the way an animal will mark its territory or attract mates with its urine.

The Greek myth of the coupling of Zeus and the princess of Argos, Danaë, could be interpreted as him giving her a golden shower, though it might be semen rather than urine, as the consequences of the story suggest. Danaë's father, Acrisius, had been warned by an oracle that one day she'd have a son who would kill him so he locked her away in a bronze room, ruling out all male contact and, therefore, pregnancy. Then Zeus, god of gods, fell for Danaë and no bronze room was going to keep him out. He came to her through the roof as a golden shower, landing in her lap and making her pregnant with a son, Perseus. Artistic interpretations of this myth vary, with some coyly interpreting the golden shower as rays of light, and others such as Titian, Tintoretto and Van Dyke as a downpour of gold coins which are promptly gathered up by a servant. Coreggio's 1532 image is not so tame. It shows Danaë on a rumpled bed with her legs open and an angel drawing a sheet away from her hips as a giant golden blob heads straight for her pelvis. And Gustav Klimt, who painted the image in 1907, didn't shy away from the the myth's erotic implications either, showing Danaë, cheeks flushed, lying with her knees drawn up and the golden shower—more a torrent—pouring down between her thighs.

If it wasn't for his particular fondness for watching women urinate, Havelock Ellis (1859–1939) might never have become a sexologist and campaigned for sex education for children, birth control, an end to the concept of illegitimacy, changes to divorce laws and to repeal laws against homosexuality. He struggled with impotence for most of his life, but if there was one thing that helped overcome his problem it was seeing a woman pee, a fixation he'd had since childhood when he saw his mother do it. They were walking in the gardens of Regent's Park zoo when she stopped. He heard water splashing and turned to see his mother squatting over a puddle. This was the beginning of his obsession with what he later described as 'golden streams'.

He then fell in love with South African novelist Olive Schreiner who, despite being an advocate of women's rights, was horrified to find she liked being humiliated and beaten. Gentle, romantic Ellis was never going to deliver on that score. 'We were not what can be technically, or even ordinarily, called lovers,' Ellis said later. Eventually she returned to South Africa and he married English writer Edith Lees in 1891. It's not clear whether he knew at the time that she was a lesbian but they lived apart from the end of the honeymoon, and a few months into the marriage she wrote to say she'd fallen in love with another woman.

In 1917 Ellis met Françoise Cyon, who had been translating one of Edith's books, and they fell for each other. Thirty years his junior, she was to be the answer to his impotence problems as she was completely willing to urinate in front of him (and accept the nickname Naiad, meaning water nymph). On one occasion she delighted him by peeing among the crowds in Oxford Circus, her long skirt hiding the fact from everyone but him as he watched the urine run down the gutter. Her continued cooperation ensured he remained potent and sexually active until the end of his life.

3

THE MAN, HIS MUM, HIS WIFE AND HIS LOVER

Nerves are making me nauseous as I come up the escalator from the gloom of Town Hall station into bright winter sunshine and I'm temporarily blinded by the contrast. I am here to meet Martin outside Woolworths. He'd said he was five-nine, overweight with a gold earring. Apart from a *Big Issue* seller in a crocheted beanie and the usual office workers, synthetic suits and high heels, there is a bloke who fits the bill with a mobile pressed to his ear. I keep scanning the crowd but spot the earring as soon as he puts the phone away. He's wearing a burnt orange bomber jacket, perhaps to stand out, so I pounce as soon as I can in case he spots me and tries to dive for the escalators.

'Are you Martin?'

'Yes. Sandra, hi.'

He's already decided where we should chat, a modern place on George Street, since closed, called the Cube Café.

While my nerves are only just settling as I position my recorder, irritated by repeated offers from waiters to take our order, Martin appears totally relaxed.

He's eased his belly in behind the table and is scanning the menu. As he reads I watch his straight-lashed eyes flicker across the page and notice he's deliberately left the temples of his thinning hair grey while the rest he's rinsed light auburn. He orders a chicken panini (no chips) and a Diet Coke.

I thought meeting Martin would be mainly so I could get a look at him and am not expecting too many more sexual revelations over lunch. Wrong. After thirty-five minutes I am suffering from information overload. We've covered his childhood sexual abuse at the hands of his aunty, his mother dressing him as a girl, his confused sexuality, psychotherapy, an aborted attempt at a sex change, and his ongoing affair with his GP.

He said his mother was extremely disappointed he was born a boy and so she dressed him as a girl until his sister was born when he was five. This matter came up about three years ago when he was seeing a psychiatrist.

'Then I started seeing a gender counsellor in Newtown. She suggested I was a woman inside a man's body. I thought okay, I could go along with that. For six months I had hormone therapy, convinced that was the way to go. I spoke to a surgeon about gender reassignment surgery. I was seeing a psychiatrist and a psychologist and I guess what brought me to my senses was when the psychiatrist suggested I tell my wife. I thought it was probably a good idea, because after six months of hormone treatment the drugs were starting to take effect. My nipples were so sensitive, just a shirt rubbing against them was outrageously erotic. My testicles started to shrink, my breasts started to get bigger and I started to get very emotional.'

Martin said his wife 'wasn't too impressed' when he told her what was going on. He was angry with his psychiatrist for leaving him in the dark about the effects of the hormones and sacked her.

'I finally found a psychotherapist who I can really trust with everything. My predilections for BDSM [bondage, discipline, sadism, masochism], waxing and shaving, she's quite happy with that; we can talk openly about it without her being judgmental. I've stopped the gender reassignment treatment. I've worked out I was doing it for all the wrong reasons, subconsciously to please my mother, to be that girl she always wanted. How sad is that? What a profound impact. At this stage of my life to think that that could still happen.'

Martin's mother's still alive but they're estranged.

'I haven't seen her for about two years and I don't intend to either. She knows how to press all my buttons.'

He is a straight talker and not for a minute do I think he is lying. When he tells me about his 'extremely small penis' I know I am right. Surely a liar would scale up, not down. Rose the GP finds it very satisfactory both orally and anally, he says. The affair with her started when he became aroused during examination for a groin injury.

'I grabbed her breast, which was not appropriate but she didn't mind, and that led to very brief sexual intercourse, after which we both apologised. But I still went and saw her and now I see her whether I'm sick or not. She's married, got a couple of kids. She knows all the gender therapy went on because she had to do the ongoing referrals and monitor the drug levels. She's a very good friend as well.'

Together they experiment sexually and swap their patient/doctor roles using her surgical equipment for added realism.

'I have half-hour appointments at her surgery each week. The good part about that is it's on Medicare, she gets paid for it. It's a multi-doctor practice, there are six of them and her surgery is right at the back of the building. There's no reason for anybody to walk by.'

He doesn't think his wife suspects anything and honestly believes his behaviour hasn't been particularly risky. He admits there was one occasion when he was working overseas that could have got him into trouble.

'I went to this party in the States, had a few drinks and joints, and got whipped. But I didn't realise how hard I was being hit because I was so stoned. I had shocking welts on my bum for three weeks after I got back. I had to undress at night in the dark, or if it was light I'd have to walk backwards out of the bedroom so Maria wouldn't notice the marks.'

My head's spinning and Martin has finished his sandwich, so I wind up the interview. He's a nice man, easy to be around, polite and totally unthreatening. I'm just amazed he's told me so much, so quickly. He wants to pay the bill but relents when I insist and heads back to work for a few hours before his assignation with Doctor Rose at four.

He calls later that afternoon to thank me for lunch and to make me an offer—to come and watch him in a session with a dominatrix, Mistress J. She has a degree in psychology and is one of the best dommes around, he says. Initially I don't know how to respond. Then I figure I have to say yes—there aren't likely to be many opportunities like this coming my way—but we have to sort a few things out first. I say that if I come along I want to witness a 'real' session, whatever that might be, and I don't want anything staged for my benefit. That will be fine, he assures me, and says Mistress J would be happy for me to ask questions throughout if I wish.

4

WAY TOO CLOSE FOR COMFORT

Dean is waiting for me as I walk around the corner from the car park to meet him outside Best & Less at Mascot. He's fairer than I expected, with a strawberry blond thatch and coarse red skin. He hasn't yet changed from his jeans and flanny into work clothes for the afternoon shift in the airport hangars. He looks like he's had a late night.

After our initial greetings I ask if he knows a café where we could go and chat.

'Oh, I don't want to talk about this kind of stuff in a *café*,' he says, his voice soft, sort of muffled. As I cast around for a bench on the street or similar public spot he cuts in with, 'Do you want to come and sit in my car? It's just parked round the back in the car park.'

The prospect horrifies me and I'm astonished he thinks I'd agree, but he obviously doesn't think he looks like something from a police line-up.

'Yeah, well so's mine. We can sit in that if you like.'

I become uneasy as we walk towards the car and he tells me he gets turned on talking about his sex life. By now he's put his black wraparound sunglasses on and I think I detect an odd walk and increasingly uncomfortable jeans.

Once we're in the car I notice booze on his breath. This is way too close for comfort and my head fills with scenarios of a gun being pulled and a forced drive to a remote location. I should have said it had to be a café or nothing.

I rummage awkwardly through my bag for my recorder, then decide to keep the bag on my lap, wedged between my body and the steering wheel.

Dean tells me he's bisexual, not gay, and that his first sexual memory was of 'masturbatin' at the age of fourteen'. He begins to sound a bit breathless as he describes his first non-conventional sexual experience, with a male masseur when he was twenty-three.

'I rang this ad, I went around, he massaged my back, he went down to my arse and underneath, and I turned over.' He keeps pausing as he speaks, losing track of his sentences as he relishes every detail of the memory. 'He massaged my front and worked his way down to my cock, I suppose. Then he masturbated me.'

Best change the subject I think, glancing at the keys in the ignition. He then tells me he's an exhibitionist. About five years ago he noticed the girl in the flats over the road was scanning his block with her binoculars, so he 'decided to give her a bit of a show'. He wanked at the window that day and has since had sex with women while she's watching.

He's also into B&D as 'both slut and master', and likes both roles equally. He's not into too much pain but likes a light session, with role-play which is 'more mental than anything'. He gets turned on by being controlled and watched.

'I could show you if you like,' he offers.

'No thanks. No.'

'Are you sure? I'd like to.' He's being pushy and I'm wanting him *out* of my car.

'*No*. This is a straight interview, nothing else.'

But he won't let up.

'It'd be easier than *talking* about it.' He lets out a goofy laugh.

Again, I say no and steer him on to when he first got interested in B&D. He wants to tell me the *full* story.

When he was in his late teens, he had a girlfriend who was into it and wanted to be his slave.

'She came over and I told her to wear a skirt and top and that I'd walk out the door for five minutes. So when I walked in she was on her knees in the slave position and I told her to stand up. Then I put her over my knee and I told her she was a naughty girl and I was going to spank her. I pulled down her panties so her pussy was exposed. She loved that, she was so wet it was unbelievable.'

He's squirming in his seat, his breathing's changed again, and my nerves are spiking.

'And then I told her I'd be walking out again and she should be in the missionary position naked when I came back.'

I calculate how quickly I can push him out of the car and start the ignition. 'Then I ran my fingers up and down her crack and I ended up putting her on the kitchen table. I tied her wrists to her ankles so she was totally exposed …'

'Okay, got the picture!' It's time to wind this up; I bring him back to the moment by asking him about his current partner and thank him for his time.

'Not a worry,' he says, rubbing his blunt-fingered hands along the tops of his thighs. He makes a final offer to show me what B&D's all about, then gets out of the car.

Idiot! What was I thinking, getting into a confined space with this guy? My hands are trembling as I reach for the ignition and my arms suddenly feel weak. I want to just sit and wait until the jitters subside before I start driving but I'm afraid he'll come back or tail me if he gets the chance. So I lock all the doors, breathe, and find reverse.

5

THE ULTIMATE SLAVE

In our first phone call, Pierre, a retired architect, had told me he was a slave but had tired of the Sydney BDSM scene because so few people understood his desire for extreme submission. I meet him, as arranged, at a bookshop café in Paddington. We spot each other immediately, shake hands and he offers to get the coffee. I ask him to choose a table and he points to one close to others by the window. This surprises me—I thought he'd want a more isolated spot.

He's slim, about five-eight, with white hair swept back from a square face and a closely cropped white beard. In his sixties, he's a bit James Mason and looks relaxed in a finely checked sports jacket and open-necked shirt—until I produce my recorder. He looks at it like it's contaminated so I turn it off and push it to the side of the table. For the first ten minutes of our conversation he keeps glancing at it and wants to check that it's really off. When my assurances aren't enough I remove the batteries.

KINK

I strain to hear his voice at times and struggle with his French accent. This isn't made any easier given that his voice drops to a whisper whenever he says the word 'slave'. There are hilarious quirks in his pronunciation—he speaks of worshipping his first girlfriend when he was an 'a*dolly*sent' and thinks men who feel they must dominate women may have '*dev*ilopped' feelings of 'ina*dick*wassy'.

He won't talk about himself but wants to stick to the history of sexual slavery, the birth of chivalry and platonic love, and refer me to books.

'It would have been different perhaps if in 732 Charles Martelle hadn't beaten the Moors in the city of Poitiers, but he did and they never went further than that. When Ferdinand and Isabella started kicking them out of Spain that was the last chance they had to make any imprint at all.' Dispatching the Moors, who were never big on worshipping women, led to centuries of peace and wealth when Europe progressed into the age of chivalry, he said.

'It originated in the fifteenth century in what is now France but was actually Burgundy at the time—the most sophisticated, wealthiest court in Europe. So they had time on their hands and they discovered the beauty of women.' Chivalry dictated that you should never nail an opponent from the back but fight according to strict rules of conduct, a notion that soldiers would put aside to slaughter 100,000 Muslims abroad in Antioch.

'But back home they believed that Platonic love was the most extreme and most advanced form of human sentiment. And so the age of chivalry was alive and well. Today a captain of industry can be an absolute bastard, a swearing standover man who torments people by offering them a high salary and have them kissing his boots and, at the same time, being a slave to a lady,' he said.

I manage to extract from him that his mother was a tall, striking woman from the bourgeoisie and his father was working class. He won't be led on whether or not she was dominating but I suspect his own worship of women began with her.

His eye contact is steady and only breaks when I stray into personal territory. Mine's less steady as I'm distracted by the broken capillaries in his nose and his small, yellowing incisors.

His eyes moisten as he quotes one of his male philosophy teachers: 'A man should never hit a woman, not even with a rose.'

He's free with his own views, too; young men today spend far too much time playing sport when they should be practising their cunnilingus, and a male slave should relish performing oral sex on a woman who is menstruating heavily.

Whips have varying degrees of severity, he says. He offers to take me to a sex shop to show me and asks if I'd be too shy to go. I mumble that I wouldn't be but avoid making a firm time.

He's well educated, academic and slightly patronising. He can't believe I haven't read *Venus in Furs* by Leopold von Sacher-Masoch or *The Story of O* by Pauline Réage. After an hour or so he tells me I'm very beautiful and says, if I could stand the thought, perhaps I'd like to have dinner with him. He says he likes me and would like to see me again, quite apart from any research I might be doing. Again, I mumble a non-committal reply.

A few weeks later I call Pierre to follow up a few points I'd missed—I'm hopeless working without my recorder—and he's much more open on the phone than face to face. It turns out that he doesn't just love a golden shower, he's partial to a golden schooner. By this stage of my research my perspective had become so skewed that when anyone rang and said they were into golden showers, I'd suppress the urge to hang up because it had begun to seem so commonplace.

'The concept behind golden showers is punishment, it's a matter of humiliation. I know that of all demonstrations of dominance, women absolutely *love* dishing it out. And I can tell you that if it's dished out in the mouth and it's swallowed, it's totally harmless. In fact it seems a very clean thing to have a woman piss in your mouth.'

Every time he had sex with his last partner, a big drink delivered from the 69 position was the climax.

'She timed it very well and had good control of it and I drank a bladder full of her pee. It's always very nice. To me it's a nice expression of humility.'

The taste and the smell don't worry him because he reckons women don't stink the way men do.

'Women don't reach those extremes, they have different pheromones. There's that old saying: "Horses sweat, men perspire and ladies *glow*."'

This insistence on the superiority of women is fundamental to Pierre's view of the world.

'I've always had a great admiration for the world of women. I found women to be ever more resourceful, sophisticated, gentle. They smelled nice, they felt nice. I never doubted my sexuality.

I never had to prove anything. Even when I was in my early twenties I always felt that to impose oneself on a woman was not a sign of masculinity. Most men were incapable of appreciating femininity properly. I felt women were marvellous beings, a gift from God, different from us and to be nurtured and taken note of at all times.'

He believes one man in every thousand has a true disposition to slavery and the worship of women, a characteristic he first noticed in himself when he was a child.

'If at the age of eight you can reach a feeling of elation, of having accomplished something worthwhile, by giving a little treat to your favourite girl, you begin to know that this is the way. I gave her a bar of chocolate, she ate it and I was elated, I thought it was beautiful. It is pertaining through all of our culture but it is not necessarily understood. Why do we offer flowers to a lady, why do we open a door for a lady, why do we serve the lady first? There are some cultures where this doesn't exist, where the man walks in front and eats first.

'Decadence and freedom of expression don't exist in the Sudan, they don't exist in Islam. You can't have the concept of the subservient woman as well as its opposite—Sacher-Masoch's ideal, where she's wearing boots and fur and dragging a whip.'

For a man so devoted to women I'm surprised he's never married. But it seems he could never quite fit it in.

'What you see and hear is one particular facet of my life. If I was a great writer or photographer or an artist and you were interviewing me we probably wouldn't cover the fact that I might have prostate cancer or that I might have insomnia or diabetes. And it wouldn't cover the fact that I might have been in a war when I was twenty and a merchant seaman when I was twenty-two and went bankrupt at twenty-five and went to jail at thirty and came out at forty-two. You know, the circumstances of my life were very extreme. I've led an adventurous life. I was always very independent. I haven't worked for anyone else for the last thirty years, mostly because I wasn't employable, but I also resented the authority of men.'

He says he's survived financially because he's been 'reasonably successful' in property development.

'What did you go to jail for?'

'I didn't say I did!'

'Yes you did.'

'Did I? Oh, that was a rhetorical thing. Well, if you really want to know, yes, I have been to jail. It's one of my past experiences. I've been mixed up with crime at one stage. But that's just part of an interesting life.'

He makes it clear I'm not going to get any more detail than that, which leaves me frustrated, intrigued.

Pierre's type of slavery is 'lifestyle', as distinct from simply sexual, and he appears to consider anything less than total devotion a pathetic imitation of the pure form. He's contemptuous of the BDSM scene and its players. One man, known as 'Mat' because he likes women to walk on him, gets a special mention.

'He has a very dull personality. He could not express himself if his life depended on it. He is as articulate as a geranium!'

I mention that I might try to find him for a chat.

'If you want to interview someone with the personality of an 'amburger, then talk to Mat.'

Pierre doesn't go to very many 'play' parties nowadays—'They're full of so-called dominant males who, in my opinion, couldn't get themselves a fuck in a woman's jail'—so he practises his slavery in private, where his submission is absolute. And if his mistress decided the relationship was all about her sexual gratification and not his then, officially, he'd have to accept that, though he added, 'It would have to be worked out.'

The matter of possible exploitation doesn't faze him because it's simply not an issue.

'That's the idea with the personal slavery thing. There's nothing wrong with that. I wouldn't object to doing *everything* I was told. Of course there's the limitation of time and it's not always possible.'

He knows a married couple who can't wait for their daughter to leave home so they can fully indulge their lifestyle without her asking tricky questions about why her father is doing all the housework. But the satisfaction of being forced into all the drudgery escapes me.

'It's the self-discipline and the fact that you have pleased your lady. You are her *slave*. It's her wish. It's her demand. She has all the rights. The reward is in the relationship. The fact is that most women like straight sex as well, and that would be part of it. She might want it at three in the afternoon, or every night before she goes to sleep, or first thing when she wakes up, or her feet sucked when she comes home from shopping or dancing.'

The titillation continues around the clock, not just around foreplay, in this kind of relationship, a feature he believes makes things much more interesting.

KINK

'Where a normal couple would say, "Well that's it, we've had sex three times, we're finished", the dominatrix–slave relationship never stops. It continues after you've made love three times in the afternoon, on your way to dinner, coming home, on a country drive, a golden shower with lunch—it never stops.'

He's never seen slavery as the way of a deviant but believes the slave is someone who can express love 'at ten times the strength and honesty of anyone else'. It's a sophistication born of the age of chivalry, he says, beyond the reach of prehistoric, and many modern, men.

'How often have you heard women complain that after they've had sex, their man turns over and goes to sleep? That is, to me, the primal male: he's run across the valley, had a quick root before some bastard hits him over the head with the pre-historic equivalent of a baseball bat, his seeds have already gone up the uterine canal, competing probably with another bastard's seeds, so the next generation will be assured when he dies at the age of twenty-five, killed by a bear. That's what genetically is in us.'

I'm about to thank Pierre for his time when things take a turn into difficult territory.

'You have never ever told me, during our two long conversations, where are *you* situated sexually?'

This topic's out of bounds, so I remind him about my policy of not discussing myself under any circumstances.

'I know, you've said that. But it would be nice if I knew which way you are oriented.'

'Why?'

He says it will help him gauge my level of 'comprehension'.

'If I am talking to a martian who has no concept of sexuality, well …'

'I think I'd rather stick with my policy. You can assume that I have a certain level of knowledge.'

'But I'm not talking about knowledge, that's irrelevant. I'm talking about your likes and dislikes.' He asks if I could imagine myself in a relationship with a shoe fetishist, or a man who falls asleep straight after sex, or one that likes to be—literally— walked all over, like Mat. Then he gets to his point. 'Could you imagine yourself in a relationship with a person like me? Somewhere along the line you must be able to say, "Yes I could" or, "No I couldn't. I'm a strictly lights-off, missionary-position girl."'

I don't think that's fair but I'm not falling into this trap.

'But for the purposes of my research it doesn't really matter what I'm into.'

'I know. This is purely outside the research thing … With female domination, it is the romantic ideal pushed to the power of ten. Would that concept be acceptable?'

'Well, I think I'd have a much tidier house!'

He laughs. 'Well, I can tell you, not if it was left to me without very strong guidance! I am *lousy* at it. The spirit of it is very appealing. The execution is very difficult, for both parties.'

The terms of a relationship (and the housework standards) must be worked out early on, and if they're not met then the woman punishes or humiliates her slave, he says.

'Imagine that you have been given, by the supreme authority in the sky, power that says: "You, Sandra, are not a psychopath and we believe that you will not kill your slave. From now on, that man is totally in your power." Imagine if you are married to that man, the house will be in your name, the car, the bank account. You will be his goddess and he will live for you.'

He's trying to make the scenario sound delicious and I have to admit the domestic slavery concept does appeal, but having a spineless man around the place, scurrying to obey my every command, would irritate the hell out of me. And how could you love someone you couldn't possibly respect? But he pushes on with the pitch.

'In a normal relationship women nag, nag, nag to the despair of the men who desperately want to watch the football in peace. Well, slaves don't watch football unless they are so authorised. And slaves don't go out drinking with the boys. They are home kissing your feet or doing your housework or giving you a massage or oral sex. Unless you are a vanilla-sex lesbian, which I don't think you are, the concept of female domination and total slavery must come to your mind sooner or later.' He suggests I try it for a year, as practical research, with him. David has been pretty unimpressed with my project so far—I wonder how I'd sell this idea to him.

An early image of female domination from 1503, just after the time of the Court of Burgundy, can be seen in the drawing *Phyllis and Aristotle* by German artist Hans Baldung Grien. It shows Phyllis riding the aged Aristotle side-saddle. He has a bit in his mouth and she, holding his reins in her left hand, wields a whip with her right. The image, depicted by many artists, including Lucas Cranach the Elder, was popular in Renaissance and Reformation Europe and was meant to tell a cautionary tale: even a man as wise as Aristotle, when driven by lust, could be duped into submission by a wily woman. When the pair was discovered by Phyllis's husband Alexander (who was also Aristotle's pupil), the older man admitted his stupidity and warned that if it could happen to him, it could happen more easily to a younger, less wise man.

A private collection of drawings, paintings and etchings which belonged to scholar and political activist Eduard Fuchs gives a good overview of how female sexual dominance has been portrayed in western culture. The combined works known as *Die Weiberherrschafft in der Geschichte der Menschheit* (*Women in Domination*) was a two-volume edition published in 1913 and the commentary by Alfred Kind argues that the way dominant femininity—and submissive masculinity—as perceived in western culture is somehow consistent and permanent:

> When an erotic motif in folklore or myth is shown to be evident from the Far East to the Far West and in all periods of history … it may be deduced that the individual erotic motif transcends time and space, or in other words that the diverse motifs of the sexual-instinct have, taken individually, not changed (as have manifestations of fashion, including sexual fashions), but that they have, in the course of human history, remained constant. In this sense, the stories of Salome or Aristotle are of the same documentary value as the detailed case studies of a 'sadist' living today, or a 'masochist' living today.

There's definitely something in the notion that female sexual dominance has been around, if not since the beginning of the species, at least for an awfully long time. Havelock Ellis cites A. Wiedemann's *Popular Literature in Ancient Egypt* to support the idea:

> Oh! Were I made her porter, I should cause her to be wrath-
> ful with me. Then when I did but hear her voice, the voice
> of her anger, a child shall I be for fear.

These words come from a love song in which the male wants to be subjugated by his lover, experiencing pleasure when she treats him as a lowly slave. Ellis believed that the status and independence of the Egyptian woman at the time may well have offered many opportunities to the ancient Egyptian masochist. Perhaps it was Pierre's French background that made him claim the concept of female domination as a product of the court of Burgundy.

6

MISTRESS J

I'm running late on my way to watch Martin in his session with Mistress J. At about five past eleven I pull up in front of the anonymous, slightly shabby terrace in Surry Hills and ring the bell. I hear Martin ask someone if he should answer the door seconds before he appears.

'Hi, Martin. Sorry I'm late, I missed the turnoff.'

He nods but doesn't reply. Odd behaviour, I think, for a man who a week earlier was chatty over lunch. I step inside to find the downstairs converted to a slick office with white walls, polished floorboards and glass and metal furniture. Mistress J, a handsome Canadian in her mid-forties, introduces herself and tells me to take a seat. She sits opposite me and extends her fabulous black-stockinged legs, the skirt of her dress falling open to show a long stretch of thigh.

I've sussed you don't speak unless spoken to with Mistress J, so it's not until I'm asked that I tell her I want to observe the session as it would be without an audience. She understands.

'All right, Martin, you can go upstairs now. Take off your clothes, *hang them up neatly*, and be waiting for me in the slave position.'

'Yes, Mistress.'

With bowed posture Martin walks up the stairs. The penny's finally dropped that the reason he's not saying much and avoiding eye contact is because he's already adopted the sub-servient role.

We give him a minute's head start then stand up. Mistress J drops her dress at the bottom of the stairs and begins the almost vertical climb to the bedroom cum 'dungeon'. I'm a pace or two behind, watching her dimpled bottom move as she ascends. Seeing her stripped to bra, G-string and stockings is when it really dawns on me I'm about to witness something incredibly intimate. I begin to feel apprehensive.

Martin is naked, on all fours, when we enter the small bedroom.

'Oh good, you're ready,' she says, giving his arse a sharp slap. 'Now get up and stand over here against the wall.'

'Yes, Mistress.'

I'm glad he doesn't acknowledge my presence and, forget-ting he's had public sex before, am surprised he shows no sign of embarrassment that I'm there.

Mistress J points to a plastic folding chair in the dim light and I go and sit on it. It's inches from the action. Normally she'd play her *Music for Dungeons: Bound for Pleasure* CD, but because I'm recording she decides not to. An electric blow heater has already warmed the room and neutral carpet softens her spike-heeled footsteps. Martin has hung his clothes—neatly, as ordered—on a hat stand and left his white lace G-string on a chest of drawers. Apart from a few pieces of simple wooden furniture and the utilitarian dungeon equipment the room is pretty bare. A rubber rat the size of a wombat, with red glass eyes, crouches under the bed.

Mistress J attaches leather cuffs to Martin's wrists and ankles, parts his legs, raises his arms and hooks him with double-ended dog clips to a metal grid on the wall.

'I like to start off being gentle with you because it doesn't take very long to *increase* the pressure . . .' she says as she begins wrapping leather thonging around his penis.

The dialogue between them is playful, and they stay in character the whole time. She includes explanations throughout partly for my benefit and partly for Martin's titillation.

'There's nothing like a leather lace, strategically placed,' she says as she pulls firmly on his bald scrotum.

'That's very true, Mistress.'

She grapples with the leather, trying to tie it around his balls, but she can't get any purchase.

'Those testicles of yours are escaping me again. They do this to me *all* the time. I think I'm going to have to get out my bolt cutters.'

'Not again!' he says in mock horror, and they both chuckle.

She gives up and selects two cock rings from a shelf above the bench containing various torture instruments.

'Just simple metal rings, available at your local hardware store,' she says, showing them to me before pushing them onto Martin's penis. The first ring, slightly larger than the other, sits at the base, and the smaller one is pushed up against that. I make a mental note to look for the aisle marked COCK RINGS next time I'm at the hardware store.

(Later that day I Google cock rings and find they're meant to keep an erection harder for longer. Depending on the material of the ring, they are usually put on a flaccid penis; the blood flows in normally, producing an erection, but is restricted from flowing back out along the external vein. Some cock rings encircle the entire genital package so the scrotum as well as the penis is pulled through the ring. Whichever style is chosen and whatever the material—rubber, leather, metal, silicon—the desired effect is a pleasantly throbbing, long-lasting erection. If the penis turns purple it's time to take the ring off. Martin's soft little penis is a lousy ad for cock rings. Maybe he needs a smaller size.)

Mistress J repeatedly flicks Martin's dick with a small vinyl whip, which might explain his never-quite-raging erection. It doesn't look like very thirsty work, but every so often she skols from a big plastic water bottle.

When she's worried about the circulation in Martin's arms she unties his hands and gets him to lie on a black iron bench covered with a thin black vinyl sheet. Once he's horizontal she blindfolds him, ties a rope around the head of his dick, loops the other end into a pulley and cranks it up. She's trying to take him to the edge of his pain threshold and he quickly reaches it; Martin screams with the final crank, lifting his hips to create some slack.

'Oh, stop complaining!' she snaps, winding the rope back a bit.

Mistress J steadily works her way through her repertoire of torture. She presses a metal-spiked disc into the palm of my hand, telling me it's an ancient Mayan torture implement, but it's more like something you'd drop into the bottom of a vase to anchor wayward flower stems. She then presses it into Martin's nipples, drips black candle wax onto his nipples and scrotum (black wax is the best because it's easier to see where it's landing in the dim light of a dungeon), and follows up with the pinch of half a dozen tiny clothes pegs on the same tender spots. It seems to hurt when she squirts alcohol down into his penis with an eye dropper, but within seconds he's loving the warm sensation it creates. If I was listening at the door I'd be convinced by Martin's ecstatic groans that he was having a fantastic time. Somehow his frequently flaccid penis isn't sending the same message. He'd said he could stand *days* of titillation and loved holding out, so maybe it was all about lasting the distance.

But it's not just torture. There's quite a bit of affection between them and she alternates the painful with the sensual, doing things that even a sexually conservative man would love. At one point she kicks off her shoes, hops up on the opposite end of the bench and massages his balls with her stockinged feet. Later she lies on top of him, her knees pinning him at the hips, and nibbles his ear lobes as she runs her feet along his inner thighs. She's an incredible tease, coming so very close to having sex with him but never kissing him, and chastising him when he squeezes a breast or thigh.

I cringe as my stomach starts rumbling loudly during the session and I start to wonder where around here I can get some sushi.

After about forty-five minutes Mistress J releases the pegs and Martin screams with pain as the blood rushes back to the surface. She then patiently picks all the wax off his testicles and nipples, and unclips his restraints.

'All right, Martin, you can go downstairs now. You know what *that's* for, don't you?'

'Yes, Mistress.'

Martin springs off the bench—he's remarkably agile for a man built like a rhinoceros—and we follow him down, out through the kitchen and into the bathroom. She stands in front of him and tells him to remove her knickers. Then she runs the hot water in the shower recess to take the chill off the tiles and tells him to lie down in it. She stands over him, still in her stockings and stilettos, and slowly starts to wee (so that's what all the drinking was about). He's focusing on her crotch but his expression is distant as he lies there wanking furiously. She controls her stream but holds back the full release until she knows he's about to come. She turns to me mid-stream and tells me that this is a golden shower. That much I knew.

When it's all over she tells him to have a 'proper' shower and we leave him. I'm overwhelmed with the need to bolt from the premises and don't really know why. I tell myself that Martin will be embarrassed if I'm still there when he comes out and that he might want a few quiet moments, unobserved, with Mistress J before he leaves. There's also the seamy matter of payment that I don't need to witness. I'm relieved he hadn't engaged with me at all through the session. It's been utterly surreal rather than embarrassing or shocking but, for whatever reason, I can't face him. I take Mistress J's card and fly.

7

CHICKEN SOUP, HOLD THE SEX

Gary's a conservative middle manager from the Bible belt and has sex with his wife once a fortnight. He's a rhapsody in puce the day we meet—shirt, tie, face, all subtle variations on the theme—and when offered a coffee says, 'Sen*sational*!'

I'm relieved when, after a minute, I realise his frequent, rapid lip-puckering is a tic and not a come-on. It's very Kenneth Williams, but he's not trying to be funny.

He says the sex with his wife Julie started to get stale ten years into the marriage when they were trying to conceive and they had to do it by the clock. He'd deliberately stay up watching TV so she'd be asleep when he came to bed. Now the relationship itself is quite sound, and sex isn't the most important thing in their marriage. But something was missing earlier on, because he started visiting brothels just after they married.

'I went to A Touch of Class. I was incredibly nervous but I had a very pleasurable experience—it was all very forbidden—

and that was the beginning. I came away thinking that was sen*sational*. In those days I had no idea what to expect. The bordello was absolutely very classy, with a very classy lady. That was the first step on the journey but it wasn't a plan.'

He couldn't be sure that Julie wouldn't indulge his sexual curiosity, but they had reached a point in the marriage where he didn't dare suggest anything different and risk arousing her suspicions.

'Now there's no turning back, you just keep going down that path.'

Seven years ago Gary started to look at Julie differently.

'I got diagnosed with lymphoma, which was a bit of a shock. These things aren't meant to happen. But all of a sudden you step back and you see how good the relationship really is, in terms of all the support. The cancer didn't change the sexual relationship with Julie at all. It was bad before that and it made no difference. The lymphoma was low grade and not aggressive so I didn't need any treatment.' So she's good on chicken soup, but she still doesn't turn him on.

He says he's become kinkier since the diagnosis and Julie still has no idea. He once blew $3000 on an afternoon of group sex at a particularly sen*sational* brothel but generally only spends about $200 a fortnight.

'You can go up to $1000 for one girl but at that price it's a rip-off. It's hard to tell the difference between that and a $250 one, particularly when you can get some sen*sational* women in sen*sational* settings for that price.'

The good salaries he and Julie earn mean the money he spends on sex isn't noticed and work-related travel provides cover. 'I've had singles, I've had doubles, I've had triples, I've had guys involved, I've had anal penetration with a dildo. But we're a normal, conservative, Hills district family.'

8
JUST LOOKING

I got a few calls from classic voyeurs who said they liked nothing more than 'a good perv'. One even had the clichéd gravelly voice and sounded alarmingly like he was getting off on the phone. When that same distinctive voice called back a couple of weeks later he denied having called before and hesitated before giving me his name—it was 'John' this time. I said I had finished interviewing and didn't need to speak to him but he wasn't going to be put off. Sounding almost panicked in the seconds before I hung up he babbled about wanking in his car next to crowded buses and squirting chocolate sauce onto his balls and getting his dog to lick it off.

I arranged to meet another voyeur, who didn't sound as creepy, at a local café. He rang the day we were meant to meet saying he couldn't come because that time didn't suit his wife. I'd been delighted he wanted to bring her; I was fascinated to see how she'd be talking about her husband's obsession with naked strangers. A week later I rang and we agreed on another time, but in the end he came alone.

Keith is a softly spoken labourer wearing a fluorescent lime-green top. He is balding, with a yellow scalp condition that looks like cradle cap, and he is covered in a fine film of dust. I fear he might be reticent, suspecting the postponement because of his wife's busyness might have been an excuse, but he is great. He'd thought a lot about the interview in the previous weeks and offers, like a pro, to begin with his childhood.

His first memory of anyone touching him sexually was during an examination from a school nurse which he describes as 'wonderful'. Then, when he was about nine, he found other ways to have fun.

'I'd cut a hole in my pocket and pull my penis through it and say to a friend: Put your hand in there. So I had this feeling of getting this done to me, and I liked it.'

At thirteen a school friend introduced him to a paedophile. The man was about forty and regularly paid Keith to submit to oral sex. Looking back, Keith has somehow made a distinction and decided this man wasn't *really* a paedophile but rather a 'dirty old man'. And, as abused children often do, he also feels guilty about the relationship.

'After a while I got found out so I got away from it. I really had to get away from it because I knew it wasn't right. My parents gave me a good talking to. My father knew the gent but he didn't take any revenge out on him or call the police. I said, Look, okay, I've done wrong. And I was only young. My excuse was I was going to the shop for him, he was paraplegic or crippled or something. They worked out it was a lie and they just said don't go back there again … No wonder I didn't do too well at school. Never mind.'

It's easy to imagine Keith as a painfully shy teenager because he still struggles to speak audibly and make eye contact. But he's also honest, painting himself as a complete failure with girls. At sixteen he was hanging out in milk bars 'trying to find someone to have sex with' but had to wait until his older brother offered to pay for him to visit a prostitute. At that point he realised 'girls were the way to go' but rarely had any luck with them.

'At about nineteen I got a car and I tried to have sex with a girl in the back seat of it when I was taking her home. It didn't work.'

When he moved to Bondi from the western suburbs in his early twenties Keith's voyeurism took hold.

'I was down the beach a lot. That was another scenario altogether because there were a lot of bathing beauties down there.' He recalls lying near a girl on the beach who was wearing just a see-through bikini bottom; they got talking, and went back to her unit for sex. 'That was a really great experience. I think that was the only real time when I've got on to a girl and it's worked.' He says he 'just left afterwards'.

Apart from that the only sex he got came from prostitutes—when he could afford them on apprentice wages—and voyeurism filled in the gaps.

'When I was living in Bondi, I found myself looking into units, and you could watch people showering. I wouldn't go and rape or assault anyone. For me it's just a matter of having a good perv.'

Since he's been married Keith does most of his perving at nudist beaches on weekends, an activity his wife Gita knows about but has no interest in sharing. She and Keith met when he answered her ad in the paper for a pen pal. He went to Fiji to meet her in 1996, they married a few years later and she got a residency visa.

'She's Hindu and she's not brought up that way. I have explained it to her. She's rung me on the mobile phone when I've been there and we have a bit of a joke about it. She says, "Be careful, don't let anyone come too near to you."'

Keith adheres to a strict unwritten code at these beaches, one that prohibits masturbation in public.

'No, I wouldn't masturbate to *come* at the beach. I'd get out of the water, I'd probably get me towel and wrap it around me penis and me balls and give 'em a bit of a rub.' He says he enjoys his erections being noticed by women nearby. 'And I get the feeling they're probably here for the same reason I am, to perv.'

So would it be considered bad form to masturbate at the beach?

'Oh yeah, definitely. But if you're a naturist, you can go there, have a bit of fun. I take binoculars and perv. Then I'll go for a swim, dry myself down, get me suntan oil, rub that all over me, on me cock, try to get it hard, turn around, someone's there watching, give it a few more rubs. Beautiful.'

Keith also likes going to nudist camps, but because Gita isn't interested he goes alone.

'I went to a resort north of Newcastle. I was lucky I got in as a single gent because it was family-oriented. I was laying down there and I got a hard-on, and I've had to go into the swimming pool to hide it, and this happened a couple of times. And the manager's come over and said, "This can't go on any more. I'm going to have to ask you to leave." I've had a hard-on so many times it's embarrassing for other people. So I came back the next day and he said, "No, there's too many men here at the moment." But I enjoyed my stay there, even though it was only for a few hours. Swimming pool. Log cabins. Volleyball. Ocean beach.'

People he's met at the beach have told him when he can watch them have sex on webcam.

'That was exciting. I was in the study and me wife was in the lounge room and I said, Come over and have a look at this. And then she got me worked up a little bit, showing them what she could do. I'd dropped me trousers but they stripped right off and got into it doggy style.'

But Gita's losing patience so Keith restricts his webcam viewing to when she's sleeping or at work.

'She complains to me that I'm on the computer a lot. Usually I put the camera away now so she doesn't suspect anything but she knows that I do it. She got mad the other day because I'd used up a whole box of tissues.'

Poor Gita. I hope her residency visa doesn't rely on her sticking with Keith.

There's a level at which voyeurism is pretty mainstream and isn't going to alarm the cops or the neighbours. It's the innate interest in others' intimacies that makes Bill Henson's photography so compelling, albeit controversially, and that has made striptease so perennially popular. This skilful removal of clothes, which is calculated to arouse, panders to voyeurism in the same way topless waitresses and pole dancers do. In fact the enjoyment of any kind of sexual imagery—in movies, books, magazines or the internet—amounts to the same thing and has been served generously since the invention of photography. But even kids are partial to a bit of a perv, even if the result is hysterical giggling rather than frank arousal. Think of primary school boys trying to spy into the girls' toilets (or vice versa) or kids desperate to see what an older teenage brother is up to with his girlfriend.

Voyeurism has been depicted in art through the ages, perhaps most famously in Jean-Honoré Fragonard's painting *The Swing* (1767). This frivolous, late rococo image shows a heavily petticoated woman high on a swing as a man hides in the bushes below trying to get a look up her skirt. And literature is filled with stories of Peeping Toms. Just pre-dating Fragonard's painting was *The Monastery Gate* (1745) by Jean-Charles Gervaise de Latouche, the story of a young peasant boy, Saturnin, who peeps through a hole in the wall at his mother having sex with her father confessor. He masturbates then tries to rape his sister, Susanna, who resists but tells him that she has already learned the delights of lesbianism from a nun. At this stage both siblings are aroused and, after spying through another hole at another couple having sex, Susanna gives in to Saturnin.

Then there was Henri Barbusse's *L'enfer* (*Hell*), a novel from 1908 based on the true story of a waiter who is prosecuted for boring a peephole in the communicating door between two hotel rooms, one of which was reserved for honeymooning couples. In the real case the waiter masturbated as he watched the goings-on in the next room and handled the penis of a boy who looked through another hole but Barbusse is coy about this. His narrator describes a woman undressing alone in the next room and, despite detailed erotic imagery which clearly arouses him, there's no reference to anything as crude as masturbation.

> What had just fallen on the bed softly, slowly, in a billowing strip, was the bodice which had pulled her in so tightly at the waist but left her open at the neck … The cloudy petti-coat opened, and slipping to her feet, lighted her up, very pale in all the darkness … I saw the outline of her legs. Or so I imagined, for my eyes could hardly serve me, not only because the light had gone, but because I was blinded by the profound travail of my heart, by the pulsing of my life, by all the presences in my blood.

He knows that his eyes 'injected with blood like two pale mouths' would betray his craving for her were she able to see him and considers bursting through her door to throw himself on her. He rejects the idea when he considers its consequences—infamy, jail, destitution—then fantasises that once her terror had subsided she might happily submit to him. This is where his obsession becomes complex, fuelled by her unattainability.

> No, again no! For in that case she would be a prostitute; and of such there are as many as one desires. It is easy enough to find a woman to do what one wants with, there is a tariff

for that sort of sacrilege. There are even places where by paying, it is possible, through holes in walls, to see love in the act. Were she a prostitute, it would no longer be she— divinely alone … Her solitude makes her shine forth, but it also protects her utterly.

Unlike Barbusse's narrator, Keith is not *attracted* to a woman's unattainability—if he could attain her he would. Years of sexual failure have helped Keith develop his voyeurism into concrete sexual gratification without having to be sufficiently attractive or articulate to actually get anyone into bed. It's the perfect solution for him; he sticks to the rules to stay out of trouble while getting sexual 'access' to any number of good-looking women, women who in any other circumstances might well be out of his league. And it's free.

9

THE PUNK-SWING CROSSOVER

Jimmy's an ageing punk in his early forties, with a dodgy bleach job through black hair, streaking it like exotic avian plumage. Slim, with a deep vertical crease down each cheek and a gap in his front teeth, he looks like Jeremy Irons' less attractive younger brother.

Sexually and professionally, Jimmy is multi-skilled.

'Currently I'm a social worker but I have done other things. Cook. Brake mechanic. I work with young people doing aerosol art. I've worked in mental health, but mostly with young people.'

He speaks slowly with a broad Australian accent, which makes him sound pissed or stoned and stupid. But he's none of these, especially not stupid.

Playing doctors and nurses with the twin girls next door as a kid was Jimmy's first sexual memory.

'It was after me mum died when I was eight and I was living with me granny, so I must have been nine. Dad was a street bum. He just took off and left me and me sister with me granny.'

He says he was 'sort of' well looked after.

'Yeah, we were, by me granny, but me grandfather was a violent alcoholic. He used to beat me up every day, basically.'

Jimmy has only recently found out that his father had been sexually abused at a Christian Brothers school in Sydney's inner west.

'I was lucky I reckon. Me grandfather just used to beat me up. I think the physical abuse is easier to deal with.'

He lost his virginity with a girl in a park at about sixteen then had oral sex with a man soon after. That same man started Jimmy making porno films with girls, paying him in heroin and cocaine, and, apart from thinking it was all a bit weird, Jimmy was okay with the deal.

'Then one night I was walking along Liverpool Street and this prostitute was sitting in a doorway and she yelled out to me across the road, "Sid Vicious!" I used to get that all the time because of me hair. She just called me over and said, "Hey, do you want a fuck?" and I said, "But that costs money." And she says, "Nah, nah, come inside." And it was just like curtains and beds. It was *really* tacky. And I ended up having a relationship with this woman for about three or four months when I was eighteen.'

Meanwhile, his punk band was playing in gay clubs because there was nowhere else to play.

'I s'pose being a teenager I was exploring the gay sexuality thing, which a lot of guys don't do; they probably should, and they wouldn't be so homophobic. But I probably wouldn't have been exposed to that if I hadn't been into the punk music because I wouldn't have been going to the gay clubs for a start. I would've just thought, Well, why would I go to a gay club? I'm not gay.'

Supporting a bad speed habit in the eighties, he went to work in a sex club in London's Soho. His first and most lucrative job there was working on the door, selling the £2 tickets to the 'live sex act' downstairs and giving change for the peepshow. He sussed that by swapping a few of the pound coins for 5p pieces, which were the same size and shape, he could make a killing.

'We'd be giving change for the wanking booth. So the compulsive wankers'd be feeding all the coins in at once with one hand so the light'd stay on and, because the floor was rubber, they wouldn't hear the odd 5p coin hit the ground. At the end of the shift I'd go and mop the booth up with what we called the Spunk Bucket. But you'd have the gloves on and you'd pick up all your fives and you'd disinfect them and you'd just use the same fives over and over. Like, even though you'd cleaned them you'd never put em back in your pocket. They were the wanker's five ps. One shift I walked off with £400.'

After a spell working behind the bar, Jimmy's Maltese mafia bosses asked him to do the act on stage. Patrons, having paid their two quid, would have to wait around for ages in the dimly lit room, being fleeced for weak drinks and buying cigarettes for girls at £15 a pack. Finally it was show time.

'There'd be a mattress on the stage and you'd come out in your jocks, the chick'd come out in a bra and panties, and you'd get on the bed and you'd dry hump, basically. That was it. It was a total rip-off.'

Once back in Sydney he met Anita. Theirs was an open relationship lasting fifteen years, but five years ago they broke up. He's still pretty cut up about it and, despite his years of pleading, she's still keeping his dog.

'We used to do a lot of "swinging", I suppose. That sounds so seventies. "Partner swapping." It all sounds so *tacky*.' He laughs often, the creases in his cheeks deepening, his wiry body rocking.

Anita suggested he try cross-dressing and she'd help him with the nail polish, makeup and wigs.

'She used to get a kick out of it as well, taking photos and stuff.'

They advertised for other couples in a swinger's magazine.

'We'd say "young couple"—as we were—"looking for similar aged, broadminded couple. Male is into cross-dressing."'

Jimmy knew swinging was risky but said nothing ever went wrong except when alcohol was involved.

'There was this bloke who didn't respect limits. He wanted to be rougher than anyone else. And it's really hard. In a situation like that, it's totally removed from any other social context. When you're all standing around naked, it's not like you're at a normal party. You don't know anything about these people beforehand. You go and meet them, you talk a bit and you decide where to go. I suppose for some people that's part of the thrill of it, the possibility of danger. It gives it an edge.'

He's been having sex with a married couple, Michael and Sally, for two years, evidence that his good gut feeling about them was right. When he met Sally at a party, she said Michael loved watching her being fucked by other men. But they always do it at Jimmy's place or a motel, away from the couple's three kids.

Despite things going well for two years, Jimmy still has reservations about Michael.

'I've just got this little niggling thing in the back of my head and I think I'll always have it. It's weird, these guys are married and they want to share their lives with me. He'll have gang bangs with Sally and have fifteen guys fuck her. She's up for it. It's not like he's forcing her or I wouldn't be involved in it. If it's something like that I'm even more alert and aware. I'm sure Michael's not as conscious about the dangers of that sort of thing as I am. Some of those guys may know each other and it could turn into something ugly. I mean, look at the mentality of a football team. Sometimes I feel like I've got more respect for her than he has, but that's part of their relationship; they wouldn't be able to do it if they weren't really committed to each other. The same as me and Anita wouldn't have been able to. Your relationship's got to be pretty sound to be able to do the swapping thing.'

So far it's just a niggle about Michael and on balance he's satisfied with the relationship.

'It's really hard to meet good people like them. There just seem to be so many people into weird shit, like dogs and things. That's non-consensual as far as I'm concerned. It's like molesting kids and stuff. With the bestiality it's not a power imbalance like it is with kids. With paedophiles it's about power and shit but I don't know what it is with the animals. I just don't get that. But fruit? Yeah!'

He's seeing an ex on Saturday who's double-jointed and really into fruit, especially bananas and mangos.

'Yeah, mangos are awesome …You eat the fruit and you rub the skin all over you and lick it off.' I naively predict shopping difficulties because it's not mango season.

'You can get them all year round, if you *need* to,' he says, cautioning that mango seeds, once inserted, can get stuck.

'I used to work in an emergency department and I've actually seen the vacuum cleaner thing, and the fucking excuse they use is "I was vacuuming nude"! It's just impossible! No one's dick is that long! It's never in the metal tube, it's always in the little plastic handle bit where you put the tube. It's an adrenalin thing. If you're caving or something and you get caught in a confined space you swell up as soon as you panic. It's the same thing if you get your dick stuck in a vacuum cleaner and you turn it on; you don't expect the sucking power to be as strong as it is, you panic and your penis probably engorges more or whatever. I dunno. Like, I've never gone there. That's *weird*. Like, you're sittin' around at home, what would possess you to do *that*?'

10

SOAP STAR SACHA,
THE SOLO PERFORMER

It was during a preliminary phone interview that Sacha revealed his particular fetish is an obsession with his own penis. Maybe I seemed less than amazed at this, believing the obsession affects most men to some extent, but he argued that his kink was as intriguing as any other.

'I'm a supposedly high-profile person so I've found it very hard to express my sexuality. I've done virtually everything you could possibly imagine so I think I would qualify as an interest for your research.'

His voice isn't familiar but I can't help trying to work out who this high-profile character is. He's partial to a bit of self-analysis and, with a rising inflection in his speech, seems unsure of how he should phrase things.

'When I was about fifteen I used to do martial arts and I used to sit in the splits for hours and gradually I began to be able to get down to the area of my penis and, being a Roman

Catholic, shock, guilt, horror, I became aware that I could actually auto-fellate myself.'

Classes teaching that trick would be sell-outs, I reckon, and Sacha's clearly not the first man to have thought of doing it. I found a reproduction of an ancient Egyptian painting depicting the earth and sky as ithyphallic gods. The earth god is on the ground, supporting himself on his shoulders, bottom pointing skyward and enormous penis stretching down to his mouth with its tip resting on his lips.

'The Roman Catholic church has got to answer for the guilt I felt. I just felt like the devil was going to take me the next day.'

Sacha was living at home with his parents, brothers and sisters so the only private time he had was in the bathroom, where he gradually became more flexible and more adventurous with this new skill.

'And that's affected my sexuality in a lot of ways. I think it's interesting with the Roman Catholic thing as well that later on I became very much involved in the B&D scene—not in the traditional tie-up-and-whip way, but more in role-playing and sort of cock, um, torture? I'm not talking about extremes or anything like that. I mean the guys at the pub would probably think putting a cock ring on was cock torture, you know what I mean? But I'd use various forms of penile restraints, which progressed to being whipped and having candle wax dripped onto me.'

I ask him whether he's gay, straight or bisexual.

'I'm straaaiiight but, um, like, I was really horny one night and there was this transsexual that I picked up and I thought,

Bugger it, she can just have oral sex with me and that's it, but when she took her clothes off, her penis was virtually the same as mine in size, shape, everything. So that created a curiosity in me and I found myself performing oral sex on her and it was sort of like I was doing it to myself. It was taking me back to the days of being fifteen years old. And with the cock torture I'm wondering if that had something to do with the guilt of being able to auto-fellate myself. So I suppose my fetish is my own penis and then—I'm not getting off here, okay?—then it became the intake of my own semen. So yeah, I would say I became obsessed with like, yeah, with my own cum? And even though I lost my agility and flexibility there are certain positions in a room with a bed that you can use to ejaculate in your mouth.'

How would that be then?

'Imagine a bed, right? Sort of like doing a false handstand, you just push your legs up the wall and keep pushing and pushing and, although I can't get my penis into my mouth any more, you can get to a position, particularly with somebody watching and encouraging you, to be able to ejaculate either onto your face or into your mouth.'

It was the auto-fellatio trick that made a meeting seem sensible. I had to check if a) this was pure fantasy, or b) I had Gumby on the line.

So I arrive at the big inner west pub he's suggested by four o'clock and size up a good spot for a quiet chat. There's no one fitting his description here yet, just a few lone male drinkers at tables near the windows and some old blokes in the back bar watching the races. It's still early so the main bar is fairly empty with pockets of dim lighting and others of brightness. I go and sit in a fluoro-lit, raised area opposite the entrance and wait.

He'd told me he was a very well-known, albeit unemployed, actor who'd had a prominent role in a long-running Aussie soap. I wouldn't know *Neighbours* from *Home and Away* so I'd asked him to describe himself so I could spot him when he arrived. When he shows up, about twenty minutes late, he's anxious that I might out him. I convince him I won't (I haven't recognised him anyway) and swiftly go to the bar to get the beers. When I return with the drinks he smiles, relaxes a little and downs half his schooner.

He starts by paraphrasing a quote about it being great to be rich and famous but lousy to be poor and famous. 'That's where I'm at. Normally I'd buy a lady a beer but I can't.' The usual warm-up small talk involves him trying to guess the subject of the biography I've written—Male or female? Alive or dead?—and tries for Michael Hutchence. Not quite! I'm keeping schtum.

'You guys [the media] are the worst! I haven't really got on with the media. I didn't play the media game and that's why you don't recognise my face. There were people in the show that I did who were only in it for two or three years and are now splashed across the media everywhere. It was my purpose to fly beyond the radar but at least I've got my integrity. Unfortunately integrity doesn't buy you beers.'

He's more tragic than bitter and, rolling a cigarette, explains that he's bi-curious, not bisexual. Sacha reckons that if he was in a bedroom with a guy nothing would happen, but if there was a woman present as well, urging him to have sex with the guy because it would turn her on, then he would. He thinks under those circumstances he could almost look at it as a straight act because he'd be doing it for her.

'Is it an excuse? I don't know, basically I'm just a slut. Mind you, I've only penetrated about five women because that, to me, is something sacred. Planting my seed in somebody is different. Look, I've been very sexual, promiscuous, and to this day HIV, Hep B, C, whatever, my blood is totally clean and it's because of the fact that I get off more on outercourse than intercourse.'

He stresses he's never penetrated or been penetrated by a man either, partly because he's a self-confessed hypochondriac and is terrified of getting AIDS. Rummaging in his backpack he hauls out a large photo album and plonks it between the beer glasses. It's full of old photos of him at bondage parties— one of him being fucked by a mistress with a strap-on and several of him in various stages and tensions of penile restraint. These cock rings and leather trussings really look like they'd hurt and I wonder why you'd subject yourself to this kind of torture. But I don't get the pain thing. I hold the album against my chest as the pub's glass collector comes around behind me clearing debris and wait till he's gone before I ask Sacha why he likes it.

'The juxtaposition of pleasure and pain, very much so. Mind you, amphetamines play a part in it. They talk about oysters as an aphrodisiac but to me speed can keep me like that for twenty-four to forty-eight hours,' he says, indicating an erection with his right hand.

I ask him if he's ever had a kinky sexual advance rejected.

'No, never. It's the way I do it. Jokes are good, like, "If you do that again I'll spank you." One time at a nightclub this Pamela Anderson lookalike was there and we were dancing and holding hands. Then I put her hands behind her back and held them there while we were dancing—I mean, read the signals. She got the idea that I wasn't going to be a normal fuck.

'But I'm such a contradiction. Although I'm into BDSM, if someone tied me up and whipped the shit out of me I'd fucking punch their head in. And I don't like to be tied up. I'm such a slut I don't *need* to be tied up.'

11

STUMPY.COM

I joined a chat group for people who are turned on by amputees, thinking it was going to be a brilliant way of learning what makes them tick. It didn't really work on that score but it did fill me in on details of the kink. I learned that people who lust after amputees are known as 'devotees' or 'devs', while those who desperately want to be amputees themselves are known as 'wannabes'. The wannabes who wanna because it'll help them get turned on have a kink called 'apotemnophilia' and those who lust after amputees have one called 'acrotomophilia'. There's an element of submission, sexual or otherwise, among wannabes just as domination of their partners is often what drives devotees. (I recall a documentary in which that very dynamic operated between a man and his already morbidly obese wife, who he continued to feed because he loved having to do everything for her. She was so vast that she was more disabled than most amputees, which meant her husband not only had to wheel her around but wash her mammoth body, lifting great swathes of flesh to ensure all crevices were clean and dry. Her helplessness turned him on in the same way the disability and immobility caused by foot binding in China was considered desirable.) A small percentage of the wannabes have 'body integrity identity disorder' (BIID), a psychological condition that sees them fronting up at surgeons' rooms begging to be lopped and being sent home with a referral to a shrink. The BIID cravings for amputation have no link with sexual arousal but have more to do with the thrills of legless daily living.

What was interesting was discovering how potent this amputee attraction is. Much of the discussion centred around sharing tips on how to get an amputation when faced with a medical system full of surgeons who steadfastly refuse to come across with the goods. Apparently it's simply not good enough to go and ask to have your left leg removed—even if you're prepared to pay for it. Many public hospitals actually ban the surgical removal of a healthy limb because it conflicts with the fundamental medical ethos of *Primum non nocere*—'First, do no harm.' You have to go to violent lengths, like laying the unwanted limb on train tracks and waiting for the 3.15 from Redfern to do its worst. Alternatively you can bury your legs in dry ice and hope the burning will be so severe that the hospital will have no choice but to slice them off. Frustratingly for some wannabes, this technique doesn't usually work. One posted a warning that he'd tried it but, thanks to advances in skin grafting, he endured weeks of agonising treatment but still walked away on two legs. Guns and mechanical equipment have also been tried, with mixed results.

Devotees and wannabes invariably have firm ideas about their preferred amputation. Legs are the most popular in both groups but it's more specific than that. Chat groups are full of code, with people saying things like, 'Phwoaarr, I saw a really nice DAK at the mall yesterday. Why aren't there more of *those* around?' Others will chime in with their views that SBKs can be just as hot but has anyone thought outside the square and checked out a DAE. I was bewildered until some kindly co-chatter filled me in: DAK = double above knee, SBK = single below knee, DAE = double above elbow and so on. An amputation at the hip or shoulder, leaving no stump, is called a disarticulation, so a left hip or a right shoulder disarticulation would be an LHD or an RSD respectively. You get the idea.

I then came across a group modified by an irritating young wannabe girl from Malaysia called Kiree, who clearly had way too much time on her hands. She posted a photo of herself, casually dressed, all pert breasts and ironed hair, and whined about what a drag it was having four working limbs. She flirted with slobbering devs and asked for their views about which bit she should have chopped off. Some of the more computer-savvy members of the group then proceeded to perform 'electronic surgery' on her image and then proudly posted their artwork, telling her how with these modifications she'd be even more of a babe.

Next thing Kiree posts the most extraordinarily detailed descriptions of amputating her digits, not all at once, but in tiny stages, gaining pace with confidence and experience. She says it's pretty easy, except for the fact that you have to be flexible if you're doing it to yourself and 'Once you start you have to have enough guts to not stop and chicken out in the middle of it.'

Sterilisation and pain relief are dealt with up front, then she lists the tools required and advises that, if you can't get suturing needles, you sharpen standard needles on a stone because the skin is surprisingly hard to pierce. She must have spent hours studying surgical texts if this is what she managed:

> *I did the second thru fifth toes and the right ring finger this way and made them as short as I could, just about enough left to barely move. I used a rubber band at the base and started cutting carefully at the next joint out, leaving plenty of skin to work with for closure and carefully cut until I found the artery and vein and when I found them I clamped it and pulled it out as far as possible, then tied it off. This was just a simple loop around it and tie a knot and trim the ends, then cut it off about 1/8 inch past where it was tied off. Everything I read in the med books said this is the preferred method for small arteries and veins.*
>
> *Once this is done, the rubber band can come off, there will be a little bleeding but not much, then for a short stump the suture line should be from top to bottom of the toe or finger, not side to side. Next the bone needs to be cut as close to the base as possible. A word of caution here, the bone should be cut with a real fine saw, not cut with a chisel or diagonal cutters, as this just cracks the bone and that takes a long time to heal. When closing the wound do not make the skin tight, try to pull the skin together and get an idea of how much to leave for fairly loose flaps and as you suture it will tighten up a little.*

She reckons this method is better than just 'lopping it off with a chisel' because it minimises pain and speeds up recovery. Still, she advises doing it on a Friday, after work, to give yourself the weekend to get over it before fronting up at work, presumably not as a typist, on Monday. But just in case anyone was thinking this was going to be a walk in the park, she had this to say:

No matter how bad you want something off, you may suffer some mild depression or weird feelings for a couple of days afterwards. I guess it is the normal reaction to the trauma the body has had. I know I had it every time and I wanted them off so bad I could hardly stand it, so don't be surprised if it happens to you also. It does go away pretty quick and soon you can have all of the phantom pains and feelings that I have enjoyed for years. I do not think most of the feelings should be called phantom pains, because most of them are not pains at all, they are more like sensations that are much different than any normal person can feel and I like them.

Of course Kiree and her exploits could have all been utter baloney—we are on the internet, remember—but if she really did exist and was doing this stuff, as I guess some people do, then I had a newfound admiration for her. She had balls—*and* the skills to chop them off. Or maybe she was just a 'pretender', which is an ideal option for the pain-averse wannabe. These are people who bend the chosen limb at the joint, bind it with bandages and get on with the day pretending it's been amputated. Many just do this in the privacy of their own homes but the brave venture out. The forums are where pretenders share tips on binding and how to manage with the disability. One man liked pretending he had a left shoulder disarticulation but really needed help with binding both arms onto his torso so he could pretend he had both left and right arms lopped at the shoulders. He also wanted to go out like this so needed help getting around—buying bus tickets and pushing shopping trolleys were going to be major challenges.

These forums regularly run polls which, although perhaps not scientifically conducted, give some idea of preferences and motivations in the dev/wannabe community. *If you could amputate a limb, right now, no questions asked, which would you choose?* was a great question, but before I could see the poll results I had to vote myself. Without giving it too much thought I clicked SAK (single above knee) and, with first-time punter's luck, picked the winner. Twenty-one per cent of respondents, including someone called 'oneshoeonly', wanted a SAK. The next most popular amputation, at 14 per cent, was a DAK, with 'wantmyownstump' being first voter off the mark in that category. 'Stumplover' and 'looking2blimbless' were among the 11 per cent that wanted all four limbs lopped off, while least popular, with only one vote, was the quirky, asymmetrical SAE/SBE choice.

Most forum contributors talk cheerily about their kink or boringly about just about anything. But there was a poignant posting as well from a troubled man who was tiring of the drivel that dominated the forum.

> Ya know what pips me the most is the fact that here we have a real chance to connect with like-minded people and all that ever really seems to happen is pointless pics and file swapping.
>
> A one-sided BIID relationship has a tough time of surviving unless the hearts are truly there for the long run, and that's putting it mildly.
>
> Personally, I just want to start something REAL, and without

hiding my BIID from a potential partner. I refuse to drop such a fact on them well into a relationship when I have this chance to make it clear. I've seen it happen and it's a hard thing to deal with for all.

I want to do it right, from the start, with someone else who is in the same boat. Maybe then we can support each other and not just sink each other's ship when in deep waters.

All I want is a friend, a partner, a lover and consort. My other half.

I wondered whether the pun in his final sentence was meant to be funny.

12

THE SUBURBAN BROTHEL
WITH MARTIN

A 1960s orange brick building in Kogarah is where Martin and I meet next. There's a vet and a poodle parlour downstairs on the Princes Highway street frontage and Amanda's premises off the back lane, upstairs. Martin crosses the greasy concrete driveway ahead of me and, from behind, his head appears to be sinking into his body. He presses a button on the wall with a thick digit, a buzz releases the screened security door, and I follow him up the dimly lit stairs. They're thinly carpeted in grubby Berber and smell like Elastoplast, but as we reach the top that smell is overpowered by the fug of sickly scented candles.

Amanda, who's waiting in the hall, is attractive, in her forties, with tousled, streaked hair and a solarium tan. You can see the standard issue G-string, suspenders, stockings and half-cup bra through her black negligee. Where Mistress J was a bit intimidating, Amanda's warm and likeable.

In stark contrast to the rest of the shabby building, the first room off the hall is a sunny, renovated bathroom. We walk down a long, dark hallway, past a table with a red lava lamp and a mini sound system, and into Amanda's big 'play room' at the end of the corridor. I quickly scan the portable hanging rack of costumes but only have time to make out an adult-sized school uniform and a few feather boas.

She's concerned when Martin rejects her suggestion to have a shower.

'Are you *sure* you're clean? Okay, well if you'd just like to pay me now . . .'

He hands over $250 in cash and she leaves the room with it. When she comes back she wants to know what my agenda is and gets angry when I produce my recorder.

'Oh, I wish you'd have told me about this earlier!' She's quite nervy and looks like she might call the whole thing off. 'That's like bringing a video camera in here. I can't be recorded. I lead a double life and my voice is quite distinctive.'

I agree to put it away but, still not happy, she asks me to leave it outside the room. Now I'm worried someone might nick it once the door's closed but at least she's been appeased.

'Should I just sit here?' I ask, pointing to the beige vinyl sofa against the wall.

'Yeah, but I might get you to come over and have a closer look later.'

By now Martin's stripped down to his G-string. Amanda drops the negligee and tells him to caress her breasts, which are barely contained by her bra. When she pushes his head down so he can suck her nipples it starts to look a bit more like vanilla sex than the dominatrix thing, where he'd never have been invited to do that and would have been slapped if he tried.

She then tells him to bend over a massage table in the corner of the room and spanks him a couple of times, commenting on the butterfly tattooed on his right buttock.

'We're going to have a bit of bum play today, aren't we, babe? Did Martin tell you that we were going to do a bit of anal today, Sandra?'

'Yep,' I reply, not quite sure how to deal with the way she's keeping me involved. Mistress J ignored me as requested so I didn't have to say or do anything. Here I'm part of the conversation and hope I'm not being rude by giving monosyllabic responses.

'But it's not a bum, it's a *cunt*, isn't it, babe? And you're just a *slut*, aren't you?'

'Yeah,' Martin says, a little unconvincingly.

She makes him stand up, sucks his balls, then his dick briefly—*without* a condom. I'm horrified. She then tries to put a vibrating cock ring on him. His balls retreat again, just as they did when Mistress J tried tying them up, but she manages to get one of them through the buzzing contraption. He loves it. There's something of the nurse about her as she tells him to go and lie on the bed and prop himself up against the pillows. Her tone is kind rather than bossy, the whole dominatrix role quite obviously new to her.

She grabs her 'tool box' containing dildos, rubber gloves, lube, tissues and clamps, puts it on the bed and sits facing him with her legs open and threaded underneath his. My eyes are straining in the half-light so I come over to the side of the bed for a closer look. Rather than raunchy, bordello-like red satin sheets, this bed is made up with cheerful candy-striped cotton ones in turquoise, hot pink and white.

'Sit down on the bed here if you like, Sandra,' Amanda says as she lubes up a rubber glove.

I perch awkwardly on the edge of the bed, careful not to make contact with Martin, but I'm acutely aware I'm still within reach. This is bizarre. I almost feel part of a threesome.

'Just open your legs a bit wider for me, babe,' she says as she works a gloved finger into him. 'Ooh, you're still quite tight, aren't you, babe? Look here, Sandra, I'm just sticking my finger up his arse.'

Yup, that's what it looks like. Apparently there's no inventive sex-worker lingo for the old *finger up the arse* move.

Once she's sure he's sufficiently relaxed, Amanda takes a small orange dildo and a condom from the box with her free hand then asks for help.

'Hey, Sandra, could you just put a condom on this dildo for me?'

She registers what I can only assume is a look of horror on my face because she quickly stresses that everything's sterilised between clients. I'm uncomfortable with being so hands-on but she's taken me by surprise and she genuinely needs help. It reminds me of the way I've blindly complied with orders in other alien situations—like giving birth or dealing with mechanics—simply because my inexperience grants them authority by default. I'm also trying so hard to take all this in that I can't manage an argument. So I fumble with the serrated edge of the packet and roll the greasy sheath onto the toy.

Amanda tells me to come around to the other side of the bed so I can see the video silently running on a big screen near the bed; it's coming up to the bit where a lesbian reveals to her partner that she has a penis.

'That's *real,* y'know. It's amazing,' she says. 'I didn't know about those hermaphrodites until about a year ago. I mean, it's great now, she's making money, but imagine as a child. The poor thing!'

I'm now being Helpful Spice, fetching tissues, putting condoms on a double-ended dildo and a blindfold on Martin. I'm grateful he doesn't involve me and I still wish Amanda would cut it out. She shows Martin the double-ender and they decide it's too big for him so the double fuck she'd planned is abandoned. Instead she goes down on him, and within seconds he lets out a little warning moan. She stops sucking, sits up and pushes her palm against his penis and balls, urging him not to come. Too late. It's only twenty minutes into the hour-long session and he's quietly pissed off.

'Oh, babe, do you think we're going to be able to get you back up again?' she asks, stroking his belly and sides with broad sweeps. He looks at his watch. 'Don't worry, I'm not watching the clock,' she says.

Hauling himself off the bed Martin says, 'Yeah, well I am. I think we might call it a day.'

As soon as he trudges down the hall to the shower Amanda whips off her bra. 'Jesus, I *hate* wearing this stuff!' she says, releasing her breasts. She admits she should probably have given Martin a more passionate, active session but she's hurt her back. We chat about some of her weirder customers as she shows me a full-length hairy magenta coat that was given to her by a client with a mohair fetish.

This time I'm determined not to flee so I hang around to see how Martin behaves once he's out of the shower. He's completely normal, as unself-conscious as a child as he drops his towel and pulls on his little red undies, his G-string now packed away. He seems okay with Amanda but there's a slight distance and she tries to close it, perhaps to shore up a return visit.

Later that day Martin emails me to ask what I thought of today's session. He did this after Mistress J as well and I'd rather he wouldn't; I keep my answer fairly neutral, telling him it was 'interesting'. I think he wants to engage in a more detailed discussion but I don't want to risk turning him on.

He says he was disappointed he came so quickly but 'being watched by two beautiful women' was too much for him. That's a bit creepy because as far as I could tell he behaved as though I wasn't there. Although he obviously enjoyed being sucked off without a condom, he didn't like Amanda's lack of 'sexual sophistication'. He thought she was too 'prostitute-like', and there wasn't enough friendly banter or affection.

I'm fascinated by that. It's true, she was an attractive, friendly woman, but she wasn't sophisticated. The playful rapport he had with Mistress J, who was obviously much more his intellectual equal, was lacking with Amanda. And there was I thinking it was all about the sex.

13

CATHERINE AT THE CROSS

It's freezing and windy as I race from Kings Cross station up Darlinghurst Road for my appointment with Martin and Catherine. He'd decided to go on up to her apartment rather than wait for me on the street, and by the time I get out of the lift he's in the shower.

I'd actually chosen Catherine from two sex workers Martin described to me when he needed help deciding. Here were the options he emailed (from his *work* email address I might add!): *Catherine is very uninhibited and loves to experiment, is into multiple fantasies and fetishes, likes French and Greek* [which I took to mean oral and anal], *enjoys porn poses, has numerous toys, a mirrored bedroom and a digital camera.* Melissa is: *A wanton woman who likes to pour honey over herself and watch herself masturbate in front of the mirror.* Catherine sounded *much* more interesting.

Catherine looks like a corporate woman who hasn't quite finished getting dressed: black blazer, subtle makeup, pearl earrings, stockings, heels—just no skirt. She tells me she's a journalist from Melbourne and comes to Sydney every few months for sex work.

We sit down in the small lounge room while she smokes and reads the declaration she's asked me to bring, stating that I won't reveal her identity or reproduce the recording other than in text. This place looks nothing like a knocking shop—not that I'm an expert. It's an expensive one-bedroom apartment in a glossy nineties building, but it's grotty. Magazines and newspapers are stacked up all along the walls and heaped on glass-and-brass bookshelves. The cat has shed its fur on the corduroy armchairs and there seems to be a film of dust and fag ash on everything.

'Ooh! Naked man!' Catherine calls as Martin heads from the bathroom towards the bedroom.

'G'day, Sandra, how are you?' he says as I rat through my bag for my recorder. This is my third appointment with Martin and I still think it's weird chatting about weather and train delays with a naked man who's about to have his brains fucked out.

After Catherine's inspected Martin's penis and put a condom on him, they proceed to bonk in various positions, sticking dicks and digits into every orifice. Like some kind of PE teacher, she issues instructions throughout: 'Now, look at my boobs bounce while you're fucking me.' 'Don't open my legs too far or they'll break off.' 'Watch your fingernails!' and 'Different finger now!' as he swaps anal for vaginal poking. As she rides him she smiles at me, her expression more benign than lascivious, but I'd prefer to be ignored. She dismounts, lies on her back, and as he re-enters her she hands him the camera from the bedside table, already on the macro setting, to capture extreme genital close-ups.

Maybe I'm getting jaded after three sessions with Martin, but for all Catherine's spicy promise I felt the session, compared to previous ones, was a bit ordinary. When the sex is really kinky I find a clinical detachment that makes me feel like a researcher, not a pervert. But when it's more conventional, in a Freedom-furnished bedroom with practical built-in wardrobes, first I feel like I should give them some privacy and then I get bored.

I'm hugely impressed with Catherine's time management. Martin paid $300 for an hour *of her time* but only got half an hour of sex. She ran the session so efficiently, factoring in showering before and after sex and a little post-ejaculation breather for him (to the relaxing melodies of Wendy Matthews), that by the time she closed the door behind him she'd given him sixty minutes exactly.

Later that day Martin surprises me with an email of the digital photos from today's session—the least erotic images I've ever seen. The magnification spares us nothing, not even the tiny red shaving bumps on Catherine's fanny. His favourite shot is the blunt end of an orange dildo protruding from between his arse cheeks. Again, he wants to know what I thought of the session. I tell him that I could see he had a better rapport with Catherine than with Amanda but that I thought the session was a bit vanilla and not so useful for my research. He knows what I mean and says that although he enjoyed it, he would have liked a bit more pain.

A couple of days later, as though he's been issued a challenge, he emails me to ask if I'd be interested in watching him have sex with a trannie. I'm tempted but meanwhile he's made an appointment for us with Mistress Alicia.

14
FLICKING THE SWITCH
TO VAUDEVILLE

It looks as though Mistress Alicia has put her red wig on in a hurry this morning, neglecting to slide it back to sit flush with her natural hairline. She's only poked her head around the front door, concealing her black leather corset and stay-up stockings from passersby. She warmly, but swiftly, ushers me inside.

Alicia has a lilting, babyish voice that I find soothing and she nods reassuringly whether she's speaking or listening. Her heavily pencilled eyebrows are drawn a bit lower than they should be—to compensate for the wig placement?—and she's slapped her rouge on with a very heavy hand.

Martin is already in the bathroom awaiting his 'intestinal cleanse' so he can take a dildo. He's taken plenty of dildos without enemas before so either Mistress Alicia is particularly fussy or this is a bonus treatment.

She's clearly used to making guests comfortable and I feel safe and welcome. Asking me to wait in the 'dungeon'—the second bedroom off the corridor of this single-storey terrace—she slips away to attend to Martin. The cloying smell of incense nearly knocks me flat but I begin to suspect something's needed to mask some pretty foul odours in here. Apart from the usual bench, cage, rack and stocks there's a Perspex commode with a white plastic toilet seat. There's a hinged door in the front of it, presumably so the coprophiliac can stick his head inside and look up while Mistress shits from above.

It's been a while since this particular dungeon was decorated. Three walls are shabby duck-egg blue and the fourth is wallpapered in a floral regency stripe. Part of the fifties-style abstract carpet is covered with a cheap Persian rug and a bare light bulb hangs from the middle of the ceiling. The oddest item in the room, though, is spread on the four-poster vinyl bench: a crocheted Granny blanket, its multicoloured squares lending an oddly nursing-home feel to the room.

Alicia returns from the bathroom alone, leaving Martin there to deal with the after-effects of the enema. It proves a good opportunity for her to explain the psychology behind her job to me.

'I request that the men leave their external demeanour at the front gate. Once they've knocked on the door, the session has commenced and they're in that servile demeanour. A lot of them internalise those aggressive, extroverted characteristics that predominate during their day-to-day work and they come here to relinquish control.' Her smiling and nodding is contagious and I find we're both doing it now. 'It's the essence of supreme vulnerability at the behest of an imperious, dominant female that appeals to them. My attire is all part of the imagery, and imagery is *vitally* important.'

KINK

Sometimes it can take fifteen minutes or so for that external identity to be subjugated, she says. 'But I find that a rigorous, lascivious spanking gets that under control.' Smile. Nod.

When Martin knocks on the dungeon door, Alicia calls, 'You may enter!' As he bounds in, naked and intestinally cleansed, Alicia reverses out the door, promising, 'When I reappear, ladies and gentlemen, I shall be in dominant mode!'

Alicia's brief absence gives Martin and me a chance for a bit of small talk—my new haircut and parking difficulties featuring among the topics. Within minutes Alicia's back and she orders Martin to set things up.

'Now, slave, could you put that chair in the corner for our *esteeemed* observer?'

'Yes, Mistress.'

'Slave, has that candle gone out?'

'No, Mistress, it's still burning.'

'Oh, good. Well, here's another one to add to it.' She turns to me. 'Slave has requested that Mistress uses burning candles at some point. Oooh.'

When she's satisfied he's lit the candles properly and she has everything she needs to hand she says, 'And now, slave, you may position yourself in a suitably servile pose.'

He drops to his hands and knees but that's not sufficiently servile.

'Head on the floor, slave. Do you recall what Mistress said the word is, slave?'

'Yes, Mistress.'

'What is it?'

'"Mercy", Mistress.'

83

'Slave knows to utter the plaintive plea of "mercy" if at any time he finds my ministrations unpalatable.' She slaps him sharply on the bottom. 'Or–' slap '–too extreme' slap. 'Isn't that correct, my sweet?' Slap.

'That is correct, Mistress.'

She gets him to his feet, straps his hands to an overhead beam and attaches his ankles to a 'leg spreader'—a sturdy piece of wood with eye screws in each end for latching cuffs on to. She begins striking him lightly with a soft whip on the buttocks and back, then adjusts his position so he's giving me the full frontal. As usual, he doesn't make eye contact, for which I'm grateful.

She circles him like a bird of prey and turns to me. 'What I love about slave's body is that it is denuded of hideous pubic hair. Slave has a wax, the current vernacular being a back, sack and crack wax. Have you heard that? Isn't that superb!' Martin and I both laugh and she snaps, 'I wasn't addressing you, slave!' She starts fingering his chest. 'Another thing I love about this wanton slave's physique is his stunning nipples. They are plump, inviting and they *beg* Mistress for attention.'

Martin's knees almost buckle as Alicia sucks on each nipple in turn.

'I always commence a session in a sensual way and gradually intensify the severity of the activities, don't I, slave? Slave naturally craves the seductive sting of my luscious lash, don't you, slave?'

Alicia encounters the usual problem with Martin's retreating balls.

'There are times when genital bondage meets with success and there are times when it's just not viable, isn't that right, slave?'

Later, when she attempts to put him in the stocks for some nipple torture, she finds his thick neck won't fit. She locks his wrists in anyway, tells him to rest his chin on the top beam, and chooses her next weapon from a rack against the wall. She picks a couple of heavy silver balls the size of large plums which hang from serrated bulldog clips, and attaches them to his nipples. That lasts about a second and he's begging for mercy. But that's nothing compared to the agony she causes him later when, with an accidental tilt of her wrist, the gentle drip of candle wax onto the tender skin of his perineum becomes a torrent. He bellows like a wild boar and she backs right off.

I'm beginning to think that if you're into pain with your sex it has to be controlled pain and closely linked to erotic sensations. Accidents with candle wax or dildos are just as scary and unpleasant for a masochist as anyone else. This is so much about trust and vulnerability, albeit in pseudo form, and the game won't work unless safety is guaranteed. A slip-up signals danger and when that's real, it stops being fun.

You also consent, through prior negotiation, to a certain level of pain and, although you can rarely calibrate this exactly with a new sexual partner, any major deviations are obviously unwelcome. In *The Mastery of Submission*, John Noyes explains it like this:

> The masochist seeks controlled scenarios in which fantasies of being beaten and humiliated can be played out. This is something very different from wandering aimlessly into dangerous situations. The masochist makes sure that the

person who administers the beatings knows the rules of the game and knows when to stop.

Columbia University's coalition on bondage, domination, submission and sadomasochistic play, Conversio Virium, states that the very act of referring to any activity as BDSM defines it as being consensual. Any lack of mutual consent means the acts are sexual assault or rape. Abuse is no more likely to occur in BDSM relationships than it is in vanilla relationships, they add.

Apart from the occasional miscalculation, Alicia's performance is hilarious and she obviously relishes playing this role. She might not be as much of a comedienne with all her clients, but because Martin likes the tongue-in-cheek approach she turns the session into vaudeville.

Pushing a dildo up his arse she asks, 'Does Mistress give good enema, slave?'

'She gives good *everything*, Mistress.'

'Oh grovel, *grovel*, slave!'

15
A DYNAMIC DUO

I work myself into a lather of anxiety at the prospect of ring-ing April, a submissive who organises B&D parties for a couple, Graham and Rita, in Clovelly. I want to book a ticket for the next party but worry she'll ask me where I got her number. What if she clams up and won't speak to me? What if she tells others not to as well? I *always* do this and the waste of energy infuriates me. I ring, get her voicemail, but don't leave a message.

Next I stress out with all the same questions before I ring Graham's number. I've been told he's a lovely man who makes exquisite leather gear, hosts B&D parties for lifestylers but doesn't really get involved at them. I gather the leatherwork is a fetish for him. When he answers the phone I blather on about being a writer who's researching unusual sexual interests and fetishes and I'd heard about his interest in leather.

'Yes, I'm working on it about twelve to fourteen hours a day at the moment. It's quite an obsession!' he says. He's happy for me to interview him any time and we make an appointment for 2 pm this coming Friday. He's delightful, gives clear directions to his house and asks no questions.

Graham and Rita's house is a big scruffy two-storey place behind a high wall in the beachside suburb of Clovelly. I shove open the gate, wooden slats cross-braced with studded black metal, and knock on the door. While I'm waiting I notice the central feature of the front garden is a massive phallic cactus towering high above the wall. Everything else is a mishmash of plants and concrete sculptures.

Rita, a tall toothy blonde in her fifties, comes around the side and asks me to follow her down the path to the back. I'm nervous, but she gives me no reason to be. In the living room, Graham is sitting on a badly sprung leather sofa and he struggles out of it to shake my hand. He's sorting pieces for a 'bring, buy and swap' party on the weekend.

He looks like an old bikie—bald on top with the remaining grey hair pulled back into a long ponytail. But the vehicle parked out the front is not a motorbike—a burgundy Magna wagon is more his speed.

As Rita returns from the kitchen with strong tea in pottery mugs, Graham tells me that fourteen years ago they were complete bondage virgins. They went with friends to a party at the Threshold Club in Surry Hills, and got right into the scene for years. Their regular visits to this and other clubs uncovered sides of their personalities they didn't know were there. Rita said she thought she'd be a sub, but found in the scene she was 'getting a bit dommy'. Graham figured he'd be 'a top' because he was quite dominant in business, 'but I couldn't whip anybody'.

Rita still plays the domme for certain clients and one, a middle-aged legal professional, has an unusual kink.

'I get all dressed up in my elegant mistress look—long strappy black evening dress and stilettos—and give him the naughty schoolboy treatment. I give him a paddling, then a spanking, then a caning and, once he's had enough of that, I lean him over a chair on the lounge. Then I light a cigarette so he can see me, either directly or through the mirror, and I do it in a Greta Garbo kind of way.' She affects the star's imperious expression. 'And then I go behind him, I've got a glove on, and I spread his cheeks, put the burning end of the cigarette inside him and take a drag. Meanwhile, he masturbates and he gets burned. That's his thing. Then afterwards we sit down and have a nice old chat!'

'I've spoken to him and it takes him three months to recover,' says Graham. 'Rita should use one of my cigars and it'd take him *six* months to recover!'

Another of Rita's regular clients likes role-play with a murder theme, which Graham says has been much easier since an undertaker mate of his gave him two used body bags. Rita laughs as she describes what she does.

'The first time he came around, I shot him, the second time I killed him with a samurai sword and rubbed tomato sauce all over him. Both times I kicked him around the floor and I finally pushed him into the body bag. I said, "Oh good, I think he's dead now. He deserved it." And I checked to see if he was breathing. I love going through all the role-playing. Then I just zipped up the body bag, went out and left him there for a minute, came back and dragged him through the house and left him again for about five minutes. Then I came back and said, "How are you?" and he said, "Oh *thank* you, Mistress!"'

Until I started this research I'd always thought a whip was a whip, but not in Graham and Rita's world. On a rack in the spare bedroom are about thirty in fibres of different weights, strands of different lengths and studs of different density. Graham used to import human hair from 'Red China' in the fifties for whips, long before he tried BDSM himself, and I ask what the effect of these is.

'They don't really hurt but they can be nice and stingy all over. It depends on how you use them. It's really nice if you just get them with the ends and do the whole body,' Rita says.

'And if you wet the last few inches of the strands you get a sting with cold and wet,' Graham says, his mouth almost watering.

There's one with round strands of black rubber that look like liquorice and another with a thick, heavy handle and short strands that Graham calls a 'thudder' because the weight of the handle comes through on the stroke. They encourage me to squeeze handfuls of strands to get an idea of their impact on skin; the fibres' edges pressing into the flesh of your palm give a fair indication. The whips made of thick plastic strips that crackle like electricity scare me the most.

Graham hands me a medium-weight leather whip and urges me to try it out on him.

I refuse.

'Go on, it'll be fine,' he says, bending over, gripping his knees. 'Go as hard as you like. I won't feel a thing through the jeans.'

Okay, I should give this a shot. I swing the thing slowly in his direction, the strands flopping against the seat of his pants.

'Come on! Get into a rhythm! One side then the other!'

I stand back a bit and make a few slightly less pathetic, more rhythmic strokes while they tutor me on avoiding bony structures like spines and hips and vital organs such as kidneys. They both cry for more pace but I don't want to hurt him.

'Yes, you do!' Rita says. 'You're *loving* it!'

Well I'm not, actually. It's doing nothing for me, so I thank him and stop.

We spend the next half-hour or so going through the wardrobe looking at rubber dresses and platform boots, many of which belong to a friend, Chris, who likes to dress women up for parties. They have a close circle of friends from the scene and are particularly fond of Mat, a guy in his thirties so named because he likes women to walk on him; Pierre had mentioned him to me. We go downstairs and Graham points him out on 'the wall of shame', a collection of photos in the lounge room, and wants me to note how Mat's face becomes redder the longer he's walked on.

'Sometimes Mat will come round here and he and Rita will go down to Clovelly beach and within about five minutes he's got some woman walking on him! And he's such a quiet bloke.'

There was a similar case in sexologist Richard von Krafft-Ebing's 1886 text *Psychopathia Sexualis*. Krafft-Ebing, who defined hundreds of fetishes, including masochism and sadism, in this work described a man as 'a model husband, very moral, father of several children', who visited brothels to get his trampling. Like Mat, he liked a few women at once and would choose two or three of the largest, but he liked it altogether rougher.

> He bared the upper portion of his body, lay down on the floor, crossed his hands on his abdomen, closed his eyes, and then had the girls walk over his naked breast, neck and face, urging them at every step to press hard on his flesh with the heels of their shoes. Sometimes he wanted a heavier girl, or some other act still more cruel than this procedure. After two or three hours he had enough. He paid the girls with wine and money, rubbed his blue bruises, dressed himself, paid his bill, and went back to his business, only to give himself the same strange pleasure again after a few weeks.
>
> Occasionally it happened that he had one of the girls stand on his breast, and the others then turn her around until his skin was torn and bleeding from the turning of the heels of her shoes. Frequently one of the girls had to stand on him in such a way that one shoe was over the eyes, with its heel pressing on one eye, while the other shoe rested across his neck. In this position he endured the pressure of a person weighing about 150 pounds for four or five minutes.

It was believed by his doctor that he'd become impotent for sex with women, that this trampling was his equivalent turn-on, and that 'when the heels drew blood, he had pleasant sexual feelings, accompanied by ejaculations'.

Graham and Rita don't mention whether trampling is quite this thrilling for Mat and I'm reluctant to ask so they go on to describe another pal, Greg. He's in his late forties and, when he adopts his slave persona of 'Wendy', he's particularly useful after a party, Rita says.

'I often have slaves coming here to clean up. I get my feet rubbed. Last time Wendy was here she was dressed up in a girl's skirt, stockings, corset, blouse and a wig, and I had coffee made for me, my feet massaged, the phone picked up for me and brought over. Highfalutin guys, they want to be on their hands and knees, crawling.'

I get the impression Graham and Rita seem less interested in BDSM within their own relationship than they once were. They like the social side of the parties, the accessories and the money they make on door takings, and they're genuinely fond of certain players. But nowadays, between themselves, I suspect they can take or leave all that whipping caper.

It's time for me to go, but before I do Graham wants to give me a few accessories he's made: a thick black leather studded choker, leather earrings that look like tiny whips, which I love for their dangly elegance—one pair in black, another in red—and two pairs of earrings made from metal chain—one silver, one gold. Excellent. This has put quite a different complexion on my hitherto conservative jewellery collection.

While some people actually get turned on by the feel, smell and sight of leather clothes and accessories, leather is, as importantly, a way of signifying a person's sexual dominance, orientation or membership of a sexual subculture. It was appropriated from the biker culture by some gay men after the Second World War, and provided a suitably macho alternative for those who didn't fit with the camp, showtune-loving part of the community. It's also a good, durable material for whips.

Whipping's been popular for centuries though in the past it was considered more a treatment for erectile dysfunction than a masochistic kink. It was believed that whipping the buttocks could remedy flagging potency in older men, the idea being that it encouraged the coursing of blood through the veins and therefore was an effective way of attaining an erection. There's an eighteenth-century English copperplate, *The Cully Flaug'd*, which shows an elderly man, pants down, leaning over a chair and being whipped with a thick bundle of birch twigs by a young woman. It is captioned thus:

> What Drudgery's here! What Bridewell-like Correction!
> To bring an Old Man to an Insurrection.
> Jirk on Fair Lady Flaug the Fumblers Thighs
> Without such Conjuring th' Devil will not rise.

Two centuries earlier, English poet Christopher Marlowe described similar purposes for the practice.

> For his lust sleeps and will not rise before
> By whipping of the wench it be awakened.
> I envy him not, but wish I had the power,
> To make his wench but one half hour.

In John Cleland's *Memoirs of a Woman of Pleasure* (1748–9), Fanny Hill describes in some detail the service she provides to a client, Barville.

KINK

Seizing now one of the rods, I stood over him, and according to his direction, gave him, in one breath, ten lashes with much good-will and the utmost verve and vigour of arm that I could put to them, so as to make those fleshy orbs quiver again under them; whilst he himself seem'd no more concern'd, or to mind them, than a lobster would a flea-bit. In the meantime, I viewed intently the effects of them, which to me at least appear'd surprisingly cruel: every lash had skimmed the surface of those white cliffs, which they deeply reddened, and lapping round the side of the furthermost from me, cut specially, into the dimple of it, such livid weals, as the blood either spurt'd out from, or stood in large drops on; and, from some of the cuts, I picked out the splinters of the rod that had stuck in the skin … And at length, steel'd to the sight, by his stoutness in suffering, I continued the discipline, by intervals, till I observ'd him writhing and twisting his body in a way that I could plainly perceive was not the effect of pain, but of some new and powerful sensation.

So she suspects the flogging is turning him on, but still regards it as a physiological potency stimulant. She's confused though, because Barville doesn't fit the usual profile of men lining up for the service.

But what yet increased the oddity of this strange fancy was the gentleman being young; whereas it generally attacks, it seems, such as are, through age, obliged to have recourse to this experiment, for quickening the circulation of their sluggish juices, and determining a conflux of the spirits of pleasure towards those flagging, shrivelly parts, that rise to life only by virtue of those titillating ardours created by the discipline of their opposites, with which they have so surprising a consent.

Even though society tolerated the fondness for whipping in the eighteenth century, the fact that one needed it to aid potency was viewed as a weakness of the flesh and was therefore enough to make Barville wish he didn't. Fanny notes that Barville was in an 'habitual state of conflict with and dislike of himself for being enslaved to so peculiar a taste, by the fatality of a con-stitutional ascendant, that render'd him incapable of receiving any pleasure till he submitted to these extraordinary means of procuring it at the hand of pain'.

When the proprietress of an English flagellation brothel in London's Portland Place invented a stand 'to flog gentlemen upon' it was a licence to print money. Theresa Berkeley called her invention the 'Chevalet' or 'Berkeley Horse', and it looked a bit like a padded modern-day massage table except that it stood upright like a fold-out stepladder and not only had a cut-out panel for the face but two more aligning with abdo-men and groin; it was at these points that Berkeley's assistant, usually a younger girl, would provide pleasurable sensations to compensate for the pain administered by Berkeley from behind. There was a little ledge with recesses for the toes on which the customer stood and rings at strategic intervals down the side for fastening restraints.

Henry S. Ashbee, a Victorian cataloguer of pornography who wrote under the name Pisanus Fraxi, described in his *Index*

Librorum   Prohibitorum   (1877)   the   implements   Berkeley
employed.

> She had a dozen tapering whip thongs, a dozen cat-o'-
> nine-tails studded with needle points, various kinds of thin
> supple switches, leather straps as thick as traces, currycombs
> and oxhide straps studded with nails, which had become
> tough and hard from constant use, also holly and gorse and a
> prickly evergreen called 'butcher's bush.' During the summer,
> glass and Chinese vases were kept filled with green nettles.

Ivan Bloch, a German sexologist, quotes a letter from an 'ill-
behaved young man' who informs Berkeley of his impending
visit to London on parliamentary business. Word is out about her
'famous apparatus' and he offers her 'a pound sterling for the first
blood drawn, two pounds sterling if the blood runs down to my
heels, three pounds sterling if my heels are bathed in blood, four
pounds sterling if the blood reaches the floor and five pounds
sterling if you succeed in making me lose consciousness'.

Clients were clearly happy to pay generously for her services—according to Reay Tannahill, she made a profit of
£10,000 in eight years using the Berkeley Horse. But why
was it so popular? German physician and sexologist Magnus
Hirschfeld (1868–1935) believed it was a simple matter of conditioning, and cites the case of a man who fancied the rod ever
since he was caught masturbating by a sadistic governess, who
then beat his bare buttocks with a cane.

> It burned my behind like fire, but at the same time prick-
> led so pleasantly, so delightfully. And it was the blows that

did it; it had never been so nice when we masturbated ... Later, I noticed that the governess's hands, during my now regular chastisements, frequently strayed between my legs and stayed there.

This shows simply that sex can become linked with anything that brings it repeatedly to mind. And maybe there's a hereditary component to it. The famous composer and pianist Percy Grainger had a serious sadistic, as well as masochistic, streak and so had his father, John. A graduate of Westminster School, John had been regularly beaten and, as an adult, was frequently drunk and violent. That's when his wife, Rose, would chase him from the house with a horsewhip. The two divorced when Percy was eight, leaving mother and son to develop an extraordinarily close, neurotically protective relationship. Even with John gone that whip still came in handy; Rose would use it regularly on Percy if he tried to shirk his piano practice.

Percy began whipping himself when he was sixteen, the bloodstains on his shirts alarming his mother. And although he never developed into a criminal, he was obsessed with sex, pain and evil as he told a friend, Cyril Scott, in a letter in 1956.

The fact is that I really worship evil and find everything else un-worth while. But it may (nay, must) be said that all my worship of cruelty cruises only around sex-instincts. Apart from sex I am not such a bad fellow. But as I am really not interested in anything else but sex it just boils down to this: that I hardly think of anything but sex and that all my sex thoughts are full of evil and cruelty.

He fancied one of his pupils, Karen Holten, and wrote trying to persuade her to try getting whipped.

> You shouldn't have a single stitch of clothing on your body, but I, 'as a man', must be allowed to wear a shield for the tediously easily destroyed parts of a man's body. I think it must be furiously painful for you to be whipped on your breasts, don't you think?

She did end up submitting to him, as well as biting him as requested, but he wasn't happy with her technique. He later wrote telling her, 'It's good to roll or grind the teeth over already grasped flesh', and advised her to practise on herself.

It's extraordinary that Grainger ever managed to compose anything, let alone become one of the twentieth century's most prominent composers, given the amount of time he spent wallowing in thoughts of kinky sex.

> Everything that deals with sexual matters absolutely knocks me over. I love to simply wade and swim in a sea of over-wrought, ceaseless sexual thought. I feel the hot parched wind from the Australian desert has entered into my soul, and with a fury of heat I must go through, burning up myself and others. This is how I live, following my lusts, and composing now and then on the side. And no sadist can call life poor or disappointing who can realise his cruellest, wildest dreams.

He married a gorgeous Swedish artist and poet, Ella Strom, but his taste for whipping and his expectation that she participate meant that it was often a troubled union—it just wasn't her thing. He became increasingly obsessed with thoughts of incest, which might explain why Ella never bore him any children. He had written about these ideas to Karen Holten.

> I wish to procreate independent children ... I propose this: Never to whip them till they are old enough to grasp the meaning of lots of things, then say to them: Look here! I want to ask a favour from you kids. I want to whip you, because it gives me extraordinary pleasure. I don't know why it does, but it does ... Don't you think the children'd let me? I have hopes. Then encourage them to whip each other ... You know I long to flog children. It must be wonderful to hurt this soft unspoiled skin ... & when my girls begin to awaken sexually I would gradually like to have carnal knowledge with them ... I have always dreamed about having children & whipping them, & to have a sensual life with my own daughters.

Flagellation was a hard-wired kink with Grainger; he placed mirrors all around his bedroom so he could photograph the process from all angles. He then dated the images, noting the camera settings, and filed them along with explanatory notes in the hope that one day they'd be studied by scientists exploring the motivations of creative Australians. They're all there in a parcel in the Grainger Museum at the University of Melbourne, marked PRIVATE MATTERS—DO NOT OPEN UNTIL 10 (TEN) YEARS AFTER MY DEATH.

Another of Grainger's obsessions was sport, and he believed it served a similar purpose to flagellation.

KINK

I feel that flagelantism (like boxing, football & some other sports) is a means of turning the hostile, harsh & destructive elements in man into harmless channels. Much of civilis-ation consists of turning hostility into playfulness.

It seemed to work for him.

16
THE HALLS OF LEARNING

The ability of smells to transport you to the past is incredible. Stepping through the glass doors of Sydney University's Fisher Library for the first time in over twenty years and inhaling that warm, musty air rockets me back to my academically undistinguished university years in the early eighties. I'm here now to scour the shelves for volumes on sexual disorders and head next door to the quiet of the research library.

One volume with a particularly high comedy value is Clifford Allen's *Textbook of Psychosexual Disorders* (1969). Fellatio, it declares, is a perversion in both the giver and the receiver which stems from a fixation with breastfeeding. There's no acknowledgment that anyone might perform it simply to give pleasure to a sexual partner or that the partner may want it simply because it feels good. No, a woman performing fellatio has plainly 'regressed to an oral level'. And when a man submits to it 'it simply represents suckling at the breast'.

Allen has some pretty interesting ideas about gay men as

well. He says, 'It is difficult to understand why, for instance, homosexuals are frequently attracted to men in tight breeches until one realises that the buttocks beneath the stretched cloth represent breasts.' And a homosexual performing oral sex 'seems to have [the suckling at the breast] wish reversed. He turns round his wish and desires that someone should suckle at his breast (i.e. penis) … There is the possibility of course, that the passive protagonist of oralism in the case of a male submitting to fellatio, may be suffering from a very early fixation which occurred before the child had an opportunity of differentiating himself from the mother and that the lack of differentiation has caused this behaviour.'

Honest officer. I'm sure if Hugh Grant had explained that to the LA cops in 1995 they'd have let him off.

I end up reading about the daddy of all kinksters, the Marquis de Sade, and find that many of his sexual antics were driven by a pathological hatred of religion and author-ity, and a lust for the forbidden. He was also a spoilt brat, as this autobiographical passage shows: 'As soon as I could think, I believed that nature and fortune had joined hands to fill my lap with their gifts … It seemed to me that everything ought to give in to me, that the whole universe should humour my whims.' Being a brat and being sent to a Jesuit boarding school at nine could well have started the religious hatred which, according to writer Colin Wilson, made him 'one of the most consistently inventive blasphemers of all time'. But the late eighteenth century in France was a bad time to diss religion, as Sade discovered when he landed in jail for it, his first of many incarcerations.

It was 1763 and Sade, then twenty-three, had asked a twenty-year-old fan maker, Jeanne Testard, if she believed in God. When she told him she was a Christian he hit the roof. He declared he'd already proved there was no god by inserting a communion wafer into a girl's vagina before he had sex with her, then challenging God to avenge himself. God, apparently, didn't seem to mind. Just in case Jeanne wasn't yet clear on where Sade stood, he masturbated, ejaculating on a crucifix while cursing God, forced her to listen to him read atheistic poems for hours, and tried to persuade her to submit to sodomy. Finally, he made her promise to take communion with him the following Sunday, so they could pollute the hosts inside her.

Jeanne reported Sade. He was subsequently arrested, interrogated and imprisoned for two weeks, a light sentence considering the standard penalty for blasphemy at the time was death. Penitent letters encouraged his father, a count in the diplomatic service, to intercede on his behalf. He was freed but banished to the country.

Without recounting his entire life story, Sade spent many years in jail and asylums, mostly for sodomy. He was also partial to whipping, both giving and receiving, but this was common practice in the eighteenth century, when every brothel had a stash of birch rods and bondage gear. In his *Sexual Life of England*, Ivan Bloch points out that the English were so keen on flogging that it was known on the continent as 'le vice anglais'.

It was while Sade was in prison that he wrote the stories upon which his reputation for cruelty and evil was based, stories which were presumably fuelled by the sexual frustration of lengthy incarceration. And this is where things become absurd.

So keen was he to shock, to be the bad ass, and so dependent was his arousal on ever more forbidden pleasures, that his writings become, ultimately, comical. I find myself alternating between eye rolling and chuckling at the ridiculousness of it all. It's not enough for one of his novel's libertines to seek pleasure in the deflowering of a virgin. The virgin has to be a child. And it has to be done anally. By her father. Then ideally she should be shared around by her father's debauched mates and murdered when they've tired of her, preferably thrown onto a fire while they all laugh. And it gets sillier.

One of Sade's characters, a president of the court, tried to procure a little girl but her parents had rejected all his offers. The president then had the child's father convicted of an imaginary crime and sentenced to be broken on the wheel. In a bid to secure her husband's release, the mother brought her daughter to the president's house on the day of the execution, and the president got the mother to hold the child while he sodomised her during the execution, timing his orgasm to coincide with the moment the husband expired. He then threw open the shutters to reveal the execution scene. Mother and daughter both dropped dead, having been poisoned on arrival.

Other stories have characters blowing their victims' brains out as they orgasm and *Philosophy in the Bedroom*, an otherwise comparatively tame work about the corruption of an innocent girl, Eugenie, becomes preposterous at the end. The subtext, as he describes Eugenie's domineering mother coming to order her daughter home, is Sade's hatred of authority. One of the seducers tells the mother parents have no rights over their children and Eugenie tells her mother to kiss her arse. The mother is stripped, sodomised and whipped, after which Eugenie rapes her with a dildo, '... at one stroke, incestuous, adulteress and sodomite, and all that in a girl who only lost her maidenhead today'. Eugenie then proceeds to sew up her mother's vagina while the others have an orgy. Mother is then told: 'Your daughter is old enough to do what she likes; she likes to fuck, she loves to fuck, she was born to fuck—and if you don't want to be fucked yourself, the best thing is to let her do what she wants.' And with a few swift kicks, the mother is booted out.

Just when you feel his lengthy descriptions of orgies are getting a bit repetitive, with contorted bodies arranged layer upon layer, he digs deep and produces yet another taboo: an orgy in a graveyard surrounded by rotting corpses, a cannibal banquet of roast breasts and buttocks. This stuff might be more confronting if it wasn't so implausible.

Colin Wilson isn't moved either: 'All this is rather less horrible than it sounds, for the reader never ceases to be aware that this is merely a nightmare fantasy, a kind of Tom and Jerry cartoon in which no one is ever really hurt.'

Wilson describes Sade as being like 'some middle-aged hippie, or some rather old-fashioned member of the Dada-ist movement, convinced that he is still as shocking as ever, when he is in fact only slightly absurd.' I had fully expected the research library to turn up confronting material, maybe even some dreary stuff, but the ridiculous and the comedic came as a bit of a surprise.

17

SEX AND THE SUBURBS

I try April's mobile again to book my spot at the BDSM party scheduled for next weekend at Graham and Rita's. This time she answers but she's testy.

'It's *not* Graham and Rita's party. It's *my* party, at *their* place!'

Okay, already. Doesn't sound like much of a sub to me. She agrees to email me the details; I hope her mood improves before next Saturday.

hi Sandra

Drussup chris. the guy that dresses all the girls want you to call him. thanks hin. See you sat night.

April's email, although barely comprehensible, seems almost friendly. Sounds like Chris is looking for a new model and I've already seen some of his stuff in Graham and Rita's upstairs wardrobe. I call and he makes small talk at first. Then he gently broaches the question of whether I'd be interested in him dressing me on Saturday night. My wardrobe is sorely lacking in bondage gear so I'm prepared to consider it.

'I'm not part of the scene though, Chris, and I'm not prepared to wear anything too weird, with my tits hanging out or anything,' I say.

He assures me he's not into embarrassing anyone and asks me a few questions about my dimensions. When I say I'm five foot two he's surprised.

'Oh, so you're *short*!'

Okay, Chris, don't rub it in.

'It's just that you don't *sound* short.'

Together we decide that the thigh-high platform boots aren't going to be quite the look—they'd probably reach my crotch but don't look any good unless there's some exposed thigh *above* the boot. He says all I'd need to bring by way of clothing was a G-string and he'd supply the rest. When I tell him I don't own one he asks if I could get one before Saturday; it's vitally important because normal underwear is visible under the clingy latex outfits, he explains.

'Look, Chris, I'm not prepared to wear any outfit that'd be that revealing. I'll come a bit early, see what you've got and if there's nothing suitable I'll just wear my own stuff, okay?'

He agrees but is disappointed I'm not quite the model he anticipated.

When I get to Graham and Rita's, April is greeting people and collecting their money as they arrive. It's $25, which includes a buffet dinner and soft drink, but I don't want to pay the extra $10 joining fee which would give me discounts at the Hellfire

Club and bondage shops. I explain to April that this is a one-off for me, that I'm only here to meet a few people and do some research. She gently ticks me off for not letting her know about this beforehand. Rita's ready to defend me and April waives the joining fee.

Graham and Rita, in matching army camouflage gear, have already greeted me like a long-lost daughter, which may have helped get April onside. April's struggling to concentrate on anything much, let alone an argument, because a battery-powered crystal dangling from a headband is flashing right between her eyes; the ones hanging front and back from her padlocked chastity belt are giving her no grief at all. Otherwise she's wearing a long black negligee over a black bodice and fishnet stockings. She's not so much pear- as gourd-shaped, her stockings stretched to maximum tension over quivering, dimpled thighs.

By now it's about 8 pm, official start time, and I realise I haven't yet met Chris. Rita tells me he's upstairs watching the footy. I've already decided to stick with my normal clothes—black pants and wrap top with the whip earrings and studded collar Graham gave me—but thought I should meet Chris and thank him for his offer. I find him in front of the telly dressed from head to toe in black leather; if it wasn't for a very low side part and a comb-over he'd almost look cool. I tell him I'm happy in what I'm wearing and I notice a flash of disbelief on his face.

'Look, it's up to you, Sandra, but I've dressed heaps of women, all shapes and sizes. I've got this dress …'

The crowd is a mixture of ages, some in fetish gear, others who, like me, have just tarted up their normal clothes. A big, sexy young bloke in full leather and piercings is chatting with a couple in their forties about South Coast camping spots, the wife clearly nervous about being here and smiling a lot to compensate.

There are a couple of eskies filled with ice and budget soft drinks on one table and the booze brought by guests sits on another. I pour lemonade into a plastic cup and try to make conversation with a large American woman I see standing on her own. She makes no effort and doesn't seem to be at all impressed with this hokey suburban attempt at a BDSM party; Denver's hard-core offerings are more her scene apparently.

I'm rescued by Graham, who introduces me to Gloria, a baritone trannie in her sixties with Betty Grable curls. She's a sub, she says, has a mistress and has become a bit of a 'pain puppy' over the years. She's also a laugh and I could do worse than to hang out with her for the rest of the evening.

After dinner of barbecued chicken and pasta salads April taps loudly on a microphone to get our attention and runs through the rules of the evening. So far the atmosphere has been just like any friendly backyard barbecue and April's mundane 'housekeeping' announcements do little to change it. All 'games' are to be 'safe, sane and consensual', she says, and 'if anyone's giving you unwanted attention, you come and tell me and I'll sort them out. It's no use emailing me about it next week, I can't do anything about it then.' When she reminds everyone to clean any toys they've used before putting them back, Graham calls out not to worry, he'll do it in the morning.

She spots me scribbling notes and gets me up to explain my presence to the assembly. First she tells everyone that I'm a writer researching a book and that I'm not to approach anyone. I take the mike and stress that I have no interest in blowing anyone's cover by using real names or identifying features, but that I'd like to chat with anyone who feels like it.

Whether my presence is the kiss of death or the party is going to be on the quiet side anyway I'll never know, but this was feeling like a dud. I wander inside with Gloria to escape the cold and more people start arriving.

Tracy, a slave girl in her twenties wearing a pink latex halter top and black mini, is led into the room on a dog leash by her body-builder master, Adam. From her dog collar hangs a disc engraved *Anal Fuckbitch*. They tell me their master/slave relationship is 'twenty-four/seven', that they're total lifestylers and that she can't even go to the toilet without first asking his permission.

'If he says no, then tough,' she says, smiling.

The impracticality of this is staggering enough, but when she says they don't even live together I *really* think they're nuts.

She chats happily enough, admitting to peeing occasionally without phoning first for his permission when she's at work, but his quiet presence on the end of the leash is threatening. She glances at him, his eyes narrow, and I worry she's going to get a belting if she says anything out of line. His latex waistcoat strains against his huge pecs and his shoulders are disfigured by a spaghetti of bulging veins. It's not till he drops the leash to go outside that I notice his tiny matching shorts would fit a toddler.

I try to keep a neutral expression when I ask her why she enjoys this relationship, which includes her master choosing all her clothes, hairstyles and makeup and her doing *everything* he demands, including his housework. She feels safe with him, and after a hard day at the office she likes not having to make any decisions for herself, she says.

'I really like to serve, anyway, so it isn't difficult for me when he points out things I have to do.'

Most people I've met have no idea where their particular sexual tastes come from but she thinks being brought up in a strict Christian family was the key to hers.

'When I was a teenager I had constant sexual fantasies about being forced to have sex and being raped. It was the only guilt-free way I could think about sex because I wasn't choosing to have it.'

Adam, who has now come back inside and picked up the leash, is less aware of why he's so dominant.

'I've always been sexually dominant,' he says, minutely thrusting his compact pelvis as he speaks. 'I dunno why I feel the need to grab a woman by her hair, throw her down and tell her she's a fuckin' bitch. I've just always been that way.'

They invite me to one of their parties the following Saturday night but warn me they're 'hard-core'.

'If people feel like fucking, they just fuck,' he says.

Graham, on the other hand, discourages people from actually having sex at his parties: 'I don't want people thinking this place is some kind of *brothel*,' he says.

I'm not free the following weekend but tell them I'd like to go to one of their parties in the future, especially when they tell me they have lots of adult babies as regulars.

'Oh yeah,' Tracy says. 'We have the whole garage set up as a nursery with playpens and change tables. I can't change nappies though 'cause my nails are too long.'

After about an hour Adam rigs a thick chain up high across one end of the room and Tracy reaches up to hold on to it with both hands. People have started to gather around the edges of the slate-floored room in anticipation and Tracy, her back to the crowd, tries to find a comfortable stance in her platform shoes. Adam selects a thick black leather whip with a fringe that's only a couple of feet long from Graham's collection and starts a slow, rhythmic flogging. He works his way from the back of Tracy's legs, up over her bottom and across her shoulders. When someone calls out that he's not really trying he smiles and says he's 'just warming her up'.

He pauses to pull her top open and gives her breasts a quick, rough knead. After a few heavier strokes of the whip he pulls up her skirt, rips her G-string off and theatrically chucks it aside. The latex skirt stays put, leaving her bottom exposed for the next round.

Everybody moves further back when they see he's now going for the studded three-metre whip. The sheer volume of strands scattered with pointed studs make it too heavy even for Adam to wield with one hand. He gradually picks up pace, alternating from her left to her right in a figure-eight action while she moans softly, gripping the chain. About ten minutes later he stops, yanks her head back by her hair and rams his tongue down her throat. Maybe this is her reward, a deep, passionate kiss, but it looks more like another act of violence. She lets go of the chain, pulls the skirt down over her throbbing bottom and rearranges the latex halter to cover her breasts. She's badly shaken and steadies herself on the door frame before tottering into the kitchen.

She re-emerges within a couple of minutes looking less wobbly and holding a small hammer. Attended by another guest, dressed courtesy of Chris in a leather face mask, black corset and fishnets, Tracy rips open an alcohol swab from a tray of surgical paraphernalia and wipes it over Adam's shoulders. He adopts an awkward brace, bent forward, legs spread with arms clenched in a circle in front. He'd told me earlier about his needle fetish, which began with a childhood vaccination from a buxom nurse, and I'm half hoping Tracy will whack a few rusty six-inch nails into him. But it's all show. I doubt Adam, gritting his teeth and flinching, can feel anything as Tracy gingerly taps one fine acupuncture needle after another into him.

By 11 pm I've spoken to a married couple who hold swingers parties, marvelled at a tweedy couple in their fifties who look more like they should be hanging around the corridors of Sydney Uni than at a bondage party, and watched another flogging. (This time the flogger, a handsome academic, was a masochist who was only doing it so the flogee would return the favour.) Most people I chat to say they're switches—those who'll take either the dominant or submissive role—but one girl said after a couple of years she is now over pain altogether, both dishing it out and copping it. Her boyfriend, a lovely American in his twenties, likes tying girls up, and says the reason he particularly likes April's parties is because of 'the awesome food'.

The ordinariness of most of these people has surprised me and, while the conversation's been okay, I'm disappointed there's been so little action. I stifle a yawn when the masochist bails me up and offers to answer any of my questions. I politely ask a few, including what he looks for in a sadist partner.

'Oh, just the usual stuff, you know. She has to be slim, pretty and vivacious.'

I'm over this, so I take his email address for later.

Stepping past a guy demonstrating a machine that gives mild electric shocks to sensitive parts of the body, I find Graham and Rita to say goodbye. Rita hugs me, telling me she can see me fitting right into the BDSM scene, and urges me to come to another party. Graham looks at my cleavage, mutters, 'Too much bare flesh,' and drags me over to a rack containing more elaborate dog collars. He rifles through them, rejecting those he thinks are too dangerous or spiky, and insists I take one with heavily studded leather and graduating lengths of silver chain hanging from it. I may not be into the scene but I *love* the jewellery.

18

BLESS ME, FATHER, FOR I HAVE SINNED

There's been a recurring theme in my research so far—the role religion has played in people's kinks. Martin, who'd been brought up in a strict Catholic household, said 'the more forbidden the fruit the tastier it was' when describing his first sexual encounters. Tracy, the submissive slave girl—another Christian—entertained rape fantasies because it was the only way she could think about having sex without feeling guilty. And if Sacha, the auto-fellation expert, hadn't been so darn flexible he'd have been crippled by Catholic guilt over his private contortions in the bathroom.

There's an intriguing theory about all this that says religion, when people took it seriously, kept things pretty tame and fetish-free, and once it began to be questioned and undermined in the eighteenth century, coincidentally the century of Sade, it just gave people something to rebel against which in turn spiced things up. In fifteenth-century Venice, when religion still

held some significant sway, fornication was a crime and homosexuals could be burned alive, but there was no record of *sexual*
masochism, sadism, exhibitionism or anything else particularly
kinky. There was flagellation, but it was considered a religious
practice—we'll get to that.

In *The Misfits* Colin Wilson quotes *The Boundaries of Eros*
(1985), where Guido Ruggiero examines sex crimes and sexuality in fifteenth-century Venice, and deals with the sexual
misbehaviour of priests, monks and nuns, and people who
committed fornication in church.

> A man who had made love to a girl under the organ was
> reproached with having 'too little considered the injury and
> offence which he occasioned to our supreme creator.' It
> becomes clear that, although the Venetians were far from
> prudish, they took sex crimes seriously (ie incest, seduc-
> tion of children, rape) *because it might land the perpetrator in
> Hell.* Sodomy was a sin because it was condemned in the
> Bible. But we also note that seduction was considered more
> grave if it took place between an aristocrat and a member
> of the lower orders. That is clearly why there was so little
> 'perverted' sex crime in Renaissance Venice: because both
> social and religious taboos were so powerful.

By the time the eighteenth century rolled around we start
seeing accounts of a monk paying two prostitutes to make him
up and dress him as a woman, and power becoming linked to
sexual pleasure with noblemen using their servants in sexual as
well as domestic service.

According to Colin Wilson the connection between sexual

deviation and the religious climate became clear in the famous 'Affair of the Poisons', which occurred in the reign of Louis XIV.

It was revealed that priests had performed black masses and sacrificed babies. The king's mistress, Mme de Montespan, had allowed her naked body to be used as an altar, with a chalice on her belly, and a baby's throat was cut over the chalice and the body thrown into an oven. Another of the king's mistresses came to make a charm, accompanied by a man; the officiating priest got the man to masturbate into a chalice, then mixed the sperm with the woman's menstrual blood. It is clear that the idea of blasphemy had come to play an important part in the orgies described at the trial in the 'Chambre Ardente' (candlelit chamber). Religion no longer commanded the awestruck respect it had enjoyed in the Middle Ages, but it still had enough power to make wickedness seem more deliciously sinful. So it became a kind of aid to orgiastic sexual behaviour.

Wilson argues that while there was little evidence of sexual fetishes prior to this time, whatever kinks existed weren't the subject of shame. The obsession of eighteenth-century gentleman George Selwyn with executions was widely known, particularly as he rarely missed a hanging at Tyburn, the notorious London gallows. Wilson notes:

It was striking that Selwyn made no secret of his morbid fixation. When Lord Holland lay dying, he told his butler: 'If Mr Selwyn calls, show him in. If I am alive I shall be pleased to see him, and if I am dead he will be pleased to see me.' Selwyn's necrophilia was obviously talked about quite openly, as a rather amusing peculiarity. It was not until the nineteenth century that such little oddities became a matter for shame and concealment.

Indeed prior to the nineteenth century masochism, which came in religious, rather than sexual, packaging wasn't a matter for shame and concealment. On the contrary. One of Freud's pupils, Theodor Reik, wrote the first major study of masochism in social life. In *Masochism in Modern Man*, he describes the need of masochists to demonstrate their suffering to the outside world.

> The martyrs of early Christianity attached a strikingly great importance to the fact that their suffering *ad majorem Christi gloriam* was seen ... A French passional of the 15th century contains a naïve confession of masochistic enjoyment and the demonstrative character that goes with it ... A direct line leads from such behaviour to the performances of the Hindu fakirs and the Mohammedan dervishes with their self-tortures.

In 1902 Ivan Bloch wrote that masochism and sadism were 'closely linked in religious flagellantism', which he believed was a universal, anthropological phenomenon. To support this perspective, he refers to 'such masochistic religious acts performed by women as scraping the phalli and eating the parts scraped off', as well as women eating the faeces and drinking the urine of holy men in India.

There are many proponents of the argument that masochism is universal, its general thrust being that almost all cultures have repeatedly attached some kind of moral value to pain, often as part of a religious experience. The value placed on pain may vary between cultures, but the common notion is that pain possesses at least some positive ethical quality. In his 1987 work *Aspects of Pain*, Ernest Kern claims that all societies have seen the individual's ability to deal with pain as a measure of his or her belonging to the group and cites examples from ancient Sparta through to mediaeval flagellation.

Perhaps, though, it was the very religiosity of flagellation that provided a respectable cover for something that was operating on an altogether kinkier level. Surely if it was purely religious the church would have had no reason to object to the practice and yet it did, frequently. Havelock Ellis wrote that the link between religious flagellation and perverted sexual motives saw it condemned by the Inquisition, which prosecuted priests who prescribed it for penance, personally whipped anyone, had it inflicted on a stripped penitent in his presence, or made a woman penitent discipline him. In the eighth century Pope Adrian IV forbade priests to beat their penitents, and in the thirteenth century, when church-sanctioned whippings had reached epidemic proportions, Clement VI issued a bill against them.

The other important development between the time of Sade and that of sexologist Richard von Krafft-Ebing and *Psychopathia Sexualis* was that people had learned to use their imagination. It makes sense: without imagination you could not get excited simply at the thought of frilly underwear. It is the imagination that associates the underwear with the woman and her sexual parts and, through conditioning, itself becomes the source of arousal.

Krafft-Ebing had a patient who could only make love to a woman if she was fully clothed in a silk dress, petticoat and corset; a naked woman or one in a nightdress did nothing for him. He explains the case like this: 'The reason for this phenomenon is apparently to be found in the mental onanism [masturbation] of such individuals. In seeing innumerable clothed forms they have cultivated desires before seeing nudity.'

Colin Wilson elaborates by suggesting imagination and sexual frustration had combined to 'imprint' their own idea of a sexually exciting female on the mind.

> This then seems to provide a plausible answer to the question, what happened between 1740 and 1840 to cause such a proliferation of sexual deviations? The answer is that human beings learned to use the imagination far more than in previous centuries. *They learned to day-dream.*

The zeitgeist must have been right because it was in 1740 that a printer named Samuel Richardson wrote what is now recognised as the first modern novel, thus harnessing the power of daydreams. The story, *Pamela*, was about a young servant girl whose master tries everything to seduce or rape her—leaping on her out of a cupboard as she is undressing, getting a procuress to restrain her while he tries to ravish her—before surrendering to her virtue and leading her to the altar.

'For readers of the eighteenth century—accustomed only to picaresque novels and "true narrations" like *Don Quixote* and

Robinson Crusoe—the impact of this sexual realism must have been stunning,' writes Wilson, who argues that when imagination was applied to sex the result was the rise of pornography—and of 'sexual perversion'. Once they got the hang of it, people realised they could vary the intensity of their sexual response by using their imagination, as this 1793 passage from *Visions of the Daughters of Albion* by William Blake shows:

> The moment of desire! The moment of desire! The virgin
> That pines for man shall awaken her womb to enormous
> joys
> In the secret shadows of her chamber; the youth shut up
> from
> The lustful joy shall forget to generate & create an amor-
> ous image
> In the shadows of his curtains and in the fold of his silent
> pillow …

So it was during the eighteenth century, thanks to literature, that people began to use their imaginations—but it wasn't until the nineteenth century that Krafft-Ebing defined and documented the kinks that resulted from it.

Wilson observes that none of the 'sexologists' recognised the obvious fact that most of the perversions they were writing about dated from their own century. Krafft-Ebing was inclined to obscure this by talking about the sadism of the Roman emperors, or the widespread immorality of the seventeenth and eighteenth centuries, Wilson notes, yet most of the cases in *Psychopathia Sexualis* are unique and are a result of imagination producing new and strange varieties of perversity. We read of a man who masturbates while caressing a furry dog, of a man who wanted to be masturbated by a prostitute with mud on her fingers, of a girl who wants to perform anilingus on old men ... the variety is due to the fact that the imagination is free to choose what will produce sexual satisfaction. And before the 19th century, men had simply not learned to use their imaginations in this way.

I'm not so sure about this. I think the reason the perversions dated from Krafft-Ebing's own century was just as likely to be because he was writing contemporary case studies about his own and other sexologists' living patients. The thing about this evolution that delights the atheist in me is the way religion seems to have encouraged kinks and, by making them sinful, has made them more fun. There's a satisfying symmetry about the role of imagination in kink formation as well; after all, what is religious faith without the ability to conjure a view in the absence of anything concrete?

19

SPRUNG

Today I drop my bundle. Martin's found out who I am and where I live. A friend, Roger, had been drinking with a bloke at a Paddington pub who told him he'd been helping a journalist with her research for a book on sexual fetishes. This man told Roger that the journalist said her name was Sandra but he'd found out it was really Stephanie Clifford-Smith and she'd written a book on Bernard King.

I want to vomit. I have no idea how he traced me but can only assume it was through my number plate. He works for the army so maybe he has mates in intelligence.

After a few hours of nausea and jitters, I decide if any of the people I've interviewed for this research had to know who I was I'd rather it be Martin than anyone else. But the fact he's investigated who I am has overtones of stalking and it does change my view of him a bit.

Anyway, since then he's gone to ground. When Roger told him he also knew me Martin probably had a quiet freak as well, realising that his snooping was going to get back to me. He might also have realised that I do have rather a lot on him and that it would only take a call to his wife and things could get very ugly. He's not to know I'd never do it.

I haven't followed up for our date with the trannie.

It's been nine months since I heard Martin had discovered my identity and my initial fears that he was going to turn out to be a stalker have proved unfounded. I haven't heard from him in all that time and the relief I felt for the first few months has mellowed into curiosity about how he worked it out and what he'd been up to. So I email him to ask, and he says he was looking for a book on Bernard King and saw my photo on the publisher's website. It strikes me as a bit implausible because I really didn't pick him as the Bernard type—despite his penchant for bum play—but then my original theory that he'd tracked me down through military intelligence was pretty stupid too. Not that he'd have admitted to it if that's what he'd done. In the absence of anything better I'm giving him the benefit of the doubt.

Anyway, Martin's been having a rough time since I last saw him. He's been hospitalised with depression and diagnosed with bipolar disorder, conditions which he blames for his 'sexual recklessness'. I had thought it risky the way he used to email me from his work account to ask which sex worker we should visit. He says he's behaving quite differently now that he's on a stable drug regimen and only strays from the marital bed occasionally.

Sometimes the need (much like a drug addict's I imagine) gets too overpowering and I succumb but suffer no guilt afterwards. I have come to terms with the fact that my behaviour sexually is part of who I am and that I can modify but not completely control my indulgences, he writes.

I've barely touched this project for the past year. The first fly in the ointment was Martin finding out who I was. The second was that I was frankly sick of talking to people about their sex lives. It didn't matter what they were up to, it was all so tedious.

Even the discovery of another fetish—thick spectacles— is only mildly diverting. Some people like the look of others wearing them and others want them for themselves. There's a website with pictures of bespectacled women, fully clothed, smiling for the camera. No bedroom eyes or soft lighting. They're ordinary portraits shot in cafés and shopping malls. If the distortion of the cheek at the frame's edge is obvious that's considered particularly hot.

If I thought this project was going to change my status of being officially unshockable I was wrong. Or maybe I'm just officially unshockable *and* officially slack.

Anyway, with the next Hard Core Heaven party looming I've turned my attentions back to my research and joined a few kinky sex websites. I'm hoping the HCH party in ten days won't be a rerun of the dreary BDSM soiree I went to in Clovelly last year; it's the promise of adult babies that's dragging me up to Sydney's leafy North Shore for this one.

Coincidentally, as I was standing in the kitchen browning lamb shanks last Saturday night Darren called. I had spoken to him over a year ago and found him pretty uninteresting.

He said he had lots of female friends into sex with dogs but couldn't find one willing to speak to me. He told me I should ring them and get information by pretending I wanted instructions because if I was upfront about an interview they wouldn't talk. I refused and thought that would be the last I heard from him. He was beginning to irritate me anyway.

So he rings me again wanting to know how the book's going and says he has a friend who *will* talk to me. At last, a useful connection. The problem with Darren is he wants to go on and on and *on* about what a turn-on it is watching these women fuck their dogs and I'm trying, first, to get the shanks into the oven and, second, to remain polite and not reveal the nature of the conversation to the rest of the household. David, by the way, is no more tolerant of this research than he was a year ago. It's such a bummer. Yesterday, as we were leaving the art gallery, I wanted to point out a park bench where Darren said he'd been sucked off by a stranger in nothing but an overcoat last winter, but I knew he wouldn't want to hear it.

20

I LIKE MINE CANINE

Kellie, a receptionist, is in her mid-forties, has two kids and a miserable, sexless marriage. And until her dog Robby died recently, she liked having sex with him.

'I remember in high school hearing about some girl who got sprung with a dog licking her pussy and I thought, That's just rubbish. Being the naive person I was I didn't think that would ever come into anyone's realm of thinking and never thought about it again.'

Her first sexual encounter with Robby, a cattle dog cross, was an accident. She was at the computer, wearing headphones, chatting to a guy in the US and masturbating when Robby stuck his wet nose into her crotch and licked her. She'd had Robby ten years and he'd never done that before. She squealed.

'The guy on the internet wanted to know what had happened and when I told him he said, "Let him." There was a moment of "will I or won't I" but I did, and it was one of the greatest orgasms I've ever had. Much more intense than with a guy.' She said the experience 'tweaked a devilment' in her and she couldn't let it go.

'I think it was the sheer naughtiness of it in my mind and the fact that dogs have amazing tongues, and I was sharing it with someone online.'

After a few repeat performances with Robby licking her until she came, Kellie began to feel guilty that she was the only one getting anything out of the relationship.

'I didn't know anything about canine sex so it was a bit of self-discovery with me and the dog. So I wanked him off and he seemed to like it, and it progressed from there to me performing oral sex on him. I stopped short of him mounting me because I was scared. I didn't know what would happen, it was unknown territory and I couldn't control it. I was worried that if he got stuck and someone found me, it wouldn't be an easy thing to explain.'

Yuck! Bestiality qualms aside, didn't she think sucking off a dog might taste disgusting?

'Oh God, yeah! It was very tentative. Luckily he was very placid and just lay there and let me play. I tasted it on my finger first and it didn't really have much of a taste, it was fine. And when I knew he was about to come I almost pulled my face right away because I thought if this tastes disgusting and I gag then that'll be the end of it, but actually it has a really nice neutral flavour, it's not like a guy's at all. Dog cum is really runny, quite clear and it's really hot.'

At this point I realise I am no longer unshockable. Fellating a dog is something I'd never imagined, let alone discussed with someone who'd done it. But back to the animal lover herself.

Kellie works part time and is regularly at home alone during the week. She's now had time to research sex with dogs and she's no longer worried about getting stuck. She's likely to choose a Labrador-sized dog to replace Robby and she's looking forward to full penetration when she gets him.

'When Robby died I just felt a little bit lost and I didn't know how to go about doing it with another dog. I'm just not sure if I want to have sex with someone else's dog. It's a really stupid thing to be even considering but I'd prefer it to be my own. My girl dog will lick me but she's not really interested, it's too much of a hassle for her, whereas he was always keen, you know?

'I can tell you now I will not be in this marriage for too much longer and I will not have another relationship that doesn't include K9; I want it part and parcel of the relationship.'

Negotiating that will be her next big challenge but she knows the internet will be vital.

'This is the hard part; it's seeking people out who are like-minded. It's a very guarded world to get into anyway; people don't open up unless they're very sure of you. It makes it really hard to crack in, but it'll happen. I wouldn't have discovered K9 sex without the internet and then I wouldn't have been able to learn more about it without the internet—it's not something that comes up in my circle of friends, I can tell you.'

There are practical reasons for Kellie wanting a human partner involved in her canine sex.

'It's really quite an awkward thing to do on your own, especially when you're a novice. There are lots of angles and it's a bit of a workout. I let Robby up on me once and he'd thrust a bit but I stopped him because the thought of him getting stuck was just overwhelmingly terrifying. Coordinating bits is really hard, depending on how tall you are and how tall the dog is and whether it can get in close enough—some dogs don't have that natural ability to know where to put it. That's why having someone with you is the ideal way to go, someone who shares your love of K9 sex.'

Although her arousal isn't dependent on canine involvement, it certainly helps—even if the dog itself isn't there.

'I had a guy come up from Sydney recently and we played with dog cum, which was really nice. He'd brought it with him in a little bottle. Just knowing it was K9 cum was a big turn-on for me and the fact that I was so turned on turned *him* on, so it was a nice play, you know?'

Once they'd worked themselves into a lather over the contents of the bottle they had sex.

Kellie's confident this fetish is here to stay and she'll always want to do it with dogs.

'The adrenalin rush was so strong that I can't ever see me not wanting to feel that again. It'd be like feeling an orgasm and never being allowed to feel one again. It doesn't harm anyone else. I'm not out there in society causing problems for anyone else. I'm sure there's a lot of it that goes on that's not spoken about.'

It's little wonder Kellie was so secretive about her dog lust given that having sex with animals is a jailable offence in many places and, even where it isn't, it's widely viewed with abhorrence. But it wasn't always thus.

In Greek mythology gods often appeared as animals to have sex with humans, which suggests the relationships weren't totally outlawed. Beyond mythology, the notion is reinforced in classical works such as Aelian's *On the Characteristics of Animals*, written around AD 170, a work that was regarded as a scientific treatise. He tells of a groom who falls in love with a mare, consummating the 'strange union' and continuing the relationship until the mare's jealous foal kills him. Then there was the goat herder who fell for the prettiest goat in his flock and 'under an erotic impulse' lay with her. But it wasn't just, er, animal lust—he was quite the romantic, bringing her sweet herbs 'to make her mouth fragrant for him if he should want to kiss her'. The love affair ended tragically when an angry billy goat killed the herder, and this is where Aelian's moral lies: watch out for jealous animals, they can be just as danger-ous as jealous humans. There was no suggestion that sex with animals was a bad idea in itself. In fact the neighbours didn't have a problem with the herder's amorous ways; they deified the man-faced goat that issued from the union, then built the herder a fine tomb.

The many examples Aelian gives of sexual relationships between humans and animals indicate the classical view that animals are very like people in that they experience the same emotions—love, anger and jealousy—and have the same aes-thetic appreciation of beauty, even if on occasion that ideal is set aside for a less attractive partner. He tells the story of a seal who fell in love with an ugly diver, the moral being not to be surprised at this, because even people sometimes fall in love with ugly people.

The power balance was often in the animal's favour, he believed. 'Baboons and goats are lecherous, and … have intercourse with women … And even hounds have assaulted women … One woman in Rome was accused of adultery and the adulterer was a hound. Baboons are wanton and have fallen madly in love with girls and have even raped them.'

When he writes about men and boys being the object of an animal's affection he doesn't specify the animal's gender, leaving open the possibility that some of these affairs were homosexual. And there's no end to the diversity of animals likely to fall for a human according to Aelian.

> I am told that a dog fell in love with Glauce the harpist. Some, however, assert that it was not a dog but a ram, while others say it was a goose. And at Soli in Cilica a dog loved a boy of the name of Xenophon; at Sparta another boy in the prime of life by reason of his beauty caused a jackdaw to fall sick of love.

In classical times the perceived boundaries between humans and animals were so blurred as to be non-existent; gods could appear as animals without diminishing their power, and stories about the births of human–animal hybrids had a tone of the unremarkable about them. So when the early Christian church fathers wanted to outlaw these intimate relationships, they had to set about shaking off the classical heritage. The Bible, specifically Leviticus, left the reader in little doubt about the church's views: 'You shall not lie with any beast and defile yourself with it, neither shall any woman give herself to a beast to lie with it: it is perversion.' And if you needed a better reason not to do it than wearing the taint of perversion, Leviticus had one for you: 'if a man lieth with a beast, he shall surely be put to death: and ye shall slay the beast.'

There were three main precepts behind the early Christian legislation against bestiality, apart from the desire to distinguish between animals and humans. First, bestiality was seen as disturbing the natural order of the universe, a theme which Leviticus extends beyond sex with animals all the way into fashion advice: 'Ye shall keep my statutes. Thou shalt not let thy cattle gender with a diverse kind; thou shalt not sow thy field with mingled seed; neither shall a garment mingled of linen and wool come upon thee.'

Second, if Christians were to have sex, they had to be trying to make babies, not just having fun, and bestiality violated the procreative intent. So, incidentally, did masturbation, oral and anal sex, incest, adultery and rape.

And third, you could say goodbye to those cute satyrs, centaurs and minotaurs of classical times; Christian thinking held that the offspring of unions between humans and animals were monstrous, evil in themselves, or at least portentous of it. Anyone breaking the rules faced strict penalties; if you were under twenty it was fifteen years' penance for you, twenty-five years for married people over twenty, and if you were married and over fifty, you had to wait until the end of your life to receive communion. The eastern Christian rules in Greece weren't nearly as harsh, settling the matter with the occasional reprimand.

But while laws of varying severity spread across Europe, there was no reason to think it put anybody off the practice. In her essay 'Bestiality in the Middle Ages', Joyce Salisbury notes that modern surveys show a fairly consistent pattern of activity in rural areas which likely matches that in the Middle Ages. She quotes a tenth-century Spanish text describing an anecdote from the career of Yahya'b about Ishaq, who practised medicine in Cordoba, and how he managed a peasant presenting in agony.

> The peasant told the physician he had been unable to urinate for several days. The physician ordered him to place his swollen penis on a flat rock and quickly punched it with his fist. The patient fainted in pain, but pus and urine flowed, curing the peasant. The physician explained his diagnosis: 'You have cohabited in the anus of an animal and therefore a grain of animal feed was stuck in your urethra and caused the inflammation.' The moral of the story as told by the author was not to avoid the dangers of animal contacts, but instead he said this anecdote showed the brilliance of the physician to make such an accurate diagnosis.

Although Aelian's work continued to shape thinking in the Middle Ages, writers were selective about what they took from him because by then it was the Christian texts rather than the classics that laid the moral groundwork. So we find Aelian influencing works of natural history and animal lore culminating in the bestiaries of the twelfth century but, sexual animal anecdotes notwithstanding, tales of actual bestial intercourse were left right out.

That didn't stop people like twelfth-century chronicler Gerald of Wales perpetuating superstitions about hybrid creatures through his writings. He told how in the Glendal-ough mountains a cow gave birth to a man-calf after a man had sex with her, and added that the local folk were 'especially addicted to such abominations'. He reported that Irish men and women had sex with cows, goats and lions, and that they believed such unions were sometimes fertile. Which led him to wonder whether it would be murder to kill such an animal. 'Who can disallow the claims of a creature which stands erect, laughs and goes on two feet to belong to the human species?'

Sadly for quite a lot of beasts who happened to catch the eye of servant Thomas Granger, by the time the seventeenth century rolled around the teachings of Leviticus still held sway. Governor William Bradford's diary *Of Plymouth Plantation, 1620–1647* tells of the 1642 trial of Granger for bestiality. When Granger was aged between sixteen and seventeen he was indicted for 'buggery with a mare, a cow, two goats, five sheep, two calves and a turkey'. He was found guilty and condemned to death by hanging, as Bradford describes here: 'A very sad spectacle it was. First the mare and then the cow and the rest of the lesser cattle were killed before his face, according to the law, Leviticus xx.15; and then he himself was executed.'

There are lots of reasons people have sex with animals; sometimes it's an act of deliberate cruelty, or it might be teenage experimentation in the absence of a human partner. But it's a fetish when an animal is chosen in preference to a human. Krafft-Ebing, who never quite mastered the art of clinical detachment, described it as 'impulsive sodomy' and gives this case study:

A. was convicted of having committed masturbation and sodomy on dogs and rabbits. When twelve years old he saw how boys masturbated a dog. He imitated it, and thereafter he could not keep from abusing dogs, cats and rabbits in this vile manner. Much more frequently, however, he committed sodomy on female rabbits—the only animals that had charm for him. At dusk he was accustomed to repair to his master's rabbit pen in order to gratify his vile desire. Rabbits with torn rectums were repeatedly found … At the height of the attack there were sounds of bells, cold perspiration, trembling of the knees, and, finally, loss of resistive power, and impulsive performance of the perverse act … A. stated that if called upon to choose between a woman and a female rabbit, he could make choice only of the latter.

Many people I spoke to said they drew the line at sex with animals. Jimmy compared the animal's inability to consent to a child's, which ruled bestiality out for him. But Kellie managed to satisfy herself on that score, because as a woman she was the passive party in the beginning, and later when she took the active role felt she was returning Robby's favour. Even though she feels the moral issues are all in order, I don't expect she'll be bringing it up at mothers' group any time soon.

21
NORTH SHORE, HARD-CORE

I'm driving down a dark, tree-lined street in Turramurra looking for the Hard Core Heaven party and not wanting to be here at all. I'm already feeling like a fish out of water when I spot what I think from a distance is a woman in black shiny latex—the fabric everyone wears at these things—and pull over. I check my makeup (dark eyes, crimson lips, called me clichéd), put in the red whip earring I'd taken out earlier because it kept getting caught in the seatbelt shoulder strap, and hop out. I negotiate the path leading through the native-planted front garden to a screened security door. The house is a seventies exposed-brick block common to the area; I wonder if the people sitting in front of their televisions in all the neighbouring houses have any idea what's going on at number 22 tonight.

'Door Bitch', a cheerful guy in a leather G-string and boots, welcomes me and takes my $35. Tracy, in a nurse's uniform, is busy with hostess duties but stops to say hello and kisses me on the cheek.

KINK

The rippling Adam, Tracy's master, is moving silently among the guests so I say hi and he shakes my hand with a surprisingly wimpy grip. The veins spreading across his gargantuan shoulders have multiplied in the last year and he's looking like more of a freak than ever. Again sporting weeny black shorts, it's obvious all those steroids have shrunk his balls to hazelnuts.

There's a towering Swiss drag queen with huge hair and extreme makeup on the bar—her sash says BAR BITCH—and because I'm not drinking she fills a plastic cup with warm diet lemonade. Mmmm. Just what I felt like after a long drive through the treacherous reaches of the upper North Shore.

I'm chatting with a shy boy in a leather loincloth and studded harness who's overwhelmed by Sydney and just wants to go back home to the North Coast. He's worried there won't be as much work in office furniture installation up there but he reckons he'll find enough people in BDSM to keep him happy and can always come back down for parties anyway.

The smell of sausage fat is filling the yard and people are starting to queue for their dinner. Conversation is like it is anywhere—at least at this stage of the evening—and covers work, kids, holidays. Most of the women are in latex corsets in black or red and the men are in black leather. There's a very tall guy with a barrister's voice and a grey comb-over wearing thick black-rimmed spectacles and a transparent babydoll nightie. I don't know who's going to fancy him with his hairy arse thinly veiled in nylon, but then I'm probably not his cup of tea either.

I was kind of disappointed when Tracy emailed me a few days ago to say that yes, Baby Jennie would be coming, because

I really expected the hard-core adult babies would be men. Anyway, Baby Jennie obviously isn't old enough to understand gender yet, because he *is* a man. He has shoulder-length black hair tied in high bunches with pink ribbons, a short cotton sundress printed with pastel-toned teddy bears, a pink leather harness—presumably to stop her running onto the road—and matching pink leather boots. And pink plastic pants over a bulky nappy.

I queue behind North Coast harness boy and plonk ham and Waldorf salad on a buckling paper plate and sit in the garden next to Ron and Angie, a couple in their fifties. I've decided not to be as upfront tonight about being there as a writer, researching a book. I won't lie but I don't want to jinx the night either. But sure enough, the usual preliminary questions start coming my way and I have to 'fess up. They're okay with it and quite eager to talk.

They tell me there's nothing on the Sydney scene that really caters to their needs; they're after a place where they can dance, be as sexually uninhibited as they like with each other, but *not* swing.

'We went to a "scene" weekend away in the Blue Mountains a couple of years ago,' Ron says, 'and we were chatting to a couple for a while in the afternoon before the party, like we're chatting to you now. Then that night the woman came straight up to me, opened my fly, put her hand in and grabbed my balls. Whoa! I had to explain we weren't into swinging but they just presumed that if you're on the scene, you're up for it.'

An absolutely model-gorgeous man in his thirties comes over and says how shocked he was when he got the address for this party, realising it's only a block from his place.

'I couldn't believe it! Who'd have thought *this* would be going on in Turramurra! I'm keeping my eyes peeled for women from mothers' group!'

He asks what I'm into, whether I'm married and if I'm there with my husband. I tell him I'm not really into the scene at all and that this is my first party here.

'What, so you just like going to fancy-dress parties, do you?'

When I tell him I'm a writer he recoils.

'So are you here *researching*?'

I'm not using anyone's real names, I say, but we only chat for another thirty seconds—he can't escape quickly enough.

After dinner people start to move in to get a good position for the show, which Adam has been talking up all night. There's a large paved outdoor entertaining area scattered with Jarrah barbecue furniture, one side of which has been curtained off for the performance. White curtains hang from rigging with a central one dividing the 'stage' into two sections. But first, DressUp Chris takes the floor to hand out the 'best dressed' awards and to draw the lucky door prize—a fine, flesh-cutting cane. When a woman in black velvet shorts and a red velvet Jean-Paul Gaultier-style corset wins a special award for being 'our very own Madonna' of the evening, she shrieks, stands on a wooden bench, wiggles her arse and—heavy with irony— shouts, 'Like a virgin!' A predictable gag, but she got a laugh. I suppress the urge to roll my eyes.

The show begins like a badly rehearsed school play. Here's the scenario: Tracy, looking stern in her nurse's outfit, announces she is Matron. Doing her rounds she happens upon two young nurses having it off but before she really lets rip disciplining them, they rope her into the action. There's a lot of writhing, breast kneading and tortured, open-mouthed expressions before Matron tears herself away, her hat abandoned, her hair cascading and wild. Composing herself, she returns to the naughty nurses and orders one to give the other 'a foot-long enema'. End scene one.

We are diverted, stage left, with an eye-watering display of genital torture. The curtain is pulled back to reveal a patient on a bed in stirrups, her heavily pierced labia directed towards the audience. She looks a bit like a burns victim in a tight white latex hood and has both arms bent at the elbow and tightly bandaged in metres of white gauze. Her breasts are bare and enormous, scarred by rows of stretch marks running towards pierced, weighted nipples, her middle encased in a white lace corset. A 'doctor' appears in black latex pants, a tight black hood masking his face with gauzy patches over the eyes and a white cotton dentist's jacket. He produces what I realise is a dildo but it's really thick at one end and shrinks halfway down to a narrow neck—more like something you'd pull socks over for darning. It's wooden, too, so maybe that's what it really is. Anyway, he doesn't appear to be worried about holes in his hosiery, so he lubes it up and after giving her clitoris a perfunctory rub pushes it into her. So far so good, the patient seems to be enjoying herself.

Next he rummages in his Gladstone bag and pulls out a drill. There's no theatrical flourish, no Dick Dastardly moustache twirling; he just nonchalantly walks over to her, stretches her labia down over the dildo and punches studs through her flesh and into the wood. I'm not sure if he's making new holes or if he's using existing ones but she doesn't flinch. What he does next *really* hurts though. He gets several eight-centimetre needles and forces them, one by one, through her top lip and out through her bottom lip then attaches small corks to them so they can't slide back out. You can tell by the way he has to shove at this, and by the patient's wriggling feet and watering eyes, that these are definitely new holes being made. He then helps the patient out of the stirrups and up off the bed. She stands, legs astride, posing for photos with the tapered end of the dildo still protruding from her. Ta-da!

The left curtain is drawn and the right one is opened, bringing us back to Matron and the naughty nurses. Here we find Nurse 1 on her back on a bed, knickerless, with her feet attached to a leg-spreader over her head. Nurse 2 sits at the end of the bed with her latex-clad foot up to the heel in Nurse 1's arse. In hard-core Carry On style, Matron walks in and exclaims: 'Nurse! When I said to give her a "foot-long enema" *that* isn't what I meant!' Boom-boom.

The audience half laughs, half groans at this. In fact throughout the show most of them just keep chatting and drinking. Tracy reappears and, with a game-show hostess's wave towards the garage, announces that the Fuck Room is now open. Nobody moves. God, how long does it take for these parties to warm up? I'm feeling grumpy and bored and doing my best not to show it. I think it's working.

I wander over to the woman who played the patient, now sitting with friends, and ask her how her lips are feeling. I don't know why she's looking at me as if I'm being cruel until I notice she still has the needles in her lips! Oops, sorry. Don't know how I missed that and the blood now crusting around the metal.

Gloria, the trannie I met at Graham and Rita's party last year, is standing on her own and couldn't be ripping through her jumbo pack of ciggies any faster if she was eating them. I suggest we have a coffee some time because I'd never followed up on my promise last year to call her for a formal interview. She suggests her place because she needs a favour.

'I've made this bench and I need you to lie on it so I can test out all the parts.'

'Riiiight …'

'See, you lie on it with a rope around your neck and your ankles and wrists strapped in and there's a lever at the back that pulls your legs open and your arms out to your sides. It's quite simple but I can't test it myself because I can't reach the lever from that position.'

Now, either I look particularly stupid or I've given Gloria the impression that I trust her unreservedly. We agree I'll go around next week but don't strike a deal on anything else. I'm about to say goodbye when she suggests I borrow a whip and give her a good flogging. Remembering my experience with Graham I tell her I wouldn't be any good and, although a little disappointed, she believes me and lights up another fag.

It's eleven-thirty and I'm over this party. It occurs to me that I should go and check out the Fuck Room but I don't want, or need, to see anyone fucking, thanks. There are a few huddles forming by the time I leave; a tall man face down on a cruci-fix in the second bedroom awaiting a whipping, and a Keith Richards lookalike with diamante-edged eyelashes chatting up a couple of women on the sofa in the lounge room. Maybe the action was all in the garage but, with an appalling display of investigative ennui, I head for the door. My major reservation about leaving so early is that I haven't spoken to any of the adult babies, and they were the main reason I made the effort to come to this party. Maybe they're all in the Fuck Room on change tables or in highchairs, but I've already decided I'm not going in there to check.

Door Bitch asks why I'm leaving before midnight and I say I have to get up early.

'Yeah, me too,' he says. 'I've got a heap of my daughter's friends coming around for a swim in the pool at ten so I've got to get up and clean it.'

As I'm driving away I catch sight of a big pink plastic-clad bottom and realise it's Baby Jennie bending to pick something up off the street. I stop just past him and call out, 'Hi, Jennie,' in a last-ditch attempt to line up an interview. He can't make out where the greeting's coming from and calls out 'Ooh hello!' into the dark street and continues on her way back to the house. I've missed my moment.

I'm having a hard time deciphering some of my shorthand from last night's party. The phrase 'nailed labia to dildo' has me stumped for ages but we were never taught that one in shorthand lessons.

A problem emerged with my decision not to declare my agenda upfront last night; I couldn't just ask people bluntly what they were into without them scrutinising me and wondering if I was chatting them up. As a result I hardly spoke to anyone and was totally preoccupied when I did. One young man of about twenty came over and introduced himself and, although he was wearing a white blouse and tartan skirt, standard-issue girls' high school uniform, he was totally blokey, free of makeup, tits and wig. So when he said his name was Joanne it quite threw me.

'Hi, I'm Stephanie. Oh! Sorry, I mean Sandra.'

He laughed. 'Been a busy week, has it?' Then he wandered off to talk to someone less loopy. Next time, if there is one, I'm telling the organisers I'm researching, having it announced publicly if necessary, and risking everyone being timid and dull because I'm there. God knows my undercover approach didn't exactly make last night a hell-raiser.

22

LOOKS AREN'T EVERYTHING

Jason's photo on the 'alternative sexuality' website makes him look like an axe murderer—intense stare, turned-down mouth, weird swept-forward hair—so I've arranged to meet him somewhere very safe and very public. Lunchtime at the Archibald Fountain in Hyde Park had seemed like a great idea until it started raining, but I'd still rather get wet than risk going somewhere secluded with him.

I do a double-take when a gorgeous, smiling young man, *sans* axe, comes to meet me, but given his proclivity for excrement I still think the open-air, no-handshake option is the go. We find a bench under a tree, which gives us a little shelter.

He's new to the scene, likes being pissed on and really wants to try scat. His fascination with urolagnia began when he was about twelve and was aroused by a dream that he was pissed on by a group of girls.

'I've thought about it since then but I didn't really do any-thing about it until about six years ago, I s'pose. The first time was by accident. I was giving my girlfriend oral and when she came she actually peed a little bit, which I loved. So I guess that set the whole thing off.'

What's to love about that?

'That it's wrong and socially unacceptable, I guess.'

Anyway, the problem was the girlfriend was never prepared to pee on him again and it's been hard negotiating it with other women since they broke up. He usually needs a few drinks before he can broach the subject but most women think it's 'a bit disgusting'.

'I don't know if there's a subtle way of doing it, you just have to come out with it: "I'd love you to piss in my mouth" sort of thing.'

Although none of them have agreed to do it, none of them have run screaming from the room either.

'I haven't had any really bad ones, like "you fucked-up twat" or anything. It's been more like "Eeuw, no, I'm not going to do that."'

I'm figuring that once a girl is in bed with this gorgeous hazel-eyed creature, it's going to take more than a suggestion like that to make her bolt. But it doesn't matter how attractive he is, he's the first to admit that negotiating the scat thing is bound to be difficult. He'd like to try being shat on from a height, smeared, and would even try eating his partner's shit. He's unconcerned about the smell and taste and thinks that's part of the appeal.

'I've got no idea how I'd bring it up with a vanilla partner. I think it'd be ten times worse than bringing up pissing. Unless it was on the website or with a pro, no idea. You could try to use a joke, like, "I'm so attracted to you I'd eat your shit hot." Or there's the old line that's been used on really hot girls, "I'd use your shit for toothpaste".'

I think that line is hilarious and laugh when he says it, so I guess he risks not being taken seriously if he tries it. Then again, at least they'd think he was handsome *and* funny.

But for Jason the appeal of 'toilet training' (in kink parlance) is more than just its social unacceptability. It's about humiliation and submission, and it's a mystery to him where this desire came from; his parents didn't put him down, there was no delicious primary school teacher who shamed him in front of the class—he just thinks he was born 'twisted'.

Later, in an email, he said he'd

love to be spanked, sissyfied, forced by a mistress to have sex with guys. I'm not attracted to guys but guess it comes back to being forced to do demeaning things. Love to be teased. Would love to be tied up and forced to watch my partner being fucked by someone else. Get very jealous but it really turns me on at the same time.

The thing he finds weirdest about his desire to be dominated sexually is that he's not submissive in everyday life and describes his demeanour as assertive. I tell him that contrast isn't unusual and he remembers the cliché that it's always the CEOs lining up at the dungeon door for a whipping.

'I guess it's just part of the life that's missing,' he says.

Although the idea of total lifestyle submission to a mistress appeals to him, he knows lots of the things he loves—surfing, his job, socialising—would be impossible if he took it beyond the bedroom. So until he finds the ideal mistress he'll happily make do with, and enjoy, vanilla sex and occasionally switch right over and dominate his partner. In this mode he says he'll force partners to 'suck my cock, or rather have me fucking their face holding onto their hair. Pissing on them and making them swallow it. Restraining them, spanking, slapping their faces whilst they suck cock. Blindfolding, I guess, too.'

Sheesh! For a guy whose natural fit is submissive he doesn't half go hard with the dom stuff. Or maybe he just likes to keep his options open.

23

HOT RODS AND HORMONES

There's no mistaking which house is Gloria's—the hot rods being restored out the front are a dead giveaway. She's been a rev-head since long before her sex change and fifteen years of oestrogen and some genital surgery aren't about to change that.

At sixty-five Gloria still has great legs and is fond of showing them off. We're finally meeting up for that coffee, at her place, and as she's not going anywhere she's barefoot and comfortable in a mauve micro-mini and a loose pink and white checked shirt. She's still got a very male, round tummy and her breasts are apples rather than melons; but as she says, 'Anything more than a mouthful's a waste.'

She makes tea, which she serves with Kahlua-flavoured Tim Tams, and we take it out onto the patio. It's blazingly hot out there under a clear fibreglass roof and the chocolate biscuits are melting before our eyes. She forgoes the biscuit in favour of a cigarette, which is all the more desirable for having been hidden, ineffectually, by her son after her mild stroke five days ago. Settled, and buzzing at last with nicotine, she launches in.

'My first knowing thoughts of wanting to be a girl were when I was five, standing on the front lawn in a girl's dress. It had a little bib with straps crossing over the shoulders. I remember wishing I didn't have to get out of it. Then you get to eleven or twelve and puberty starts to kick in—I can remember hating that but knowing all the time that you didn't talk about it.'

That day in the dress was 1945 and Gloria was a little boy called Greg. He spent an inordinate amount of time playing with the dress-up box, a treasure trove of feather boas, beads and even little girls' sundresses. But by the time he was a teenager he couldn't get away with that any more. The upside to advancing maturity was that he could grow a beard, which he did as soon as possible at about eighteen.

'Most of my life I had a beard or a moustache or both because there's nothing worse, nothing looks sillier, than someone with a beard in a dress. It's a way of stopping yourself from cross-dressing.'

The only time Greg tried cross-dressing as an adult was at a party in 1961.

'And the funny thing was no one knew who I was for at least an hour and a half, not even the people I used to drink with. That gave me a bit of confidence; I thought when and if I did change sexes I might look okay.'

Greg married Rose at twenty-six, had two sons, but struggled with his marriage as he always had with his gender.

Mechanically inclined, he worked as a factory foreman before running the workshop at Sydney College of the Arts.

'By the time I was in my forties the urge to cross-dress was getting worse. I was giving the students at uni hell on roller-skates because every now and then I'd get really cranky. But even when I was running factories I know I had a reputation for being reasonably easily pushed over the edge. I was very aggressive. I know Greg wasn't a very nice person.'

Working at uni suited him better because his colleagues were more open-minded than the factory crowd and occupied a wider sexual spectrum. But he was still miserable and decided to have a couple of years of therapy with the college counsellor.

'I'd be able to open up to her and admit what I felt but then I'd leave work and by the time I got halfway home I'd be thinking, "I didn't say that, I didn't say that." And by the time I got all the way home I'd be ready to rip people's heads off.'

Allowing himself to admit that a sex change was what he really wanted was the difficult thing.

'You think about it, heading towards fifty years of being Greg then admitting to that. Then one day I was on my way home and I thought, Yes, I did say that. That gave me permission to move very slowly towards a way of perpetually cross-dressing— because by then I'd been kicked out of the main bedroom. You could wear women's knickers without being seen. Instead of a Chesty Bonds singlet you could put on a woman's singlet.'

He started taking oestrogen around that time as well and one of the more noticeable physical changes was super-sensitive nipples. 'I remember walking into a stiff breeze up a hill from uni wearing a khaki work shirt and by the time I got to the top my eyes were crossed and rolling—the shirt had been flapping against my nipples, and oh my God! I walked into the chiropractor's and told the receptionist, who I knew well, that I was just experiencing something she'd known about all her life. She said, "I know how you can get rid of that. Just go out in the sun and get sunburned a few times and it'll go away." Well, I can tell you my breasts haven't been in the sun since that day!'

But the hormones and the underwear weren't enough for Greg and things at home hit an all-time low before he could see a way out; Rose was on to her third affair and came home one Sunday morning having been out all night. They had a massive fight and she said she wanted to end the marriage and for Greg to leave.

'I'd thought about this on and off over the years and knew what I was going to do—I went down to the garage to commit suicide. But where I lived lots of backyards backed onto ours and there were these two kids playing outside, having fun, and I heard them. As I opened the garage door I thought, What am I about to do to my own children? So I went back upstairs and thought, Things couldn't get much worse, I'll try being someone else.'

He decided to tell his boys he was going to move out and start living as a woman and would change his name to Gloria.

'So I sat with Jared, who was eleven, for about ten minutes telling him why I was moving out and he asked lots of questions. After that he gave me a big hug and said, "Dad, everyone's got problems but boy, you've got a big one!"' Both Jared and Craig, eighteen, wanted to live with Gloria, which surprised him and resulted in Rose accusing him of brainwashing their sons.

KINK

In the beginning Jared couldn't give a hoot but Craig hated it.

'All Craig's friends rocked up here to take him drinking because he'd been done for DUI. But do you know how he got out of the charge? When he went to court he said, "I'd just found out my father wanted to be a woman and it upset me so I went to the pub to have a few drinks to settle my nerves and had a few too many." And the judge said, "Oh, you poor thing! I'm not going to charge you!" So he didn't lose his licence after all. Ooh, he's a little con! Craig's mates totally accepted it and from that he learned to accept it.'

The father of one of Jared's friends wouldn't let his son play there because he felt Gloria was a bad influence. Gloria's sisters also dropped her and her mother rang and blurted out that she hadn't been stressed during pregnancy so it couldn't have been her fault, then hung up.

Seven years later, Gloria received a workers' comp payout for a bad back and left her job at the uni. With the money, she tossed up between retiling the roof or having a sex change. She got the approval of two psychiatrists, found a surgeon and went for the operation. But all those years of oestrogen had shrunk the penis so much that it was too small to fashion into a vagina, so the surgeon used a portion of her large bowel instead. Everything works magnificently, she says, and the surgeon's quick flick of her clitoris at her first post-op examination was so intensely, excruciatingly pleasurable it had her rigid and clinging by her claws to the ceiling.

On the scene Gloria's generally a sub but it wasn't a position she chose or one that she sticks to religiously.

'I was pre-op and I went to the Sleaze Ball with a friend from uni who was a domme. She chose my outfit for the night—gold chaps, a G-string and a leather harness that crossed over and buckled at the back with eye rings on it and a see-through black blouse—and all these women in the Dyke Hall kept asking me if I was allowed to dance.'

Of course she was, she told them, but was puzzled until her friend told her she'd been dressed in an outfit with a meaning. Full of coke, speed and ecstasy that night, she experienced the pain of having her torso pierced with a horizontal circle of hooks which were then looped with ribbons through a hula hoop, and, as she told me at Graham and Rita's party, has been a bit of a 'pain puppy' ever since.

'Being a sub was imposed upon me but in a way that allowed me to find out what it was and how you had to learn to accept pain. In the beginning it was the thrill of the unknown, because pain can be applied in different ways. If I go inside and stub my toe on that aluminium door frame, I'll burst into tears and sob for half an hour. But if you hit me very hard with a flogger when I want to be hit very hard, I'll say, "Please, another one, Mistress." It's a totally different kind of pain.'

For Gloria the pain doesn't necessarily need to be followed up with anything erotic and can be pain for pain's sake.

'It can also be very cathartic. I could be so full of emotion that I could actually use a flogging as a cleansing mechanism by having a bloody good sob without the person who was hitting me knowing, and just getting rid of so much rubbish out of my mind. You could be literally refreshed at the end of the session.

Sometimes if the person who was hitting me saw I was crying it could be difficult for them because I'd be sobbing, "No, don't stop." Sob. "Keep going." Sob.'

But a whip has to be expertly wielded, so I'm glad I hadn't acted on Gloria's suggestion at Hard Core Heaven to borrow one and give her a good flogging before I left. I'm bound to have disappointed her.

'If you're going to whip me on the back, I shouldn't have thongs coming over my shoulder and hitting me on the side of the face or coming around and hitting me on the stomach instead of on the bum.'

A good domme should be able to read body language and know when to stop, even when the sub, like Gloria, has a problem knowing when to tell them to.

Sometimes, though, Gloria will switch. She'll even have sex with men occasionally, but she's choosy about which ones.

'I'm very careful about which males I'll bed. It has to be somebody that I like who has a sense of humour so the pre and the post can be as convivial as the act. Your average male has trouble carrying a conversation in a bucket. And I'll bed *them*, they don't bed *me*.'

Not long after her sex change she wound up at the home of a married couple after a party. After watching a porno movie with them she had sex with the wife and then pushed the husband down onto the sofa and jumped him as well. 'He was totally shocked, gasping for air and said, "Gloria, I thought you were a lesbian!" and I said, "I am—when it takes my fancy!"'

As I'm leaving I ask Gloria what pseudonym she'd like me to use.

'Call me anything you like—just don't call me late for breakfast.'

I used to work with a guy, Jim, whose sex change put his partner through as many hoops as it did him. When he was a woman, he was a large-breasted lesbian called Judy. She had a breast reduction because big tits looked terrible in dungarees and years later realised it had been a way of chipping away at the feminine form she hated.

Judy met and fell in love with Helen, who was a married mother of two who'd always considered herself straight. After much soul searching and angst, Helen decided that yes, she *had* come over all lesbian and that she would leave her husband and kids to be with Judy. Then, after some years together, Judy came over all butch—well, more than usual—and wanted a sex change. Years of counselling ensued but Judy had made up her mind. She started on hormones, which deepened her voice, encouraged facial hair (which s/he wore as a goatee) and introduced male-pattern baldness. Then those reduced breasts were completely removed in a double mastectomy and Jim was born.

Helen was distraught and mourned the loss of the woman she'd fallen for. After years of coming to terms with being a lesbian she'd ended up with a bloke after all, albeit one without a penis. The dismal results when surgeons attempt to fashion a penis from abdominal skin mean that the patient ends up with an insensitive tube through which he can pee standing up but that has no erectile function. Jim and Helen thought it was best that he just stick with female genitalia and use a dildo for sex. He also wore a prosthesis, which he was fond of adjusting with a fiddle and a knee bend, particularly when discussing blokey things like clearing gutterings. Last thing I heard they were still together.

24
STEP ON IT

When he was four and still living in Bosnia, Alen's babysitter, a beautiful blonde in her early thirties, discovered she could keep him quiet if she lay him on the floor and rested her shod feet on him. He's never been quite the same since.

'Later on, when we both got more relaxed and used to that position, she started to use me for other things. It was a good thing that she never ever hurt me or gave me any pain. She was bossy but caring.'

As time went on she started to get Alen to clean her shoes—with his tongue.

'She made me lick her shoes clean, including the soles, every time. Later on she realised how powerful she felt by making me love the smell of her shoes, stockings and feet. And I have to admit I did love it, I guess because that was my first touch, smell and feeling of a woman. So she used to wear the same shoes and stockings for a couple of days and then make me take them off and smell them for a long time and clean them inside.

Then she would rest her stockinged feet on my face for hours, making me smell them and clean every part of them. When I was eighteen I saw her again and she was more beautiful, too good-looking. She was in her mid-forties by then.'

Alen had seen a music video with a man kissing a woman's leather boots and recognised his own fetish. Now, at thirty-two, he's fine-tuning his tastes.

'If I like the person she could wear pretty much any kind of shoe, high heels, runners, whatever. But if I had a preference it would be for high shoes, more like smart court shoes.'

It's more than just the shoes, though.

'I have to like the person and she has to have nice feet. Some women don't take care of their feet. I like painted toenails and smooth feet. I like elegant ladies who take care of themselves.'

He gets turned on 'big time' by having a woman's feet resting on him but it doesn't have to lead to sex.

'I could spend my life that way,' he says. He still likes to clean women's shoes and act as a footrest while a girlfriend is talking on the phone or watching TV. It's a way of showing appreciation and respect, he believes. But he's not into pain so doesn't like being walked on.

Although he finds ladies' shoe shops a bit of a turn-on he wouldn't go hanging around them.

'I'm not that kind of Peeping Tom. If a lady walks by wearing nice shoes, I would have to look at them, I couldn't help myself, but wouldn't harass a woman—I'm always polite.'

I quite believe this. He seems a very sweet, gentle fellow and says when he first broached his kink with women his shyness made it difficult.

'Most of my girlfriends got to know me and, being a Scorpio, they all expected me to be kinky. I am open-minded and always honest so I say what is on my mind.'

The more he brought the subject up the more confident he became. He often tests the water with a joke.

'That gives me a good idea if there is any chance or not. By doing that it doesn't mean I am hitting on that lady.'

The approach has been pretty successful.

'Most of my girlfriends, ninety per cent, did play with me. The biggest problem is if they are in love with me they do not feel comfy by placing me under them. Some of them did it for my pleasure but if both of us are not enjoying it I am not happy. I have to admit that most women who tried it, even just for fun, started to love it and a lot of them got crazy about it. Some of them are still in touch with me and still loving it.'

Even if a woman didn't want to get involved with him sexually, Alen would be happy with the footrest role, he says.

'It could be a friend who is bored or upset and just needs to feel like a queen. Some of them could just rest their shoes and feet on me, some of them apply a bit of pressure and talk a bit dirty to humiliate me for fun. No sex, just fun for both. Some of the women are attached or still not close to me or not after sex at all, just amazed with the idea that someone can get turned on and crazy about their feet and shoes. Some of them can make me, you know, finish, by using shoes or feet on me, and that makes them feel powerful and happy.'

Alen says the gratification he gets out of these experiences goes beyond the sexual.

'Most of them do thank me a lot for making them feel

appreciated, queeny, dominant, bossy, beautiful, and so on. I understand that some of them do not get in life what they deserve so it is like a kind of therapy for them and I am glad to help. They all know that I am a strong and dominant person in life, and I am not just a mat or dust with no brain. What they like about me is the fact that they can have a nice conversation with me about anything, and most of them say that the turn-on for them is the fact that they see me as a strong person, so the stronger I am the more power they feel.'

He knows women who like to show off in front of female friends by having him come along as a foot stool while they have a coffee and chat, an arrangement he enjoys.

He's not in a relationship at the moment and knows that any woman not prepared to rest her feet on him wouldn't last. He thinks he'll always be turned on by it, has never suffered any grief from it and is happy to have it.

'Look, I've survived a war in Bosnia, I've been shot at and been clinically dead, and my way of thinking is there's life in front of you, just do it. Don't hurt other people but just enjoy it.'

Later, in an email, Alen shared with me a brainwave he had about helping me with my research.

I have an idea. You may like it or not, but you made me think: as you said you have no experience in this field but you are doing the book, I can help you to gain some experience and maybe you would understand better and actually get the real feeling. Don't get scared. I am not after you or trying to use this to get to your feet ... :)

My idea is we can have a 'relationship'. Example: when you write to me or talk to me on the phone be bossy and Lady and demand respect. When you feel bossy, or you are upset, or feel like humiliating someone, write to me, give me a call or sms me, when you are with your girlfriends do the same and see how they react. Send me as reward some pictures of your feet or shoes, or wear them or stockings and send them to me to worship them and clean them and send them back to you. See how you would feel then. Knowing that you own someone and can have him under your shoes and use him to get your frustrations out when you feel like it. I believe that would help you a lot and give you the real taste. Once again I will not try to interfere in your life or ask for anything. I'd just like to help and honestly I think that could be fun for both of us, learning and exploring together. Let me know about your decision. Wishing you best luck, Alen.

Sweet boy. He also sent me a photo of himself lying on the floor, a big smile across his broad face, captioned *happypuppy*. I emailed to thank him for his offer but to decline it. True to his word, I never heard from him again.

Much is made of the line 'How beautiful are thy feet with shoes, O prince's daughter!' from the Song of Solomon as evidence of a shoe fetish, but the rest of the verse shows the interest is far from selective:

> the joints of thy thighs are like jewels, the work of the hands of a cunning workman. Thy navel is like a round goblet, which wanteth not liquor: thy belly is like an heap of wheat set about with lilies …

and so on as the song praises the woman's breasts, neck, eyes, nose and hair. Richard von Krafft-Ebing cites loads of shoe-fetish case studies in *Psychopathia Sexualis*, all of which he believed were a form of masochism. Sometimes the shoe alone was enough, at others it needed to be worn by a pretty woman. One man wished to become a servant, 'to blacken shoes for distinguished ladies, to put on and take off their shoes for them, etc'. He described his dreams as always involving shoe scenes.

> Either I stand before the show-window of a shoe shop regarding the elegant ladies' shoes—particularly buttoned shoes—or I lie at a lady's feet and lick her shoes. For about a year I have given up onanism and gone to girls; coitus takes place by means of intense thought of ladies's buttoned shoes; or if necessary, I take the shoe of the girl to bed with me.

One man had been hooked on ladies' shoes since he saw a woman mounting a horse while an attendant held the stirrup for her. He found the shoes were the only interesting thing about a woman but, happily, had a sufficiently good imagination that he could get it up by simply looking at a drawing, done by his own hand, of a woman's lace-up boot.

That same volume describes almost as many cases of foot fetishism which seemed to originate and operate in similar ways to the shoe obsession. But evidence of the foot fetish having a broad cultural base can be found in the Chinese practice of foot binding. The resultant tiny 'lotus' feet, ideally not longer than ten centimetres, were considered enormously erotic, as was the unavoidable gait with which the women walked. While there are Qing dynasty sex manuals outlining dozens of ways to play with bound feet, the deep cleft under the arch mimicking female genitals, many men never saw the feet completely naked. The tiny embroidered shoes might be removed but usually the bandages stayed on because the deformed feet, which were impossible to wash properly, stank, thanks to infections with lively colonies of fungi and bacteria.

Freud believed the shoe symbolised the vulva and the foot the penis and, even though nobody takes Freud very seriously any more, you can see how such thinking might fuel a foot fetish. It also aligns with the idea that small is desirable; it was Cinderella, with her tiny, delicate feet, who the prince wanted to marry, not the ugly stepsisters with their oversized hooves. (That she was pretty probably helped a bit too.)

There's also the dominance symbolism of black leather boots, which reminds me of Pierre's attraction to the iconography in *Venus in Furs*. But sometimes things are less symbolic and more straightforward; some people get aroused when their feet are touched and get a tingling in the souls of the feet at orgasm. This can probably be explained by the same 'brain map' phenomenon that accounts for phantom pains, and pleasures, in amputees. In simple terms these maps indicate which parts of the brain are responsible for the sensation and function of particular body parts. The borders are not clearly defined and there is some blurring between sensations run by adjacent territories. When neurologist V.S. Ramachandran was trying to discover why leg and foot amputees often experienced sexual pleasure in their phantom limbs, he realised it made perfect neuroscientific sense—genitals lie next to the feet on the brain map, and when the feet no longer receive input the genital maps likely invade the foot maps. In short, when the genitals feel pleasure so do the feet, and if it can work in one direction the reverse suggests how foot stimulation could be sexually arousing. In his book *The Brain that Changes Itself*, psychiatrist Norman Doidge cites other erotic enigmas that fell into place with this discovery: some women who have had mastectomies get turned on when their ears, clavicles and sternums are stimulated—three body parts which are all close to nipples on the brain map. With mechanisms like that operating it doesn't take much, even without the benefit of conditioning, to see how kinks might form.

25

COPROPHILIACS MAKE SHITTY LOVERS

Most of the kinksters I've met so far say they're into everything legal *except* scat. We've all heard the rumours about the TV star who likes to lie under a glass coffee table watching while his partner shits on it. And the movie star who told his partner to wait while he popped outside for a moment, ostensibly to slip into something more comfortable, and returned smeared with his own excrement. The Marquis de Sade wrote at length about it, there were largely unsubstantiated rumours about Hitler being partial to it, but I was finding it hard to track down anyone who'd tried it. Then, through a website, I found Dolores. Anxious about protecting her identity she was never going to meet me, so our interview was a series of emails, the first of which said she's been playing with excrement since she was thirteen.

I used to play with an older cousin of mine who used to enjoy going down on me. Some call it abuse, but I wasn't treated like shit, in fact he pretty much worshipped the ground I walk on. Still does. Anyway sometimes I'd be clean, right out of the shower, other times without a shower for a day. I noticed that when I wasn't as clean, he would spend much more time down there and I wondered why. He also liked to lick my ass. So when I was playing by myself one day, I thought to put a finger in. I think it was more the naughtiness of it than anything else.

The idea of having a guy under her when she's shitting is, she believes, one of the most powerful feelings of being wanted.

Think about it, how often will you ever have a man offer himself to receive you, in any way, shape or form? Most guys don't even bother going down on you. When you find someone who gives you every freedom, then you know you have power. It's not a butch thing, it's more of a respect thing. Sounds weird, but there's no way most guys would give this much of themselves let alone open themselves to the idea.

She said she couldn't really explore scat until she knew she would be okay opening up about it. *Until then it was just a dirty fantasy*, she said.

Dolores is in a relationship but feels her partner's too vanilla to cope with her scat play.

I have a playmate who lets me be me without judgment. I stay with my partner as my playmate stays with his. We are comfortable with what we do and carry no guilt; we're just in it for the kink. Basically we fill each other's empty places while our mainstream partners are our day-to-day life. This is a kink, not a lifestyle thing.

Every now and then she'll 'receive' but most of the time she 'gives'—either way there's always smearing and always sex, which she says is *magical*. I ask about performing on demand and she says they usually hold out for a day or so before they know they're going to meet. If that doesn't work they'll use enemas, which she describes as *lots of fun*.

And what about practicalities, like cleaning up?

Yeah well when you're fucking a married guy of course you have to think about that! I think the most 'inconsiderate' thing we've done was play in a cheap and nasty hotel and left the bathroom a mess!

She thinks that's hilarious.

As she's only ever had one partner with this fetish she's never experienced the problem of misconstruing anyone's interest in it and embarrassing herself. But she doesn't imagine too many would share it.

I do know that most guys cringe at even going down on girls coz, as I've been told 'you piss from there'. My boyfriend doesn't go down coz he can't be bothered, then I get offers when I walk down the street so I dunno what's goin' on with that!

I wonder if it's all about context or whether the smell of scat arouses her outside a sexual setting.

Hmm, if I'm feeling horny and I smell it, it might make me a little more moist than usual, but it's usually when I know we're gonna fuck and I'm gonna get licked properly *that it comes into it. It's not always about shit and the like.*

Far from struggling with an obsession she can't control, she seems happy and manages to enjoy it without it affecting her relationship with her vanilla boyfriend.

I wouldn't be in it if I wasn't happy about it, and if I didn't like it, I'd just stop. Unlike certain weak-minded people, this is something I do because I enjoy it, not coz I want people to see me, or gain status from it. I don't care for that, and I don't care for people who seek that. Just coz you're into one form of sex or another, whether it be gay, straight, BDSM, whips and chains or whatever, what you do does not make you who you are. If you don't like what you're doing and you continue to do it, you're a moron. Pretty simple equation.

Irish author James Joyce had few qualms about his scatological interests if his letters to his wife, Nora Barnacle, are anything to go by. At the age of twenty-seven, when he was in Trieste for a couple of months, he wrote erotic letters to her regularly as she did to him. Hers didn't survive but his show a man filled with all kinds of lust, and only occasionally worried that his tastes were grubby or somehow distasteful.

My love for you allows me to pray to the spirit of eternal beauty and tenderness mirrored in your eyes or fling you down under me on that softy belly of yours and fuck you up behind, like a hog riding a sow, glorying in the very stink and sweat that rises from your arse, glorying in the open shape of your upturned dress and white girlish drawers and in the confusion of your flushed cheeks and tangled hair. It allows me to burst into tears of pity and love at some slight word, to tremble with love for you at the sounding of some chord or cadence of music or to lie heads and tails with you, feeling your fingers fondling and tickling my ballocks or stuck up in me behind and your hot lips sucking off my cock while my head is wedged in between your fat thighs, my hands clutching the round cushions of your bum and my tongue licking ravenously up your rank red cunt. I have taught you almost to swoon at the hearing of my voice singing or murmuring to your soul the passion and sorrow and mystery of life and at the same time have taught you to make filthy signs to me with your lips and tongue, to provoke me by obscene touches and noises, and even to do in my presence the most shameful and filthy act of the body. You remember the day you pulled up your clothes and let me lie under you looking up at you while you did it? Then you were ashamed even to meet my eyes. (2 December 1909)

The next day Joyce wrote again, this time telling her that she took the sexual initiative with him when they first met, turning him into a beast. He then quizzes her about sexual exploits with other men before she'd met him. Then, three days later, he's back on track, jealousies forgotten, though he does wonder if he's corrupting her.

I would like you to wear drawers with three or four frills one over the other at the knees and up the thighs and great crimson bows in them, I mean not schoolgirls' drawers with a thin shabby lace border, thigh round the legs and so thin that the flesh shows with a full loose bottom and wide legs, all frills and lace and ribbons, and heavy with perfume so that whenever you show them, whether in pulling up your clothes hastily to do something or cuddling yourself up prettily to be blocked, I can see only a swelling mass of white stuff and frills and so that when I bend down over you to open them and give you a burning lustful kiss on your naughty bare bum I can smell the perfume of your drawers as well as the warm odour of your cunt and the heavy smell of your behind.

Have I shocked you by the dirty things I wrote to you? You think perhaps that my love is a filthy thing. It is, darling, at some moments. I dream of you in filthy poses sometimes. I imagine things so very dirty that I will not write them until I see how you write yourself. The smallest things give me a great cockstand—a whorish movement of your mouth, a little brown stain on the seat of your white drawers, a sudden dirty word spluttered out by your wet lips, a sudden immodest noise made by your behind and then a bad smell slowly curling up out of your backside. At such moments I feel mad to do it in some filthy way, to feel your hot lecherous lips sucking away at me, to fuck between your two rosy-tipped bubbies, to come on your face and squirt it over your hot cheeks and eyes, to stick it between the cheeks of your rump and bugger you.

Basta per stasera!

I hope you got my telegram and understood it.

Goodbye, my darling whom I am trying to degrade and deprave. How on God's earth can you possibly love a thing like me?

O, I am anxious to get your reply, darling!' (6 December 1909)

Two days later he writes again, hilariously, revealing that he's not only into the occasional brown smear on Nora's knickers, he's positively wild about her wind. This particular fetish is known as eproctophilia.

I am delighted to see that you do like being fucked arseways. Yes, now I can remember that night when I fucked you for so long backwards. It was the dirtiest fucking I ever gave you, darling. My prick was stuck in you for hours, fucking in and out under your upturned rump. I felt your fat sweaty buttocks under my belly and saw your flushed face and mad eyes. At every fuck I gave you your shameless tongue came bursting out through your lips and if I gave you a bigger stronger fuck than usual, fat dirty farts came spluttering out of your backside. You had an arse full of farts that night, darling, and I fucked them out of you, big fat fellows, long windy ones, quick little merry cracks and a lot of tiny little naughty farties ending in a long gush from your hole. It is wonderful to fuck a farting woman when every fuck drives one out of her. I think I would know Nora's fart anywhere. I think I could pick hers out in a roomful of farting women. It is a rather girlish noise not like the wet windy fart which I imagine fat wives have. It is sudden and dry and dirty like what a bold girl would let off in fun in a school dormitory at night. I hope Nora will let off no end of her farts in my face so that I may know their smell also … Goodnight, my little farting Nora, my dirty little fuckbird! There is one lovely word, darling, you have underlined to make me pull myself off better. Write me more about that and yourself, sweetly, dirtier, dirtier. (8 December 1909)

26

THE CRÈCHE WITH BABY JENNIE

Having blown my opportunity to talk to Baby Jennie at Hard Core Heaven, I was thrilled when I found his email address and he agreed to a face-to-face interview. It's a Saturday afternoon and he's just back from work. He opens the door to his North Shore townhouse and apologises for not being 'in uniform'. But he is, sort of. He's in white gaberdine shorts, a pink and white striped T-shirt, his hair's pulled back in a pink plastic headband and he's in short, lace-trimmed white socks with pink sneakers. He's super confident and very—strangely, given the outfit—handsome.

We go through to the lounge room, a cluttered space that hasn't seen enough air or sun, and Jennie introduces me to his friends. There's a married couple from the scene, Barbara and Chris, and, joy of joys, another adult baby, Angelica. Baby Angelica is in his mid-thirties with grey shoulder-length hair and, although he's wearing normal male street clothes, he's already very much in baby-girl personality mode.

'Hello, Thandra,' he lisps in a tiny voice—and then curtseys!

I sit in a deep, loosely upholstered chair and Jennie sits on the adjacent sofa, leaning forward on parted knees. His coffee table is one of those carved Indonesian things with lots of tiny drawers which neatly accommodate all his dope-smoking paraphernalia. He starts to roll the first of many joints and asks if I've had a chance to read his erotic short stories, which he'd emailed during the week. I tell him I thought they were well written—which they are, if your favourite words are shaft, nub, glistening and tumescent—and he says they're read by thousands of people every week.

'Yeah, I'm highly literate and rather erudite so watch out!'

I laugh at his lack of modesty.

'No, I am! There's no modesty about this at all. I actually did creative writing at university and got high distinctions all the way so I'm actually really good at this. I only write for pleasure, because I have a skill that I make a living out of in the medical field and I'm *really* good at that. I've got a very successful practice and I've seen over a hundred patients this week.'

He says transvestism is as common among adult babies as any other fetish and most of the adult babies he knows are men in baby girls' clothes. I want to know if there was a time in his childhood where he actually stopped wearing baby clothes or if he continued from birth. He thinks he had a break from it until about five, when he realised he wanted to get back into nappies and started fashioning them out of towels and using his mother's shower caps to make plastic pants.

'I've done a fair bit of reading on this, as you can imagine. I did psychology at uni as well, which was handy.'

But it hasn't given him any answers.

'That's the confusing thing. I can remember several key points in my life when I was playing babies with children in the street, up to the age of eight, and getting told off by a father who said it was inappropriate for his daughter to be undressing me and putting me in nappies. I'd get all embarrassed and yet find it exciting. Being up in the treehouse and all the boys had to pee into the cut-off stump of the tree. And when the girls had to do it they couldn't aim and it shot everywhere, all over us. Was *that* an exciting moment! All us boys were squirming and saying, "Eeuw, girl germs," and yet I'm still into pee play. Is it from that point in my life? I can probably attribute a lot of things to a lot of things but I also know that similar things have happened to other people I know and they haven't ended up adult babies. Why so? I don't know.'

On the sly he dressed in his sister's clothes until he was about nine, when his outraged parents busted him. He fought to suppress the urge until puberty when it re-erupted and became uncontrollable.

'My parents discouraged me from it. My father was a very masculine man, ex-rugby league player, but by discouraging it all they did was drive it underground. I just made sure that if I wanted to play dress-ups I did it when they weren't around. That simple.'

When he was thirteen he started snowdropping, pinching panties from clothes lines because he couldn't buy his own.

'Then I got caught shoplifting a pair of panties when I was

about fifteen—that's how my parents found out about my dress-ups again, and spent about a year and a half going to a psychiatrist. I had group therapy; that was interesting, I met some really fascinating people.'

I totally believe him when he tells me how pretty he was as a seventeen-year-old in drag but he gets a photo to prove it anyway. Glossy black hair, long eyelashes, well-applied makeup and a white strapless dress … he really was gorgeous.

'I could walk into bars and guys would open doors for me, buy me drinks, light my cigarettes. I didn't have to say a word, darling. I'd just have to bat my eyelashes and they'd be blithering idiots.' Even his voice back then was convincing as a woman's, before it had been deepened by the ravages of tar and nicotine.

I ask him if he's always been straight.

'That's a twisted word, darling. Be careful how you use it. You mean, have I always been heterosexual. Okay, no, I've always been,' he pauses for effect, '… sexual. My preference is for heterosexual sex, I've only ever been in love with women or in relationships with women, therefore I would have to classify myself as … heterosexual. But I went to a boarding school when I was thirteen and by the time I was fourteen I was sleeping with I don't know how many guys. By the time I was twenty I had slept with about a thousand of them. That's not a lie or an exaggeration. I've slept with thousands of guys and hundreds of women. More guys than women because it was easier and more convenient. Also I was into gang banging for a while when I was eighteen/nineteen/twenty so I'd sometimes sleep with ten guys in one night.'

But why was it easier with guys? Apparently that's a dumb question because he replies like he's spelling something out to a simpleton.

'Because boys want to have sex more often than girls want to have sex. Have you noticed this? Hmmm, it's a funny thing that, isn't it? And if you put a whole bunch of guys together they'll have sex with each other.'

His tone is funny rather than humiliating so I won't hesitate to spit out my next stupid question when it pops into my head.

'I could go out on a great date with a really nice girl when I was eighteen and still living at home with Mummy and Daddy and she was still living at home with her parents, and I'd drop her home and everything would be sweet but I'd be as horny as hell. So I'd go into one of the gay saunas in the city and get the shit fucked out of me for two or three hours and go home, have a shower—"Hi, Mum and Dad." "How was your date?" "Fabulous." "You look happy." "I am."' He grins. 'They were strange times.'

By his early twenties he'd started to work out that his fetish was getting in the way of a few important goals.

'By then I was dressing in drag a lot and really getting into my baby fetish and wearing nappies in bed but I knew I was headed for trouble because I was starting to attract more guys than girls. But I'd worked out I was heterosexual and I wanted to be a parent; I really wanted to be a mother but I knew that wasn't possible so I decided to become a father. I knew I had to look straight so I divested myself of all my fetish trappings, the virgin birth that every drag queen goes through, the thrash and trash. Most drag queens go through that two or three times in their lives.'

One of the advantages of getting older, he believes, is you resign yourself to the way you are and stop fighting unorthodox urges.

'You review all that stuff. I'm never doing it again because you realise that if you truly have a fetish and you try and suppress it you will in fact go insane. How insane you go is completely dependent on your friends, your situation, your work. But you will go insane and start taking unnecessary risks to satisfy the fetish. Like walking outside in the street dressed in something inappropriate or getting drunk and doing something stupid. When your fetish is getting taken care of on a regular basis, those risky things don't ever appeal to you.

'Anyway, so I decide I'm going to get butch. I go to the gym, put on muscles, ruined myself for sleeveless gowns! Such a shame. Put on six inches around my chest, which is great if you're a guy, but it's really hard to get frocks. I'm size 10 down here and size 16 up here—and it ain't tits, baby! So I cut my hair very short, tried to grow a moustache.' He laughs when recalling that attempt because given his Asian genes he doesn't have much facial hair. Apparently he's one-eighth Chinese but I reckon he looks much more.

'Just that little one-eighth?' I ask.

'Yep, just that little one-eighth. And it's all in my bladder!'

When he was twenty-three he fell for a girl, Celeste, and desperately tried to suppress his fetish.

'I tried to get all butch and it didn't work. She was an alcoholic. She was twenty-one and we were going to twenty-first parties and engagements all the time so we'd go out and get hammered every weekend. Every time she drank she got hammered. She'd say, "Well, you smoke grass" and I'd say, "Well, yes, I smoke grass but I can still have a conversation. You drink and you fall over." I'm always going to carry a little package of guilt because I feel that my fetish contributed to her alcoholism.'

So, although she already knew he was into drag, he did eventually share the baby fetish with her. I ask how he did it.

'I told her I liked to be babied, breastfed, cuddled, that sort of stuff and she was into that. Then I told her I liked to wear nappies and she thought that was amusing. Occasionally I'd wear a babydoll nightie to bed and I'd say, "I wish I had a nappy on" and eventually I went and had them made.'

The dressmaker really didn't know what she was doing so they weren't a good fit. He calls out to Barbara, who's busy dressing Angelica. 'After you've got that pinned on can Angelica come over and show off her nappy, please?'

There's some struggling and giggling going on over at the change table and after a few minutes Angelica comes over to model her bulky pale pink embroidered nappy. She's smiling coyly, head down, eyes up like Princess Di, then with arms by her sides and hands pointing out like fins she does a slow turn.

'These are made for me by an ex-girlfriend of mine I call Mummy,' Jennie says. 'She usually gives us the embroidered pieces and we hand sew them on ourselves like good little girls.' Jennie's decided that's enough modelling for now and dismisses Angelica. 'Go put your placky pants on now, baby.'

Jennie introduced the fetish before he and Celeste married, and she still wanted to go through with it.

'I was twenty-seven and everything was cool. Then gradually things started to fall apart. I wanted to sleep in nappies at least a few nights a week and she didn't want me to. We fought and she was drinking heavily. She was a very aggressive drunk, which I had a lot of problems with.' They broke up shortly after, ending a seven-year relationship.

Jennie decided after that he would never ever get involved with a woman without letting her know about his kink.

'I'd reached the point where I'd tried to suppress it, started going nuts, doing stupid, risky things, then I realised that was a great way to ruin my life. I wanted to make something of my life so I had to get my act together.'

Then he met Angela.

'It was just after I'd graduated and set up my own practice. She was an actress, very open-minded, very playful and very sexually adventurous. I told her I liked to be babied and dressed up sometimes and she was fine with that. We had a great relationship for the next few years.'

They married, agreed to have children, and had a baby soon after.

'Shortly after we had the baby I asked her to put a nappy on me and she looked at me blankly and said, "You don't expect me to do that any more? I've got a real baby to look after now."' His jaw drops and he exhales loudly. 'My world fell apart. I tried to make a go of it and we had a second child three years later. But that was it. It was hopeless, I knew that. And then gradually we came to hate each other. Now we're amicably divorced. Well I'm happily divorced and she's almost reached the point of being amicable.'

They split five years ago and the boys, now twelve and nine, know about the baby gear, nappies and spankings. They weren't meant to find out—Jennie hid his photos on a separate hard drive of the computer—but somehow about six months ago they got into it. So how did they react?

'Oh, Jesus, this is a tough one. My boys are geniuses. I'm really, really bright but one of my boys is a genius. Taught himself to read at the age of four. Now, that's really bright, okay? And he asked me who Baby Jennie was. My ex-wife rang a few days later and said, You bastard! Those boys have seen photos of you in nappies. I said, Yeah, there's a photo of me in a baby dress on the fridge, there's also one of me in a wedding dress and another one of me in a Tarzan outfit.'

He told the kids he went to fancy-dress parties and the first time they saw him in full drag he was dressed as a 'big girl' in a mini, fishnets and stilettos. He hadn't wanted the boys to see him but they weren't asleep as planned when he was slipping out to a party.

'The older boy, the genius, said, "Wow, Dad, you look beautiful. You look like a sexy schoolgirl."'

The next time he was busted was one morning when he came in from a party at five, was having a smoke before he went to bed, and his son woke up and saw him in full baby gear. He asked if his father had just been to a fancy-dress party.

'But now they've seen the website photos and they know about Baby Jennie. I know how bright that boy is and I know he's put two and two together. I don't know if he knows it's a sexual fetish but I'm waiting for those questions to arise and they will—he's a very bright boy. And because I'm really bright myself and because I'm *incredibly* well read–' he says this with no trace of irony, '–my kids have always used me as an information source. So I'm going to have to try and answer them as honestly as I can because the worst thing you can do is lie to them. And I've already done that—I didn't realise they'd already seen the information and I was still trying to conceal it. So I'm already in the poo; they may not ask me anything for a year or two, to my regret. It's a bad incident in my life.'

He relied on a couple of salons with professional mistresses during his married years when he needed to play, but it wasn't ideal.

'It was costing hundreds of dollars and, besides, it's much more fun playing with people you like.' Barbara and Chris, long-term swingers, murmur agreement. 'Having swinging sex is okay, but having swinging sex with people that you like is *really* horny. There's an emotional involvement, an intellectual involvement, you get a better quality of sex. Everyone knows that.'

The expense wasn't the only thing narrowing his options. 'In baby play you often end up pooing your nappy and cer- tain houses have rules against that. Unfortunately it's not always the easiest thing to control, especially when you're in full baby mode.'

It used to take him a while to get into that baby headspace and to become incontinent, but now all he needs is to put on a nappy. And have a nip of alcohol.

'Angelica and I make up bottles and we almost always put a tiny splash of alcohol in them. That's all it takes to have an effect. Ecstasy works too. "Oh dear, I've wet my nappy. Oh dear,

I'll have to be changed." Angelica usually gets changed about once a night and I usually get changed about three times a night and that gives me more opportunity to play.' He gets furious with himself when occasionally he wets the bed on nappy-free nights.

I want to know how the nappies can cope with a full adult bladder so he takes me to the huge change table in the corner, with its neatly folded nappies stacked underneath, to explain. He unfolds one on the table and points out the two layers of double terry towelling with an extra layer sewn into the centre. He also inserts a toddler's extra large disposable nappy as a soaker pad. 'That is good for three seated wettings, or one and a half litres of fluid.'

So what's the difference between seated and other wettings?

'When you sit down there's more pressure in the crotch of the nappy and the flow is limited in where it can go. When you lie down it trickles out the back. When you lie on your front it runs all the way up the front. When you're sitting, like in the movie theatre, it's only going to go into one place—the bottom of the nappy. And after three wees, or one and a half litres of fluid, this will start to leak around the leg area. But if I go to sleep in one of these I can wake up in the morning, having weed four or five times, and I know this simply because of the weight of the nappy, and I'll be safe as houses because more of the nappy soaks it up when you're lying down.'

During the day he wears disposable incontinence pads for adults. 'Or I wear pull-ups because I'm a big kid now.'

He gives me the tour of his props: the adult-sized highchair with a heavy, lockable tray to trap wayward babies and the playpen, not that much bigger than a normal one but with much higher sides. He's made them all himself without any training in carpentry because, as he reminds me, he's a genius.

We sit back down and Baby Angelica, who's finished getting dressed, comes over to be admired.

'You're a pretty, pretty gell!' Barbara says in a baby's voice. Jennie doesn't bother with special voices.

'Very pretty, Angelica. You putting Mummy's shoes on again?' Jennie asks.

'Yass!'

'It was worth all the effort. You look gorgeous,' I say.

'Fank you.'

'I like the plaits with the ribbon threaded through,' I add.

Jennie checks out the hairdo.

'They're beautiful, darling. You're so clever, Aunty Barbara. We love having Aunty Barb come to visit because she's really creative with stuff like that. She makes us look like real pretty little girls. Angelica! Could you make me up a drink in my Hot Jelly cup, please? Yeah, they're all in the dishwasher. Dishwasher needs to be emptied, thanks, darling.'

Baby Jennie turns to me and says, sotto voce, 'Darling, if there's anything you want, just ask Angelica. She's a true submissive. She lives to be bossed around by women.'

'Well, I'll have to think of something I want now.'

'Or just call her over and give her a slap on the bottom. She'll get as hard as the hobs of hell!'

Barbara says Angelica was very hard when she was trying to put that nappy on, making the job almost impossible. It also explains the giggling and grunting I heard.

Jennie seals another joint and says, 'I told you, darling. If you treat her like a naughty little two-year-old girl she loves it. And she is *big*. Not the biggest I've ever seen, but the biggest white guy I've seen.'

Angelica comes around and sits on her heels on the floor next to my chair and sucks on a bottle of dark brown liquid. When I ask her what's in it she looks shy, giggles, and tells me it's 'Coke wiv a liddle tiny bit of Southern Comfort mixed in.'

So Jennie's fetish had destroyed his second serious relationship and he was miserable until he met Crystal.

'I met this beautiful woman, love of my life; she's a flight attendant, and it was just perfect. I told her about my baby fetish and she made me a nappy. She was away three days a week so although she knew about it she didn't have to play with it or deal with it very often. So I wore nappies and played babies three nights a week when she was away, and then once every couple of weeks she'd go full on and mother me. While I was with her I made my highchair. She made me a dozen nappies, a couple of dresses, really sweet stuff, they're really pretty.'

Crystal also went along with Jennie's interest in B&D, despite the fact she was a pacifist.

'She's a pure and gentle soul, she'd run from an argument. She's a wonderful woman but she couldn't beat me and part of my thing is not just being a little baby girl but being a naughty baby girl who needs to have her bottom smacked occasionally … You don't start off a pain slut.'

He shows me a very spiky domme's collar and I ask why he'd have one of those.

'Here's the thing, I'm not a submissive.'

'But you like to be humiliated and spanked?'

'Correct.'

'I'm a bit naive about this stuff.'

'That's okay. Yeah, I'm a bit of a pain slut and I like to get *fucked*, really hard sometimes. I don't know if that's because of growing up in a boarding school the way I did. I lost my virginity to a woman when I was seventeen years old. She was the mother of one of my school friends. I seduced her. Straight out. Said I wanted to lose my heterosexual virginity. She was thirty-eight. She had no choice. I just took her apart. I fucked her brains out and left her writhing and sweating on the bed and she said to me, "I thought you said you were a virgin!" I said, "I am," but at that stage I'd slept with about three or four hundred guys. I knew what I liked when they did it to me so I just turned the tables and did what I liked to her.'

But back to the lovely, gentle Crystal.

'So we lived together for four years, had a beautiful relationship, but eventually she told me she couldn't beat me. I got her to do it several times but there came a time when she actually broke down, burst into tears, threw the paddle away, stormed out of the room. She said, "I can't do this, I can't hurt you." And I said, "Yeah, but look what it's doing to me." I had this raging hard-on. She said, "But I can't do it. It makes me physically ill."'

He was by now watching his third long-term relationship unravel because of his fetish but he also knew it was inescapable. He suggested to Crystal that he'd visit dommes to get his fix so she wouldn't have to beat him and assured her there'd be no sex involved.

'And she said, But you'll masturbate, and I said, Yeah. And you'll come. Yeah. So that's sex. But there's no intercourse, nothing like that at all. She said, It doesn't matter, it's sex in your head. And if it's sex in your head then you're being unfaithful to me. And she was *right*, I couldn't argue with her. So we mulled it over for a few months and eventually I had to say to her, I can't do this, I'd rather be your best friend because I love you that much, and not sleep with you, than sleep with you and lie to you and destroy our relationship. So we had lots of tears and I moved out. She's living nearby, and we're still best friends. She still changes my nappy occasionally and breastfeeds me and makes Angelica and me these wonderful clothes and nappies and things. She's still the most wonderful woman, but she won't have sex with me because you don't have sex with babies.'

The conflict for Crystal was that she couldn't play with him as a baby and sleep with him as a grown-up. To have sex with him she needed him to be butch and adult, a problem Jennie understood.

'I'm well educated enough to know exactly what I'm asking of female partners. One of the things I've always tried to do with the women I've been with is to look after them *in extremis* because I know I'm asking a lot of anybody. Being a mummy is hard work. That's why most women give it up after a few years because it's fucking hard work. Changing smelly nappies and feeding and washing baby, they're all tasks.'

His next relationship was with a beautiful Singaporean mistress who advertised in the local paper. He booked Tammy for a two-hour session but, fuelled by coke, dope, booze and whatever else Jennie could pull out of that chunky coffee table, it turned into ten. He saw her half a dozen times professionally over the next year but not even Jennie's pain threshold was high enough for Tammy.

'Pure pain isn't my fetish. She's a sadistic little bitch, God bless her cotton socks. She actually enjoys applying the cane. We've got it all on video. Angelica's got a couple of seriously good studio-quality cameras, hand held, with an editing suite.'

Tammy went to England with a client, came back when her visa ran out, caught back up with Jennie and they started spending weekends together.

'She didn't ask to become my girlfriend or anything like that. It just kind of happened, we sort of drifted into it. In all this time I'd never ever had sex with the girl. We'd done lots of other things, most of them terribly obscene and several of them highly illegal in most states. Most of them we did repeatedly and with gusto. But then when she was interested and it came time to perform, I couldn't get a full erection. I'd never expected to have sex with this person and being called upon in that situation was really weird.'

He says impotence isn't usually a problem for him unless he's been drinking.

'As they say three drinks and I'm anyone's, ten drinks and I'm no one's. I can drink Southern Comfort till it's squirting out my ears, no problem, but three glasses of wine, gone.'

Anyway, Tammy made a fatal mistake for a professional mistress—she took Jennie to one of the private fetish parties in Sydney. Goodbye expensive salons, hello bargain-rate suburban kinksters.

'And, oh, the world did open up for me. I *knew* there were other people like me because as soon as I got a computer at nineteen I'd been searching for adult baby pornography. I'd also found some serious treatises on paraphilias and infantilism and all those other polysyllabic words which don't have much meaning. At parties I met people who said they really liked dressing up in nappies too and wetting themselves and even being bad girls and pooing in their nappies. They're the people I wanted to talk to.'

The trouble was his IQ was so high it was difficult to find an intellectual match, he says. Tammy was smart as well as gorgeous.

'Tiny waist, little heart-shaped bottom, just the kind of thing you want sitting on your face. Want to sit down? Let me clear a space,' he says, brushing his face with his open hand in two broad sweeps.

That first party was about four years ago. Angelica was there in drag as a big girl. She was desperately shy, wanted to be dressed as a baby girl like Baby Jennie, but was too frightened to try it. Angelica's feeling comfortable enough to chime in with her version of events, something Jennie says would never have happened a few years earlier. Angelica has even dropped the baby voice, though maintains a sooky demeanour.

'I followed BJ like a little puppy dog. I had my high heels on and lingerie, a nice little baby-type top and a pair of panties.' He says a friend, Mistress Brown, pointed out Jennie, saying, 'Look, there's your wet dream,' and urged him to try dressing like her. 'I'd been on the scene for some time and I'd never met BJ. She was always doing other things at parties or having people play with her bot bot during the night.'

Jennie had noticed Angelica admiring him, knew he needed help with the next step into the baby-girl fetish, so used Mistress Brown as an intermediary.

'I'd bought this dress on the internet which was way too big for me, so I said to Mistress Brown: You tell that Angelica that I have a baby dress that would fit her that she could wear whenever she wants to go out. I wouldn't give it to her, I said, but if she wanted it she had to come over here and get dressed up.'

Angelica's grinning at the memory.

'Two hours after that phone call I was here! Hee hee hee.' The baby voice is back. 'I got all dressed up in nappies and the baby-girl dress and it was sooo good I could not wee in my nappy! I had such a hard-on it took three hours before I could let it go.'

'I was pouring drinks into her and she still couldn't let go!' Jennie says.

'But when I did start to go then it went hard again so I couldn't empty my bladder properly!' said Angelica, pink-cheeked and giggling.

'The first time, Angelica had trouble weeing lying down. You have to conquer certain barriers. Letting go any time anywhere is the first one. Being able to wee in any position is the next one. Being able to wee without waking is the next one.'

'What's the fun of weeing without waking?' I ask. Another stupid question apparently.

'When you go to bed in a dry nappy and you wake up saturated, just like a baby, because you've slept *just like a baby* … and you're asking what the excitement is? Let's go through that again. Are you with me now? It's the infantile pleasure of knowing that you slept *like a baby*.'

I've been here well over an hour and although this interview ranks high in the fun stakes I really have to get going. Before I leave Jennie takes me into the bedroom to check out his wardrobe. There's an unmade bed with a copy of Bryce Courtenay's latest work on the pillow (what was that he'd said about being highly literate?) and a built-in robe full of pink, red and white confections. There's lots of satin ribbon trims, puffed sleeves, broderie anglaise, petticoats, tulle, pink gingham and seersucker. I notice a pair of crimson Mary Jane flat shoes kicked off in the corner.

'Hey, how do you get shoes big enough for your feet?' I ask.

'Excuse me, slut features! What are you saying about my feet?'

I look at them again. 'Oh, they're not *that* big, are they?'

'No, they're not. Most teenage girls have got feet bigger than me these days. Darling, I have Mary Janes in just about every colour of the rainbow.'

I've had a great time this afternoon and Jennie's been hilarious company. His massive ego is a thing of wonder but I'm left feeling somewhat disturbed by the fact that I find him kind of attractive. But that particular thought bubble is quickly burst; as we walk down the hall to the front door I notice the laundry has a mini clothes line hanging from the ceiling, festooned with large pink plastic pants.

27

THE CLUB SCENE

The door bitch at the Hellfire Club in Darlinghurst is in a purple corset and matching tutu and has one of those burgundy, short-fringed haircuts popular among women who work in publishing. She looks me up and down, assessing my attempt at BDSM dressing, and knocks $2 off the $25 entry charge. Bigger discounts go to those making a real effort, usually in latex, crinolines or high boots. 'Fetish, formal or fancy dress' is the official dress code, so I'm lucky they let me in at all. I'm all in black—nothing new there—baring very little flesh, but have trotted out the leather whip earrings and studded collar Graham gave me. The fishnet stockings don't count for much because my skirt covers most of them.

I knew I wouldn't be able to convince David to join me tonight but I gave it a go anyway. He couldn't think of anything worse. So I've had dinner with my sister, several glasses of wine, and dressed at her place. She was keeping her options open, but by the time nine-thirty rolls around she just wants to drop me off and get back home—can't say I blame her—so I've come on my own.

I order a mineral water from the bar—I'm on duty now—and, as it's still early, have no trouble finding an empty table. I sit alone, feeling less self-conscious than expected, and check out the room. Last time I was here, fifteen years ago, it was a smart restaurant, and the thick sandstone walls and polished floorboards remain. I'd lunched here with my husband and mother-in-law, a perfect meal only marred when, returning from the loo, my mother-in-law tripped and toppled down the open staircase at the back of the room, silencing everyone and knocking herself out in the process.

I shake that horrendous memory from my head and peruse the other patrons. They're all ages, shapes and sizes and it doesn't matter what that size or shape is, nobody seems to mind flaunting it. I've noticed this at other scene events and I like it—women who anywhere else might be inclined to hide beneath caftans will lace themselves into corsets, letting their ample breasts spill over the top and their bingo wings flap in the breeze.

There's a severe-looking blonde across the room with her hair pulled back into a thick cluster of artificial plaits that swing like a whip every time she moves her head. She's a taut package of red PVC with stiletto-heeled boots that stop just short of her matching mini dress and don't allow her the confident stride she ought to have. My eyes wander down to the end of a leash looped around her wrist and there's her partner, a skinny, grey-haired man on hands and knees in nothing but a collar, boots and a shiny black G-string.

A group of four who know each other from the scene sit at the table next to mine and, after ten minutes or so, ask me to join them. I drag my chair across and we talk about work, kids, partners, the stuff you'd talk about at any club. One of the men, with a shaved head and a goatee, edits a four-wheel-drive magazine. His girlfriend, tall and slim with dark hair pulled into two high bunches above her ears, is a nanny. The other bloke wears a smudge of black eyeliner, has a broken front tooth and works as a glazer. He's a gentle, tactile type who shakes my hand slowly and insists on buying everyone beers. And his girlfriend, a red-lipsticked blonde, is a chatty admin assistant. I don't know what this lot get up to in the bedroom—and I can't ask because I'm not 'fessing up to researching—but from here they're just normal, normal, normal and normal.

Which gets me thinking: I'm sure everyone here thinks they're really edgy but there is a clichéd sameness about the look in the BDSM scene. People generally restrict their wardrobe to one of two colours—black and red, and to two fabrics—leather and latex. The occasional white outfit normally conforms to another cliché—the nurse's uniform (in latex, natch). Makeup's normally heavy and dominated by black eyeliner and red lipstick—it matches the outfits. Heels are always high, stockings always fishnet.

There seem to be a lot of people disappearing down a stairwell in the corner of the main bar so I go with the nanny and the journalist to have a look. Down here in a stonewalled cellar-like space there's a dance floor with thumping music, dim lighting and alcoves around the edge housing another bar, little lounge areas and torture zones with whipping frames and crucifixes.

It's crowded and smoky but everyone's remarkably friendly and unthreatening. Whether it's because people dress up here to make a spectacle of themselves and therefore fully expect to be looked at, nobody seems to mind my wandering around just looking. Lots of people are bopping with nobody in particular so for a while I join in. Then, as I'm perched on a stool at the edge of the dance floor next to a fat Greek girl in a silver tiered skirt, I realise what a shocking fire trap this place is—lots of smoke, hundreds of bodies and only one narrow staircase as the sole route in or out. That's enough to get me back upstairs for a breather.

Leaning on the bar is Baby Jennie, in one of her frilly spotted numbers, and we greet each other like old friends. He's with Barbara and Chris, who I reckon would have got major discounts on the entry price for their outfits. Barbara's in a red leather corset with wide witch's sleeves, also leather, which is gorgeous but must weigh a tonne. Chris is pretty much basic black, leather and studs. Mistress Cath, who I'd met at Hard Core Heaven, checks me out and, ready with unsolicited wardrobe advice, tells me I need a corset to make the most of my 'assets'. I think my top looks fine but, to prove her point, she grabs my breasts, shoves them up somewhere under my chin and rams them together, creating a five-inch cleavage. I tell her she's right, that I'll buy one, just so she'll let go.

I pop back downstairs to hear cheering and applause—I'd just missed the floor show. Two shiny-skinned, near-naked women scampering off the stage is all I catch, dammit, but whatever they'd been up to must have been good.

This has been fun but it's getting late so I leave and cross Oxford Street for a cab. It's much scarier out here amid the drunks and catcallers. It's filthy with litter and the neon-lit vomitoria around Taylor Square are starting to reek.

'I want to lick your furby,' slurs a very pissed boy of about nineteen as he staggers towards me, making me laugh as I swerve to avoid him. The one thing that distinguishes the Hellfire Club from other nightclubs I've been to—apart from a heavy dose of leather and latex—is that everyone inside is so well behaved.

28
GETTING BLIND

Sarah, a very vanilla woman in her late thirties, has contacted me through the alternative sex website wanting to tell me about her first experience of being a submissive. I'm intrigued. She wasn't prepared to meet so we agreed to talk on the phone. She's not long out of a marriage that involved plenty of good vanilla sex, with neither partner taking an obviously dominant or submissive role. She'd posted a fairly sparse profile on the site just to see what happened and, although she hadn't spelled out her curiosity about submission, when she was contacted by Richard, an articulate, non-lifestyle dom who wasn't into anything too heavy or weird, she decided to meet him.

She had an appointment in town anyway and, having established when chatting online the previous weekend that he was in finance, she figured he probably worked in the city. So she texted him, she was right, and yes, he was keen to meet. He texted describing what he'd be wearing—grey trousers and a blue shirt, looking *vaguely stressed, and a bit furtive*. She laughed, texting *Ha!* in reply, encouraged by his sense of humour. On her way there she'd seen a Mediterranean-looking guy in the right clothes, apparently waiting for someone, but at the wrong end of the building. He matched the swarthy image of Richard's profile shot but was wearing a baseball cap and had one of those facial hair arrangements that looked like they'd been drawn on with black eyeliner. After she'd braced herself to ask if he was Richard she nearly collapsed with relief when he looked at her blankly, shaking his head.

So she got to the agreed spot but after ten minutes of hovering in the shadows of a War Memorial statue there was still nobody that looked anything like the dark-haired, olive-skinned character she was expecting. There was a fair-skinned bloke nearby in the right clothes and, as there didn't seem to be any other likely types around, she approached him. Bingo.

'It was a bit unsettling because I couldn't get past the fact that this guy just didn't fit the picture and yet he seemed surprised I'd taken so long to approach him. First thing he said was, "Look, blue shirt, grey trousers, what do you want?" but I just thought, This guy's posted a fake pic.'

The other slight turn-off early on was that he seemed a bit cocky; as they went into a café he told her he'd once been interviewed for a job in the same place.

'Really?'

'Yep, got the job too.'

'Good on you.'

'Didn't take it though.'

'Right.' She didn't care why, she just thought he was trying a bit too hard. Or maybe he was nervous.

Sarah ordered chai, Richard sparkling mineral water, and the sussing-each-other-out began in earnest. Not that you could tell from the outside—they assiduously avoided discussing sex, sticking instead to work and travel. But their conversation was immaterial—they were there to assess chemistry. The whole time she remained distracted by the niggling mismatch of his profile photo to reality, something he'd dismissed as a lighting issue but which she felt cast a shadow over his integrity. Overall, though, she liked him and left thinking he was a nice guy, but she wasn't overwhelmed with the desire to shag him.

That all changed over the next week. A series of increasingly exciting emails and texts showed he could write, he was funny and he had an excellent imagination. And, when she challenged him about it, he also put her mind at rest about the photo.

He seemed to understand that she was after a bit of adventure, even though she couldn't articulate exactly what that might entail, and he liked the way she was outwardly 'respectable'. He asked her about her fantasies and tried to determine her limits. How would she feel about being tied up, examined naked with him clothed, and even having two men at once, he asked.

'All those ideas excited me like crazy and I felt quite flustered! I'm much braver on email than I would have been face to face so I said that all sounded good, but I knew I wasn't really committing to anything. He outlined what might happen if we finally got together at his flat. He said he'd leave the door on the latch, I'd let myself in and he'd be in the bedroom with the door closed. Better I didn't see him at that point, he said.' He told her she'd take off her shoes and put on the blindfold he'd leave for her on the coffee table. Then 'off we go' is how he phrased it.

'I told him he'd completely trashed my powers of concentration and rendered me the most distracted woman in Brisbane!' She also knew it sounded so good she had to go through with it. So they made a time, after work, two days hence.

Arriving early, she texted to check he was home and it was okay to come up. Getting out of the lift, she saw the door ajar across the hall and went in, checking it was closed properly behind her. She scanned the small, open-plan flat, noticing the closed bedroom door to the left where she knew he'd be waiting, and the bathroom to the right.

'I thought about going to the loo but I was too nervous so I went straight to the sofa, sat down, took off my shoes and put on the blindfold,' she said. She'd only ever worn airline eye masks before, which you can spy out of from gaps around the nose, but this one was utterly blinding. 'It was thick black sheepskin against my face with black leather stitched on top and firm elastic holding it in place. I fiddled with it a bit, trying to make sure the elastic wasn't pushing my ears out or messing up my hair, and then I just sat still.'

She waited for what was probably only a few minutes until she heard him come in.

'He was moving around the room behind me, fiddling with the stereo and checking his email or something. It's incredible how sharp your hearing becomes when you can't see.'

He'd said he wouldn't say anything much at the beginning and he didn't. He came over to the sofa, stood in front of her and just said softly, 'I need you to stand up.' Holding on to his hands, she rose. 'Now, just take a couple of steps over here to your left and put your hands here. I don't want you to fall over,' he said, guiding her hands to a kitchen bench.

The idea of not seeing him was, he'd said, so she would have 'the lingering thought that it was a complete stranger taking liberties with [her] body'. And as much of a turn-on as that thought might have been, she knew it was him and his voice alone was doing it for her.

'I could feel him moving around me, hear him breathing. He also made these primal little grunts which might not sound particularly attractive but were incredibly sexy at the time,' she said, laughing.

She felt his finger trace the line of her cleavage then circle her left nipple. Apart from his breathing, the only clues to where he was were the parts of her body he touched next—a buttock squeezed, a thigh stroked, a collarbone kissed.

Raising her arms she let him pull her top off then slide her skirt down. He reached around from the front to unfasten her bra, making her breathe in and pull her shoulders back, then he slid her knickers off.

'I surprised myself with how composed I was even though I was seriously turned on. I'd been so nervous but the blindfold made me focus on what was happening. It also stopped me feeling self-conscious.'

After a few more minutes of examination, when she could feel him hard behind her, he told her to spread her legs, lean forward and rest her elbows on the bench.

'I held my breath and he stuck a couple of fingers into me

and twisted them around. He said, "Ah, so you *are* enjoying yourself after all." I'd been so calm he hadn't known if I was having a good time, but that convinced him.'

Once he'd wiped his fingers on her thigh he took her by the shoulders, told her to take a step backwards and sit down. 'It felt like a padded office chair, with vinyl upholstery—which was sensible under the circumstances!' She heard him rummaging in a drawer behind her then he came back and strapped leather cuffs onto her wrists. 'He got me to put my hands around the back of the chair then somehow latched the cuffs together.'

He'd planned to tease her by playing with her nipples but realised they weren't particularly sensitive. Too much sun and breastfeeding, she said. So he unlatched her, leaving the cuffs on, and led her, still blindfolded, to the bedroom.

'There's a bed behind you. Sit down. Good. Now just lie there,' he said, guiding her down and turning her ninety degrees so her head was on the pillow.

She heard more rummaging and rattling, then he put leather cuffs on her ankles like the ones on her wrists.

'He straddled me and I could feel he was naked now. He took my left wrist first and threaded rope through a metal ring in the cuff and tied that to the bed head. I lay there while he did the other wrist and then he hopped off, parted my legs and did my ankles,' she said.

Any hopes she may have had for gentle teasing were dashed then as, again, he stuck his fingers into her. 'Sometimes it was two fingers, sometimes three, and he'd twist them around, pushing them in and out really fast. It was a bit like a really vigorous internal at the gynaecologist and it wasn't really a lot of fun.'

She shifted up the bed a bit, trying to make this experience more comfortable, and then he said, 'I want you to come for me now.'

'I said there was no way I was going to come like this, and that he'd have to be a lot more gentle and pay some attention to my clitoris. He said, No, I'm going to release one of your hands and you can do that while I watch. So I said, Okay, but make sure it's my right hand!'

She wasn't sure she'd be able to manage an orgasm while being watched but, despite the rough treatment, she was so turned on it only took a couple of minutes.

'Again the blindfold, which actually slipped off just as I came, made a huge difference,' she said.

'It was so weird. I finished, opened my eyes and said, "Oh, hello," to this guy I'd only ever actually *seen* for half an hour over coffee a week earlier.'

He then untied her, leaving the cuffs on, and said she could have 'a little rest'. The next couple of hours were great fun, though largely vanilla. But I take back everything I said about being sick of hearing about other peoples' sex lives. That business with the blindfold struck me as the most intensely erotic thing I'd heard in years.

29

THE TOUGH NEGOTIATOR

If it's the right consistency—firm to hard—Godfrey will eat a whole rectum full of Regina's shit. He's contacted me because he wants to set me straight on a kink he believes is widely misunderstood and, with his vast experience, he says he's the man to do it.

Even while we're communicating with pseudonyms through the website he's ultra cagey when I try to line up a phone interview, though eventually he agrees to call me at an agreed time.

His relationship with Regina is normal and 'neutral' he says, with neither one of them dominating the other. The scat play isn't a lifestyle thing, it's just an activity they like. The thing I'm always most interested in is how they started doing it, who brought it up, and how.

'We had been involved in the swinging scene which, to be honest, is probably something that I initiated. We'd been in that for a long time and then came to know people in the BDSM scene indirectly through other business connections. We ourselves were not really interested in that scene at the time but I think, with mutual inclination, we got involved in the golden shower scene. That lasted a while and then the excitement of that seemed to wear off and it was a progression, I guess, to suggest we try scat. Probably once again that was my suggestion. It's got to the point where we now exclude any golden shower activities from the scat activities. It just doesn't seem to fit too well together, I don't know why.'

Just going on this version of the events with Godfrey suggesting, Regina accepting, I've got a picture of her being a bit long-suffering. She's not initiating any of this stuff and I wonder how much she really likes it. He confidently intellectualises the whole thing and, although I'm careful with my questions, he sometimes sounds a bit defensive.

'I don't regard it as a perversion because that's a term on which one assesses something according to the professed norms of others. I suppose in terms of the professed social normality it could certainly be called a fetish, but then what's a fetish? It's a like. Alcoholism in a sense is a fetish but so then also is a woman's fetish for long, brightly coloured fingernails if she insists on having them all the time. One will say it's a fashion statement, one will say it's something she likes, but examined, it's really some form of fetish.'

But doesn't it have to be linked to sexual arousal if it's defined as a fetish? I ask.

'Oh no. If you want to be purely Freudian in your thinking everything has to be linked with sexual arousal, but if you look at it from the point of view of other psychologists a fetish is defined more as a compulsive behaviour. One could argue about the terminology day in, day out.' He waffles about obsessive compulsive disorder but realises it's not where he really wants to go.

'If you wanted to talk to someone who had a compulsive sexual need to play out a submissive role to an Amazonian mistress and be denigrated and defiled you've got the wrong individual here. Or if, on the other hand, you're looking for someone who wants to be the great overbearing dominant, inflicting pain and harm and degradation on people, then you've also got the wrong guy. I'm generally regarded, if one wishes to apply such an epithet, as very dominant, but I also enjoy practices which are normally regarded as extremely submissive. So I do not see these epithets as being valid. Someone did say to me once, "Ah, you enjoy these submissive activities because you can top from the bottom"—I'm sure you've heard the expression. And I suppose there's an element of truth in that. I do top from the bottom. I like what I like and I say how I like it.'

When he and Regina first got together there was nothing kinky about their sex life. He suggested swinging about two years into the marriage and I want to know if she felt threatened by the idea.

'Ah, it was a little different because the first occasion was with a close girlfriend of hers that she'd known long before I met her. So that was fun. But then yes, for quite a time there was an element of fearing to be threatened, not *feeling* threatened but *fearing* to be threatened—there's a difference. If you feel threatened you have a belief that you're about to be damaged or lose something. If you fear to be threatened you think that maybe it will lead to a situation where that may occur.'

His semantics are lost on me but it sounds like she didn't really like what was going on. So how did she cope with the golden showers?

'She had a very conservative religious upbringing so she thought it was a bit odd, but it was something out of the ordinary, a bit of excitement and she was happy enough to try it.'

I want to know how it went the first time.

'Ha ha! It was very amateurish and therefore very messy and, from that point of view, unsatisfactory. But as one overcame one's inexperience with it, it was very often fun. You get to the stage where a woman knows what she drinks will give a certain taste.'

'Really? I'm quite interested in the practical side of things,' I say and he laughs.

'There's only one way to find out about the practical side of things, you know.'

'No, there's more than one way,' I say, also laughing. 'What do you mean by amateurish?'

'I think we're probably quite neat and tidy individuals and when you get stuff splashed over the place where it shouldn't be then the normal household drudgery comes into it. Then you hear people say, "You climb in the bathtub and do it." Well, I can tell you there's nothing less sexy than climbing into a cold bathtub in whatever position with a naked body and trying to indulge in some exciting act!'

I tell him you can use a rubber sheet on the floor but he's dismissive.

'Oh yes, you can go and buy a plastic drop sheet at your local hardware store if you like but with liquid you still have the problem of run-off. It depends what people are into. Some people like having it sprayed on them, some women like standing over someone and giving them a hose down, other women prefer that it's consumed without one drop lost. You know they say for a woman to have sex she has to find the man interesting, for a man to have sex all he needs is a place!'

A prostitute whom Godfrey had helped with a business matter told him about a client she had who was into scat.

'This fellow used to bring his electric toy train set with him and set it up and she would have to squat over it and do her business into one of the little goods carriages. He would then run the train around and around while he masturbated. Now you see *that* is a real sexual fetish. That's odd, that's odd.'

I find it interesting that just because this bloke used a train set and was turned on by the turd in the carriage Godfrey finds him so peculiar. I wonder what the train enthusiast would think of Godfrey eating a couple of logs of his wife's shit as she strains to deliver them straight into his mouth. I'm also surprised he's so fussy about the taste of urine when he's prepared to eat shit. I ask him what a person should avoid drinking if they're planning to give someone a golden shower.

'I have the distinct impression that you're trying to probe me for ideas that you can actually use!'

I assure him I'm not.

'Apple cider tastes good, strong coffee is bad, strong tea is bad, some beer is bad, red wine can be bad, it just depends. It also depends how much water is consumed with it. I'll never know how Gandhi carried out his routine of drinking the first urine of the morning.'

I'm still bewildered; I mean, it'd *have* to be better than shit.

When I try to work out rough time frames he's evasive because he doesn't want to hint at his age.

'Let me just say I'm extremely experienced in this field and the reason I wanted to speak with you is because there's so much nonsense written about this. If someone's really going to write about this it might be interesting to write about the "normal" side of it, if one can call it a normal side.'

That's fine by me—I couldn't care less about his age—but I do want to know how this all works in their relationship.

'It's a question of an extremeness of intimacy. Other people don't necessarily see it that way but that's almost one hundred per cent of the way we see it.'

The issue of Regina's interest in scat play is still plaguing me so I ask Godfrey if he's ever pushed for something she hasn't wanted to do.

'My wife is a typical woman, a typical well-bred, nice woman, and there are very few such women in this world who, when they first approach these things or are induced to approach them, are not to some degree disturbed by it because their upbringing gives them feelings that somehow this is not right. There are women, and I've met them, who want to indulge in this of their own volition. We have a young friend who's many years younger than we are, who's a delicious and delightful young woman, but she discovered this scat business all on her own, and she's almost a fanatic about it, she can't get enough of it. They do exist. But for 99.9 per cent of women in the world that's not the case.'

'So is this young woman in a relationship with you and your wife?' I ask.

'Yes, yes, she is. More principally with me but my wife is always there and always present.'

'Do you and your wife both give and receive?'

'No. No, no, no, no, no, she gives only. And that's my preference. I have no desire to deliver it onto someone else. If I were pushed and asked to do so I would have no difficulty in doing it but I have no desire to do it. I have advanced from the point of just the touching and the playing to the point where I simply prefer to be a "consumer".'

'Eat it, you mean?'

'Yes, but I'm also fussy, so it has to be of a certain consistency, taste. The person giving it has to be a certain attraction physically as well as perhaps otherwise. Compatibility. There has to be a sort of sexual energy between the people. There doesn't have to be a great deal because I'm a male, after all—we only need a place! But there has to be some of that, I can't just do it indiscriminately. Probably if you walk down the main street of any city, of all the females it would probably be one in every five hundred or a thousand who'd be into it anyway, so that's fine.'

'When you consume, do you consume directly from the woman?'

'Yes, directly and only directly, that's the only scenario I have any interest in.'

'What is your preferred consistency?'

'Very firm to hard. There are, of course, other individuals in this world who prefer it at the other end of the spectrum.'

'Would you consume the whole quantity or just a tiny bit of it?'

'That would depend on consistency, taste and the person involved.' (Speaking of taste, I read in *Psychopathia Sexualis* about a coprophagiac who supported his mistress in high style on the condition that she ate nothing but marzipan. A coprophagiac, as distinct from a coprophiliac, is someone like Godfrey who loves to eat, not just play with, poo.)

'One also has to keep a clear head about the health risks and so on. But there is no health risk inherent in the substance itself, only if the person themselves has a disease. I have established over many years and with incredible frequency that there is no danger or risk to health in the substance itself. I have never suffered a problem and there have been periods of a year or two when I would consume it almost every day. But then again that was with my wife and when you live with a person you know they're healthy. And when it's a firm consistency there is very little mess to be made and that is my preference.'

'So you're not into smearing and that sort of thing?'

'Oh, I have been known to, but only when consistency and everything else fails and there's not much else left to do with it and one's desperate to get some relief.'

Godfrey says he's never been vaccinated against hepatitis but has never become ill from scat, something he puts down to luck and careful selection of partners.

'With our young friend, in her early twenties, I know her, I know her background, I know what she does, the kind of friends she has; she is very careful so with people like that I really don't have a concern. I've consumed hers on many occasions without problem and in fact she has a greater drive for it than I do. We've stayed overnight with her and the next morning she gets up and says, "I'm ready for a coffee," but actually she's got something *more* ready for me! And she is not the creature from the black lagoon, or Godzilla. She is really a very attractive, highly educated young woman doing a master's degree.'

He doesn't play with scat daily, as he used to, but then most things sexual are less frequent nowadays, he says.

'And when I think no, I shan't, I shan't, I shan't, eventually I feel I have to. So it is in a sense an addiction, but then sex is an addiction.'

'Has the scat play dropped off because your sex drive has dropped off?'

'No. I had a period of stress a few years back when my sex drive dropped off, but if I had any drive it was bound to this. But now my sex drive has picked up quite a lot. My wife sometimes complains that it's now back to where it was so many years ago! I don't know how to describe this without being crude but I went from a position when it was very high to a point where I didn't care if it never happened and back to a point where I can now manage three times a day. Which isn't as good as it was but, well ...'

'It's not bad.'

'Well, you know, I'm sure there are better.' He's obviously an intelligent man but I wonder if he believes in the mediaeval 'shit as aphrodisiac' principle. European witch trials recorded all kinds of things being consumed for arousal and one document tells of a woman who drove several abbots mad with love by feeding them her faeces.

'You say you've fought it. Does it concern you?' I ask.

'Only from this point of view: I'm getting older and every-body says that if you indulge in this practice it will do all these dreadful things to your health, you'll die of some withering disease in a corner of some squalid place, which I don't believe, but I wonder, is there really any health risk? But then I start again and I indulge lots and I'm as fit as a fiddle.'

'So it's not guilt or disgust?'

'Guilt? Forget it. And disgust? Why should I be disgusted by something I like? That's a psychosis brought on by guilt. I enjoy a good red wine. Should I be disgusted by it? I enjoy a great meal. Should I be disgusted by it? I enjoy looking at a lovely woman. I enjoy doing *more* things to a lovely woman. Should I be disgusted by it because it goes into one different avenue or one step further? I certainly don't look at children—that *is* dis-gusting. And although I've had many experiences in the BDSM scene I certainly abhor brutality and any non-consensual force or pain. And I have children, so force as far as children are con-cerned is the lowest of the low.'

'Do your children know what you're into?'

'No. I have a very firm philosophy that parents have an obli-gation and a duty to bring up their children in the worldly norms in such a way as to allow them to make their own informed decisions. Our children know nothing of our predilections. I assume they know I indulge in sex with my wife because they exist. But they know nothing more. We take great pains [to conceal it], even to the extent of not indulging in things we'd like to because it may be noticed by them. Some people bring up their children letting them know they're swingers or what-ever, but that's simply imposing your lifestyle, which may or may not be right, on your children. I don't say that my lusts or fulfilments are right. They're right for me but that's a subjective judgment; I don't say objectively they're right for anyone else. But my children have a right to develop themselves as they see fit in this world using their own intelligence, and I trust I've brought up intelligent children.'

I ask him if I can email him with any further questions.

'If you think you would like to gain the knowledge to enable you to write really accurately about the subject then send me an email and let me know.' He chuckles.

'Was that some kind of an invitation?'

'It was indeed! I thought it was nicely phrased, though.'

'It was nicely phrased.'

'Well, how can you write about something you have never experienced?'

'I'm writing about it through the words of people who have experienced it.'

'Yes, I know that. But how can you write about driving a car if you've never driven one?'

'I suppose I'd interview people who do drive them.'

'Ah, well, never mind. My invitation was simply to offer the opportunity to view it through your own eyes.'

'To *view* it?'

'Not to view it. I'm sorry, I should have said to experience it through your own feelings … As I said, any time you wish to experience it let me know—I guarantee I don't have two heads.'

Later I email him to thank him for the chat and proceed to play one irksome, probably unethical game. This is what happened: I very much wanted to meet Regina and Godfrey together to check out the dynamics of their relationship and test my suspicion that she's being coerced into scat play. So, knowing he's into threesomes and his wife's bisexual, I comment that her picture on the website is gorgeous and that he's very lucky. The photo, which appears professionally lit, is of a voluptuous, topless woman, blindfolded, with her arms crossed in front of her. He agrees he's very lucky, thinks I want to shag his wife, and suggests we meet. Bait taken.

I wonder what you'd wear if you were going to meet a couple you were planning on fucking and possibly shitting on and, while I have no idea, I think something dark and shapeless is a safe bet. So having parked well away from our agreed meeting place in Rozelle, I walk up Darling Street in a big black polo-neck jumper, mid-calf black skirt and a long black jacket, arriving just after 2 pm. They're already there, waiting on the street.

Jesus, they're *hideous*!!!

No, not really, that's completely unfair. They're simply a casually dressed, fairly anonymous-looking middle-aged couple who look as though they enjoy a good meal, have a bit of money and wouldn't warrant a second look—under normal circumstances. But I have to pretend I'm considering getting my gear off with them, which puts a totally different complexion on things.

Regina's in a beige ensemble, trousers and knitted top with a scooped neckline, and wearing a small diamond 'R' on a fine gold chain. Large dark sunglasses sit on top of her head, holding dark bobbed hair away from her face. Godfrey's portly yet buttockless and is in neutrals too, with sporty Royal Elastic-type shoes. He's put a light auburn rinse through his hair. What is it with that?

I think I'm managing to hide my nerves and repulsion as we introduce ourselves—all using pseudonyms—and go into the café. We sit at a small round table but somehow I feel like I'm in the middle.

We order; they have coffee, I have tea, she has cake. He's confident and chatty but she's quiet and clearly finding the situation awkward. Me too. She's remote, keeps looking into the middle distance. Maybe she's embarrassed. I would be. She knows her husband has told me, a complete stranger, the most intimate, kinky details of their sex life. He's spilled his guts not only to someone who's done nothing to indicate similar pro-clivities but to a *journalist*! Was she wondering how repulsive their practices might seem to me and how they might be por-trayed? Whatever's on her mind, she's dealing with it by keeping her mouth shut.

He becomes progressively more flirtatious, touching my forearm lightly as he gestures. I sit with legs crossed, knees pointing away from him and arms folded across my body.

I try to draw her out on how she feels about him fucking other women and she mumbles something about it being okay for him to get what he wants from them because he's not going to force her to do anything she doesn't want to. Ha! I *knew* she wouldn't want to be doing this stuff. He stresses she's always there when he's with other women, trying to paint himself as a guy with nothing to hide. All it does is make me feel even more sorry for her as I imagine her plonked naked in an armchair while her pot-bellied husband cavorts around the lounge room with some internet pick-up.

He thinks it's amusing that women link sex with love and loyalty and says he's just satisfying an appetite like any other. I bet he belittles her when she objects to his infidelities, dismissing her concerns as feminine trifles. He keeps asking about my sexual experience and tastes and gets mildly irritated when I steer the conversation back to my research. I'm careful because research wasn't why I said I would meet them. He tries to bargain with information, wanting me to match him revelation for revelation. He's getting ripped off, I'm revealing nothing—well, nothing sexual anyway. He tells his wife to ask me some questions, hoping I'll open up more to her, but she won't. She shrugs, mumbles that there's nothing she wants to ask. Occasionally she challenges him, becomes more animated, wrinkling her nose unattractively. The topless woman on the website was definitely *not* her.

They're passionate anti-smokers. Surely the smell and the taste can't be a problem, not with a diet like his. He likes red wine, implies he drinks quite a bit of it and says, 'But I'm never intoxicated.' He asks me if I drink, wondering perhaps what it would take to lower my all-too-obvious inhibitions.

When we're leaving he wants to arrange another meeting.

'So when are you going to call us and let us take you for a drink or dinner?'

'Um, I don't know,' I say.

'Well, don't leave it too long, we're going away in two weeks.'

KINK

'I don't have my diary with me, so …'

'Promise me you'll call in the next couple of days, okay?'

'Yeah, okay,' I lie.

'Promise?'

'Yes. Okay.'

'We'll go for dinner or a drink. We'll have some champagne. Anything you like …'

I'd been dreading that moment but manage to slip away without things getting too sticky. They're not the types to tail me but I still hide out in the butcher's down the road for a while until I'm sure they've gone.

That night they email to say they enjoyed meeting me and that 'we both thought you were really rather lovely'. Shucks. Oh, and would I please contact them so we can arrange a date. I tell them I enjoyed meeting them too but that I've chickened out on the whole idea.

30
HEEL, BOY!

I've been going on to the 'alternative sex' website's chat group in the last few weeks trying to find a plushie to interview. These are people who are turned on by stuffed toys or by humans in animal costumes—think Humphrey B. Bear. It's probably not the right place to be looking, as the site's more about BDSM, but I thought I might find a lurker there. The thing that's astounded me about the chat group is the utter drivel everyone goes on with. I haven't been on one before so maybe this is normal, but it's absolutely nauseating. People log on, a line comes up announcing that so and so 'has entered the room' and then everyone starts exchanging greetings. When someone called The Enchantress logs on, for example, people start typing, *Hiya Chanty!* <*hugs*>. 'Chanty' then says hi to everyone else online, sometimes as a group but too often individually, scattering smilies and other emoticons throughout her speech. Abbreviations make much of the messaging difficult to decipher but you pick up speed with practice. 'Thank you' becomes 'ty' for example and 'people' is cut to 'ppl'. Some messagers even describe their gestures, like '<yawns and stretches lazily>'. To ask specific questions about kinks simply wouldn't do in this forum. You have to be able to stay online sometimes for hours and restrict yourself to saying virtually nothing. I don't think it's a rule, it's just what everyone does. You might talk about your headache, or where you live and whether that café nearby is still any good or mention that your grandparents live near Coffs Harbour too and respond to others' jokes with LOL ('laugh out loud'). Then, when it's time to go, you have to announce it and have everyone online say goodbye to you individually. As irritating as it is it's not a total waste of time. It's a good way to pick active members, view their profiles and, if they're interesting, send them emails.

Anyway I've been contacted by yet another male submissive who wants to be interviewed. I'd made up my mind that I had enough material on male subs already and was going to say I didn't need to speak to him—until I read his profile. Bob's looking for a mistress, of course, but so great is his desire to serve her that he doesn't even require any direct sexual gratification. He says he will come to her house and do all the most menial of domestic duties on one condition—that he is made to work naked except for a locked chastity device and a butt plug. I've *got* to meet him. That image is so compelling. He adds that he 'would be very interested in serving a Dominant Woman who is a lover of corsets, stockings and high heels. This slave has strong high-heel worship tendencies.' So it'll be flat shoes and a baggy jumper again for me tomorrow.

Dressed in pants and a cotton top, both loose and black, and hideous round-toed Smurf-girl shoes, I get to the café a bit before ten thirty only to find it doesn't open for half an hour. Bob appears from the car park next door, a big bloke with a grey crew cut and goatee wearing a roomy pale yellow T-shirt and baggy cotton trousers. I apologise for not checking the opening hours before we'd made the arrangements and he says, 'Yeah, I saw it was closed and I thought, hello, what's she up to?' It seems I'm not the only one showing up to these meetings feeling suspicious.

I don't fancy wandering along King Georges Road making awkward conversation while we look for somewhere to sit so I am relieved to find the kebab shop two doors down just opening for the day.

'Can we get a coffee here?' I ask the owner as he's dragging open the sliding glass door.

'Only instant. Nothing fancy. No cappuccino.'

'That'll do.'

We go in, and settle down at the chrome-topped table.

Bob starts by telling me that he's disappointed with the responses he's had from people on the website and he's been on it for four years.

'I like to think I'm a normal person but I do understand that the website and the lifestyle stuff attracts some more bizarre people. My profile comes across as pretty heavy and it's interesting because I get virtually no offers from that.'

You'd never pick him as a guy with a profile like the one he posted; there's not even a hint of kink about him from where I'm sitting. He seems like a lovely ordinary bloke who's keen to tell me his story, but not without warning me that he's inclined to ramble.

'I guess my ideal is someone who's very strong and very controlling, that's part of my get-off. It doesn't mean you've got to get beaten up every night but there's an underlying control that the person can almost play with your mind. But that's not the only thing to it. I do like the paraphernalia as well, and to get all that in combination I've almost given up hope.'

He had it once with a mistress but she moved interstate and he's never found it since. Parties aren't the answer either because, with his sensitive government job, he can't afford to be recognised in a harness and chastity belt.

He split from his wife, Brenda, five years ago, mostly because of their differing ideas about sex. He'd started cross-dressing early on in the marriage, which she tolerated as long as it wasn't anything more than heels, stockings and outerclothes. No makeup, no lacy knickers.

'I used to wax my legs and look how hairy they are now!' he says, thrusting a large, muscular limb out from under the table and pulling up one trouser leg. 'That was a pain I was happy to endure. My wife got cheesed off because she said I had better legs in stockings than she had! But as I got older, into my forties, I had to admit I didn't have the body for cross-dressing, so I stopped.

'I wouldn't say Brenda was enthusiastic about the cross-dressing but there was a sort of acceptance. In our lovemaking I started to introduce a few BDSM things with me being the dominant partner. We got to a bit of spanking, none of the paraphernalia, but I never got the feedback that it was increasing the turn-on for her. If your partner's acting like a dead fish you know, regardless of what you want to do.'

There was a small reward for Bob when he cut back on his cross-dressing.

'As I phased it out I was able to encourage her to dress more erotically—stockings, high heels, that sort of thing. She'd never dressed particularly well at all. It always amazes me how I got involved with someone like that. I suppose thirty years ago, that was the person I fell into marriage with.'

Brenda was a jeans and T-shirts kind of girl but, with a bit of coercing and Bob buying lingerie for her, she'd go along with it and use it in sexual play.

'But it frustrated me because it was always like she was doing me a favour and I always wanted someone who did that anyway, for themselves. Now I wouldn't consider a woman unless she was into heels and corsets. I don't want someone who puts them on just for me.'

He's friendly and direct and appears to enjoy being interviewed. I ask him what ultimately ended the marriage.

'I've gone through this self-analysis for years about what makes me tick. I guess the seeds of the failure were always there but as the need to satisfy myself got stronger, I dabbled on the side but that was never enough. I went out of my way to ensure the children and my wife weren't involved but that duality was just getting very, very frustrating and it wasn't until I was alone that I could pursue some of my interests.

'Another thing is I think I respond far, far better to a dominant woman than I did to my ex, who wasn't very dominant at all. In fact, although she wouldn't know it or admit to it, it was a case of two submissive people being together and each wanting the other to take the dominant role. By default I was taking the lead role more often than not and that was even worse in a sexual situation.'

I ask whether Brenda would say that was why they broke up as well. Was that mutually recognised as the problem or would she say it was because he watched too much footy on the TV or something?

'I wish! In a lot of ways I worked hard to be the model husband as far as doing stuff around the house goes. We both worked extended hours in our jobs but I always spent as much time as possible with the kids. But her claim afterwards was always that I never talked to her enough about things. My interest in submission developed over twenty years, and you can't say to someone after twenty years, Well, you come on board with me. It's a developing thing and I wouldn't have known where to start. Also, and this is not a negative about her, I had a greater hunger for erotic excitement than she did.'

He tells me about a colleague at work who didn't know anything about him other than her observations of him at work and still she picked him as a risk taker, despite appearances.

'I thought that's exactly right. I get bored reasonably easily so I was always looking for excitement. And I had a wife who was quite happy to crawl into her pyjamas on a winter's night and go straight off to sleep. This is going to sound terrible but I'd almost have to beg her to get coloured underwear. She only ever wore that nude colour or white. I was able to edge that over into something a bit more exciting. And when she did try to be exciting it was so obvious to me it was just being put on.

Which is unfair to her because she was making an effort, but it just wasn't her. It never was, never will be.'

He says his ex is 'a lovely person' but she's still not over the breakup.

'I was the one who walked out and I will feel guilty till the day I die. Luckily I've got a good relationship with my two children. She's still bitter but you've got to own your own crap at some stage.'

I ask what he'd do if he got a response from a dream domme tomorrow. How would he go about managing a relationship like the one he describes on the website?

'Obviously you've got to make allowances for work. I've got quite a well-paid job so I'd still go to work. That profile would be a starting point for discussion. We'd have a meeting and discuss whether it was going to work or not and if I didn't feel comfortable I wouldn't go ahead with anything. But if I thought it was workable and I was attracted to the person then we'd take it from there. I'd have to get some agreement that I can't be made to do anything that encroaches upon work. Plus my job would be to the benefit of both of us anyway.'

But there are some slaves who stop work, do everything for their mistress, sign over the deeds to the house. Is he too cautious for all that?

'It's called marriage or something, isn't it? No, that's something which might develop but I certainly wouldn't sit down in the early part of the relationship and say, yeah, sure, here's everything. You develop trust or you may find after six months it isn't working.'

To prove that he is capable of true submission he tells me that he flew a domme he'd met online out from Canada.

'That was pretty keen of me. We'd talked for ages. I'd get messages at six in the morning—"Get up and talk to me"—and I'd respond to that. That's the totality of it. I like that sort of contact. Not just when you're physically with someone. You might get messages saying, "I want you to be here at this time and do this and that. Or else." But I got disappointed because I don't think what she presented on the website was exactly what she was. In one sense we got on really well but we hardly played at all, she was only here for two weeks. She wanted a sham marriage to gain residency. To me it was dishonest and I wasn't interested in doing it.'

He was taking a gamble because she didn't include a picture of herself and he'd imagined her very differently.

'Now I'm guarded about people who don't put any picture at all on their profiles. I never saw any image of her till she arrived. She was considerably older than I thought. A very nice woman and we shared some professional interests.'

Although he might not be conservative sexually, he says he is in other ways in that he hardly drinks and never touches cigarettes or drugs. That turned out to be a problem.

'I don't mind people who do, I just don't do it. But she was a huge Scotch drinker and smoked like a chimney. I didn't think it'd be an issue initially but that started to annoy me a bit at one stage. You can say you don't mind these things in a profile, but you start living with someone … I was living in a flat at the time and it stank like cigarettes for a bloody month after she left. If everything else had been great that wouldn't have mattered at all, but when it came down to it that was one of the deciding factors.'

He's never found a domme too tough for him but, then, he's more into being controlled than into pain anyway.

'I can carry a bowling ball in a pretty interesting way! There are ways of doing things that lessen the pain. If you're having a bowling ball suspended from certain parts, and the attachment is gripped in a certain way, it doesn't pull as much as it could do. I've done a little bit of needle play. So that sort of pain doesn't really worry me. I've never been good at taking caning. I suppose I've always been better at the static restrictions, not so much the discipline but the bondage, being fully tied up so you can't move at all and being in a vulnerable position where you can be touched, manhandled or whatever. You're defenceless. That's where I get most satisfaction. Couple that with the mental side. I've surprised myself with how much I will conform to someone else's wishes. I could be sitting here talking to you with a chastity device on—I haven't got one on—but that type of thing when publicly you wouldn't know anything about it. That, to me, is very exciting.'

He's not really into the humiliation so beloved of many subs. 'But I have to say I don't think I'm easily humiliated. If I'm asked to do something humiliating I may not want to do it but I'll go and do it—I won't get off on it but I'm reasonably adventurous. I have no issue with being nude in front of a play group. What's the problem? I don't find that humiliating.'

I ask if he's into 'water sports'.

'No, I'm a clean freak. I've done some but … obviously not interested at all in the brown stuff. I know that isn't healthy, that's all there is to it. I can see the symbolism with water sports, but I can't drink it, I just can't stomach it. I'm not against dabbling in it but it doesn't do anything for me.' He looks slightly disgusted.

'In all areas of play, I'm paranoid about diseases and it's not just personal safety, it's a thing I've got. I've got to make sure I trust someone, that they're clean, I'm clean and everything remains clean. But as I said, I'll kill for high heels. I'm terrible, I'm really terrible.'

They don't have to be any particular colour or especially high to turn him on.

'Just four- or five-inch stilettos and I'm anyone's!'

31
THE SUPERIOR SUBMISSIVE

This girl is a find. She's young, super smart, articulate and, rarest of all, prepared to meet me for a face-to-face interview. Women, so far, haven't done that other than at parties. Estrelle and I have chatted on email a bit while she's sussed me out and, although she's another submissive, the detailed info on her internet profile shows she's going to be able to tell me more about submission than any of my interviewees to date. And she's only twenty-one.

She's suggested we meet in a café near her uni where she's studying maths and chemistry, and when I arrive she's already curled in an armchair with her mug of tea. She has a broad, fair face, an easy manner, and is dressed for uni in string-coloured capri pants and a pale blue sweatshirt. She's slim and muscular from years of training in martial arts.

We'd already started online to discuss pain and how sometimes she needs it after a day of throwing bodies onto the mat but, again, I didn't get it. Luckily she gives great email.

KINK

When you're in pain, you're expected to lose control, in some form. Your body might be well trained enough to stop you crying out or shaking for a while, but eventually anyone will break, especially in a dom/sub situation, where, in my experience at least, I've wanted to break, but haven't been able to allow myself to without that external force—the actions of the dom. I'm a naturally assertive, headstrong woman, and I work hard so that my life runs smoothly, stays under control. That means that when I meet up with a lover it's not reasonable for them to expect me to drop straight to my knees and assume the role of the submissive. My mind is still caught up in the 'assertive' frame of mind, and even though I long to be submissive with them, it's not something I can conjure myself, sometimes. That's when I tend to get insolent or cheeky, and a little supercilious sometimes, which is my cue to my dom that I need a firm hand that night. It's often when I most need to be submissive that I find it the hardest to allow myself to. That's where pain comes in; it allows me to shrug off the 'tough-girl' attitude and just be a girl. Once that initial wall is broken and I've been pushed to the point where I'll cry out from the pain, then I enter the submissive mindset very smoothly. I'm not a masochist, I don't enjoy pain, but sometimes I do need it. This is one area where the skill of the dom is paramount—push the submissive past that point and you're just hurting them; don't push them far enough and they'll be left unsatisfied, frustrated.

It sounds like the pain's a stress relief tool but, over tea, she says it's deeper than that—she needs it as part of the relationship. She also wants the dom/sub dynamic to operate beyond the bedroom.

'That said, I intend to have a good career. My decisions

about my career will be mediated by whoever I'm with to the same extent they would be in a vanilla relationship.'

But what about asking your partner's permission to go to the toilet, like submissive Tracy had to?

'There are some things I'm quite happy to have controlled around the clock—what I wear, what I eat. But things like going to the loo, that's excessive, I think. I don't think it gives anything to the relationship other than making it more strange than perhaps it needs to be.'

I'm curious about the firm hand she says she needs before she can submit.

'It can be anything. If I'm in a relatively good mood I can say something a bit insolent with a little bit of a barb in it—I'm not setting it up, it just happens. And generally, if they know me well, they'll say, "Estrelle, you're not going to speak like that," and that will often be enough, I'll be put in my place. But if I'm in a really stressed-out mood or if I'm angry at them for some reason, then I'll continue and I'll challenge them, in which case it can go further, to physical discipline, but that's much more rare. Generally I like to discuss things—but physical discipline can be fun,' she says, smiling.

She's not turned on by pain but she is by the actions a dominant would go through to inflict it, she explains.

'Very few people actually enjoy pain itself but the idea of having someone whip you, their actions and their state of mind as they do it, are arousing. It's a subtle difference and I think a lot of people mistake one for the other.'

Nobody's ever whipped her but she really fancies the idea.

'And I like having my air supply cut off a bit too sometimes.

I like that feeling of being controlled. In martial arts there are two ways to win a fight: you can lock someone on the ground or you can choke them. I tend to go for choking because being a girl it's very hard for me to lock up a man who's much stronger. The neck is a part of the body that's vulnerable regardless of how big and strong you are. And when I have something on my neck, whether it's a hand or a rope, something in me just lies down. That gives me a real physical feeling of being controlled and I do really enjoy that.'

She's had this desire for submission since she was a child but obviously didn't realise what it was at the time.

'When I was a kid I used to tie up my Barbie dolls and in my games they would always get kidnapped but never rescued. I also watched movies like *Star Wars* and *Aladdin* and there were scenes where girls would be chained and I always felt really funny when I watched them. I was aroused but as a kid you don't know what arousal is. So it's been since I was little.

'And I've *never* been interested in men my age because I was a teenager and teenage men don't understand the idea of dominance. I've always been attracted to older men, men who were smarter than me, because that brought into play a kind of natural dynamic of dominance and submission. On average they'd be about ten years older at the moment. Any older and I find it harder to be physically attracted to them.'

By the time she was sixteen, although she still didn't understand her desires, she did end up with a boyfriend five years older than her who she says was 'slightly dominant'.

'But he wasn't really into the whole dom–sub dynamic. I didn't know I was submissive at the time, I didn't know what that meant. I just knew that I cleaned his house and I wanted to please him in bed as opposed to having him please me. But it frustrated me because he just kind of went, "Oh, this is the kind of girl every man wants," and didn't give me back the things that doms should. He didn't give me any discipline at all or any of the special attention dominants give to subs, like paying attention to their behaviour. If someone's monitoring you then it means they're interested in you, which is nice. He didn't talk to me about certain things and he just didn't notice when I was frustrated. Which I was. A lot.'

What she learned from that relationship was that you can try to be the perfect submissive girlfriend, but unless your partner plays his role it won't make it the perfect relationship.

'Being submissive didn't give me any kick unless I was with someone who was being dominant. He was pretty much just an average guy and I was being *very* submissive. But he wasn't being dominant and I lost interest. Submission doesn't mean anything unless there is dominance—otherwise you're just submitting to yourself.'

After that relationship broke down she swore off men for a while.

'I've only had five lovers and most of them have lasted less than a month. Between the ages of eighteen and nineteen I didn't have any because I'd had enough of men who didn't understand me.'

Although discovering the alternative-sex website when she was eighteen didn't convince her she wasn't a 'freak', she felt that if she was at least she was in good company. But to date it hasn't helped her find a partner.

'I kind of get disgusted by all the latex and kinks—it's not me. I'm open to it but it doesn't arouse me. I also get disgusted by all the sleazy old men asking me to be their little slave girl for the rest of my life.'

But she's been surprised that some older men on the site understand things about her she hadn't yet worked out.

'One said to me once that he thought my characteristics pointed to the personality of a true slave. And my fury and disgust at the word slave spoke volumes about the fact that he was correct and that he was seeing something that I wouldn't let myself see. And over time it became clear to me, although it's pretty sad, that that was in fact quite an accurate observation.'

So what else has she found out?

'I've been coming to terms with the idea of promiscuity. As I said, I don't see men very often. I hate the idea of sleeping around. But again it's that enraged response to a concept, and I'm coming around to the idea that perhaps I'm afraid of my sex drive, which I know is well beyond that of the average woman. So generally whenever I can identify a response in myself which is beyond a calm one, then I've started to analyse it and figure out why I'm responding that way.'

She wants to be submissive but most men just can't make her feel that way.

'So the idea of sleeping around with lots of men doesn't work because I'd need to be sleeping around with lots of *dominant* men who were of similar intelligence, if not higher, who could beat me in a fight—and there's not a lot of men who fit that bill!' She laughs at how she's narrowed her options but simply won't jump into bed with just anyone.

'I value myself quite highly so I have no intention of being won over easily because I have a lot to offer. I mean, for a possible lifetime of servitude, then they can work at wooing me into bed!'

Leather and studs play no part in her vision of a perfect partner, she says.

'To be honest, that side of the scene really turns me off. I'm not into dressing up. I'm happy with the way I am. I was with a guy for a while who said he wasn't interested in doing anything that he couldn't do with his hands and I like that. And although other things can be fun, like bondage, which really is something that turns me on, I do like the philosophy behind being able to dominate someone without any tools or equipment or fancy dress. To me it's just primal, it's not something that I put on and take off.'

Having said that, she does have a corset which she can tolerate sometimes for more than an hour if she wears it regularly and gets used to it.

'I like my corset a lot. I lose six inches. I cinch well. Having a little waist makes me feel delicate. I lift weights a lot and I'm hurling people to the ground three nights a week so it's hard for me to feel delicate. I mean, if a man can really put his hands around your waist it's inescapable that you'll feel very feminine at that point.'

And heels?

'I wear heels a lot but I am tall. And if I'm not with someone who's quite tall, then there's no way I want to be taller than a man I'm with. No way. So sometimes I wear flats.'

Unlike many subs, she's not into being humiliated.

'I have a very high self-esteem. And the thing that's been

holding me back from accepting the slave characteristics is that I do want to be respected. I know that's a little incongruous.'

The wrong sorts of men approach her online all the time, despite her profile being really clear about what she wants, and they're mostly of a type.

'They're mainly older men with very high opinions of themselves. With some of them that's a well-deserved opinion, but the majority of them simply surround themselves with people who fawn over them and allow them to maintain that view of themselves. I was chatting to a guy today and he's been very keen to meet up and he sent me a photo of himself and said, "Here's something for you to drool over." He's an average-looking guy! He's married, too, and no doubt his wife drools over him.'

She also gets approached by lots of men who are switches and she thinks she knows why.

'I'm very assertive and confident and I have no problem being dominant with men who aren't my lovers in a day-to-day situation. So they're *sure* that I'm a domme, they're sure that as soon as they get me into bed and things start to get hot and heavy that if they push things so that they're on the submissive side that I'll be happy to go along with it—which I'm not. My libido just disappears. Not interested.'

There is definitely a dominant side to her and with the couple of female lovers she's had she's been 'mildly dominant'.

'I don't exclude the possibility that as I grow older I might discover a dominant side sexually with men because it certainly is in my personality, but it's in the same way that I don't exclude the possibility that I might become religious at some point.' She laughs. 'I honestly don't see it happening but I'm not going to rule it out.'

She thinks she's so dominant with men outside the bedroom because she abhors the idea of anyone taking advantage of her; hiding her submissiveness is a defence against that.

She knows it's going to be tough to find a man with all the characteristics she wants, even though at only twenty-one she hasn't been looking long.

'I want a man who's confident and who's assertive.'

That shouldn't be too hard in the circles she's looking. But suddenly she's animated, she's having a light-bulb moment.

'I want a man who's also quite *humble*. I really like humility in men, which is interesting because a lot of guys say, "I'm so dominant and I'm always right," but I'm not interested in that—I really like humility and grace in a man. I like eloquence, I like them to be well read. I like them to be interested in the arts or at least tolerate them because I'm very interested in them. I want them to be attractive but I'm not looking for a model. I want them to take some care with their health, and to exercise. I'm an obsessive gym junkie and I eat very carefully so I can't be with somebody who doesn't give a damn about that stuff.'

But it's a man's ability to beat her in an argument that really makes her swoon, and she found it once.

'I was being pretentious and ridiculous, but I didn't know that at the time, and this man won the argument. I was instantly besotted. I fell madly in love and we were together for a while, but he lived overseas. He was very intelligent and very capable of being dominant. He was pretty much perfect.

He was a body builder with a master's in applied mathematics who studied philosophy for fun. There was a *natural* dominant/submissive dynamic. It wasn't anything that was talked about. It was never "Do as I say or I'll put you over my knee". It just felt natural for me to serve and in the end I guess that's what I'm looking for, but it's so rare. I live in hope …'

Today I got an hilarious email from someone on the website with the handle 'Bilash':

> *I will help your research only if you order me to do it and be naked and maintain a constant erection for the full duration of the interview. You must be very hard on me about this.*
>
> *And I will answer all your questions.*
>
> *No touching required by other party.*
>
> *B.*

32
WHAT A DRAG

A week ago a drag queen called Marcia Switch Bitch—or Marcia to her friends—contacted me through the website, inviting me to a play session this coming Friday night. He was going to be in dominant mode and was having a couple of subs around and thought I might find it interesting. He warned, though, that I might end up as part of the action. Alas, I was going away for the weekend so couldn't make it but said I would like to meet him for an interview. This was his email autoreply:

Hi Playgirl,

I appreciate you contacting me.

I'm probably shackled to some sort of dungeon equipment at the moment, enjoying a BDSM session with my nipples in clamps, my balls in a press, my dick encased in alufoil and connected to a TENS unit with an anal probe pumping away while sending out stronger and stronger electric shocks.

On the other hand I might be in the process of a bondage

session with a large-breasted subbie girl and after paddling her rear with my hand and then with a paddle and finally with a riding crop, I am now applying the Wartenberg wheel to her bound, protruding mammaries, making her squeal whilst she is riding the largest inflatable vibrating dildo you can imagine driving her to climax after climax not able to cry out because of the mouth-gag strapped firmly around her head.

Now if you're shocked by all that then you're on the wrong website.

MarciaSwitchBitch.

Goody, a sense of humour! So we arrange to meet but before we get to that, his email set me off researching Wartenberg wheels and generally getting sidetracked, nay *educated*, about BDSM equipment. I was astounded by this stuff. The Wartenberg wheel's not particularly interesting; it's just a little spiked wheel about three centimetres in diameter, developed originally as a neurosurgical tool to test skin sensitivity. The spikes aren't sharp enough to pierce the skin (unless you press really hard) but will presumably give you a bit more than a tickle, depending on where you roll it.

The website dealing with this equipment had all kinds of penis pumps, but they also had 'pussy pumps' designed to enlarge the vulva. They come in a range of sizes and look like little glass butter dishes. The website pitched them thus:

```
The latest rage ... swollen lips! No we're
not taking about the pouty lips of Angelina
Jolie!! These are the lower 'love lips'...
the labia and vulva! Pussy Pumping! It's
```

> sexy to look at, sexy to touch and feels
> oh-so-sexy to do! Create the popular '**Camel
> Toe**'! These are designed for comfort and
> long life usage! Measurements are inner
> dimensions. Be sure to measure accurately!

I don't know who the Camel Toe is popular with; I'm only just getting my head around the Los Angeles rage for labial trimming. The photo accompanying the appliance shows what I presume is an optimally pumped pussy; it looks much like a swollen scrotum with a deep central cleft. Mini versions of the pump are available for nipples and clitorises.

But what really surprised me were the sets of 'sounds', long, thin, stainless-steel pokers to be inserted into the penis. They come in various widths, some with bullet-shaped tips, and are designed for massaging the prostate. There was a set of J-curved ones as well, *uniquely designed to fit the 'J-curve' of the male urinary-urethral tract. And don't forget the Surgi-Lube and Latex Gloves!!* the website added helpfully.

I knew men liked having things pushed up their bottoms but thought a metal rod up the eye of the penis would be torture. The things I'm learning.

Marcia doesn't trust me enough to meet me in his ordinary clothes in case I reveal his identity so we arrange to meet at 9.30 pm at a café in Surry Hills. He'll be done up and on his way to the Hellfire Club. Just as I'm parking the car, right on nine-thirty, he calls my mobile to tell me he's waiting for me. I'm with him a minute later, on the corner, where he's with his makeup artist, Gene, and two tiny whippets.

'Trust a woman to be late,' he says, only half jokingly, as I approach.

Gene, a thick-set bloke in sweatshirt and jeans, says, 'Not everyone runs on Swiss timing, Marcia.' He tries to restrain his whippets as they dance around me, which gives me a second to take in the vision that is Marcia Switch Bitch.

Marcia's hand feels like an enormous bony paddle when I shake it but I'm not going to find out what makeup man's is like; he visibly recoils from my outstretched hand, looking as though he fears catching girl germs from it.

Looking like something from *Priscilla, Queen of the Desert*— a lead, not an extra—Marcia has done everything he can to stand out. With his heels and massively teased chestnut wig he's about seven foot tall. Those heels are clear perspex on red patent-leather peep-toe shoes—but his long toes gawk, more than peep, from them.

By now the café is packed and noisy so Marcia suggests we go to the pub opposite. Gene and the whippets disappear down a side street and Marcia and I cross the road—he steps like a newborn giraffe.

It's one of those old Australian pubs with tiled floor and walls and too-loud music. We drag a couple of chairs up to a little round table and, as I'm not drinking, Marcia turns down my offer to buy him one. I'm worried I'm not going to be able to hear anything in this place and ask if he'd mind holding my recorder up to his face as he speaks. He's delighted at the suggestion and swirls it around like a club singer's mike.

I ask how long he's been cross-dressing. 'Well, I'm pushing sixty-eight years old …' He wordlessly accepts my compliment that he looks fantastic for his age. 'And I've been doing it since I was a teenager.'

He really doesn't look anywhere near late sixties in that makeup but says without it he does. He has all the drag queen hallmarks: masked eyebrows to make way for pencilled ones drawn well up on the forehead, black lip liner filled in with glossy red lipstick, and false eyelashes so long they cool the room when he blinks.

He started cross-dressing just after a weird surge in hormones triggered the development of small breasts when he was about thirteen.

'Everybody thought I was worried about getting breasts whereas actually I was wishing I had some more, and it just sort of developed from there on. I snuck into Mum's room when she was out and tried on her clothes.'

Stockings were the first things he tried because they felt the best.

'The smooth silky feeling in my hands. Just skin-coloured stockings, we didn't have pantyhose then. Then I'd pinch a bra, stuff something in it. Then I tried makeup.'

He was never caught, he says, and seems proud of his stealth.

'I actually didn't let anyone know until I had trouble with my marriage.'

He had married Wanda at twenty-five and continued to cross-dress in private, especially at work, where shifts meant he was alone most of the time. But after about fifteen years, during which time they'd moved to the outback and had two sons, his desire for cross-dressing had tightened its grip and he wanted out of the marriage.

They separated for nearly two years. The boys, who were at boarding school in Sydney, were miserable and the marriage breakdown made matters worse. So Marcia and Wanda agreed to reconcile, bring the boys home, then all move to Sydney together. But coping with all those changes meant Marcia and Wanda needed counselling.

'When we went for counselling I just had to admit why I'd wanted to get out of the marriage. I couldn't tell my wife face to face, so I asked the counsellor to do it for me.'

No dice. The counsellor told Marcia he had to do it so, sick with nerves, he confessed.

'I just had to say, "I have to tell you something. I like to dress up in women's clothes."'

Marcia might be kinky but he's also very straight and shows none of the humour face to face that he did in emails. He doesn't embellish stories. It's as though all his creative efforts have gone into his appearance, leaving his conversation depleted. Maybe all these dramatic events are so far in the past he can't muster any passion for recounting them. I find it hard to believe Wanda's reaction to his cross-dressing revelation was as matter-of-fact as this:

'Oh, she didn't react very well at the start. She said, "Well, you have to give it up." So for a while I did try to give it up, but in the end it got the better of me, I couldn't do it. I did it on the sly again for a while then eventually I said, "This is no good. This is what I have to do." Then she sort of came around and helped me buy clothes, underwear, things like that, and it got better and better from then on.'

After forty two years he and Wanda are still together

but her acceptance of his frocking up varies from month to month.

'Oh yes, she puts up with it, but she still doesn't *like* it. Sometimes she helps me buy things and other times she wants me to give it up. At the moment she's not happy about it because I went out last Friday and I'm out again this Friday. Normally we have a sort of agreement that I only go out once a month.'

I'm wondering if I've seen Marcia before or if I'm just remembering clichéd images of trannies from the media. Then it dawns on me he was the bar bitch at the Hard Core Heaven party last year—the one who handed me the warm lemonade. He confirms this. He's *always* the bar bitch there, he says, before adding incidentally that he thinks his BDSM interests grew out of guilt about cross-dressing.

He says he's mostly submissive when he plays but subbie girls love him as a domme. But I'm not clear where the arousal comes into it and want to know if he ever has sex with Wanda while he's dressed as Marcia.

'I never get turned on sexually at all when I'm dressed. When I had Jacqueline, my mistress, she once asked me to fuck her, but I couldn't get it up.'

But doesn't he play at parties and doesn't that involve arousal?

'Not when I'm a domme bitch. The feelings I get are more about power over the subbie. To know I could do anything I wanted even if they use the safe word. Also, if I do something to them that I like to have done to me when I'm in a subbie mood I imagine getting the feeling of helplessness and pain or whatever I'm making them feel. And I urge them on to take more and more of whatever I'm doing to them. Sometimes when I'm spanking I have to stop myself from going over the top. It happened twice, once at a commercial establishment, and once when the subbie could not remember the safe word. In both cases they ended up crying and there were quite a few strokes of the cane where the bruises took a while to go away.'

He says he gets turned on when he's a subbie, properly tied up and helpless and his genitals or bum are part of the play. 'But I suppose that doesn't have much to do with the cross-dressing,' he adds.

It would be a shame to trade one of his glamorous outfits for a hundred metres of clingfilm—one of his preferred bondage mediums—and I want to know where he gets them.

'Most of my outfits I have made by a dressmaker. Do you know House of Priscilla in Oxford Street? There's a professional performer, Chelsea Bun, who organises shows and she owns it. Fantastic clothes. Most women just go weak at the knees when they see the gowns and shoes and wigs. And nails. No nails for me tonight, I've got to get up before six tomorrow morning. I've got a special job on.' He is, he says cryptically, in 'postal work'.

I ask if he thinks he'll ever give up cross-dressing.

'No. I've just ordered myself a crop top from England. It's a full upper body suit with built in breasts that fastens around the neck. Flesh colour. Ideally you don't wear much at all on top so you can show it off.'

Tonight he's in a sheer red body stocking underneath a black latex corset edged with frills of white lace. From the waist down it's a black latex tutu with more white lace petticoats, red fishnets and those peep-toe shoes. Enormous diamante chandelier earrings and a choker complete the look.

Extending his legs to the side of the table so I can see his shoes properly, he tells me this is his most comfortable pair because they're the right size. 'Normally it's hard to get shoes the right size at a reasonable price.'

Given the toe overhang I think he could have gone a size bigger.

His son Sam, aka Samantha, also cross-dresses. Although Marcia hadn't told his boys that he did it, he thinks Sam found some of his gear as well as Wanda's clothes and tried those on. So how does Marcia feel about that?

'Oh, terrific!' He's not joking. 'We go to the Mardi Gras together!'

'Did it concern you at all when you first found out about it?' I ask.

'No!'

He's being defensive so I carefully explain that I was only wondering if Marcia worried about him having the same marriage difficulties as he'd had himself.

'He may have. He's divorced. Now he's got a new girlfriend who knows about it. She actually comes out with us. She thinks it's great.'

'And how did Wanda react when she found out that Sam was cross-dressing?'

'Oh, she was very upset.'

'Did she blame you?'

'No. No, no, she never blamed me. When you research why people do it there's no documentation to say why they do, whereas with transsexuals there's usually a chromosomal problem or something like that. With transvestites there's no known reason why we do this. I want to be a man but from time to time I want to dress up.'

'It's not just about clothes, though, is it?'

'No, it's the inner feeling. It just makes you feel complete. I feel great when I'm dressed up. Sometimes when I'm really hyped up I'll just walk down the middle of the road, down Oxford Street, and stop the traffic. Can't help myself. Gene sometimes tries to give me an ecky and I say, "I don't need one!" I even tried one once with my mistress and I couldn't feel a thing. I *already* felt high.'

His friends and colleagues don't know he cross-dresses and he says he couldn't let them know.

'I'd be out of a job. My job involves the public. My family in Europe didn't know until two years ago.'

'How did they find out?'

'I couldn't help myself! My sister and I have webcam on MSN so she could see me. She wanted to know who she was looking at and in the end I told her it was me. Her reaction wasn't too bad. She thought I looked terrific so I sent her more pictures. My mother doesn't know.'

His sister's reaction *wasn't too bad*? His bland choice of words astounds me because I'm sure you'd react strongly one way or the other, but he doesn't respond to probing. He shrugs, purses his lips and looks like he wants to change the subject—so I ask him if his wife has any interesting kinks.

'Not that I *know* of.' He almost smiles. Then, in a sympathetic tone, he says, 'She's not very well. She's had both hips replaced and has arthritis in her back. But I don't think she has any kinks. She's a very standard type of person.'

Deafening mariachi music starts to bounce off the pub walls just as I'm winding up the interview. He offers to walk me to my car but I'm parked only a couple of metres away so I decline. I probably should have offered to walk him somewhere—he makes quite a target.

There are examples of transvestism right throughout history and the motives for it have not always been sexual. Women would sometimes do it just to shake social or familial constraints put upon them or to do a man's job. Many women, according to the hagiography *Acta Sanctorum* (*Lives of the Saints*), dressed as men so they could become monks or hermits. Joan of Arc claimed to have been told in a vision by Saints Margaret and Catherine to wear men's clothes, which allowed her to fight against the English in the Hundred Years War, while Dorothy Lawrence, a reporter, posed as a man to become a soldier in the First World War.

There seems to have been a sexual element to Mary Frith's cross-dressing in the seventeenth century, but whether she was a lesbian, a fetishistic transvestite, a hermaphrodite or a latent transsexual remains unclear. Known as Moll Cutpurse, she always hated feminine clothing and the 'mincing obscenity' of female behaviour. So, at great risk, she abandoned the clothes of her own sex, which she considered 'Finicall and Modish excesses of attire'. In turn, she gained notoriety among her contemporaries. Mary struggled with her transvestism and was acutely aware of how farcical her life seemed: 'let me be layn in my Grave on my Belly … and that as I have in my LIFE been preposterous, so I may be in my Death.' She declared, 'It was my Fate not Me; I doe more wonder at myself than others can do … when viewing the Manners and Customs of the Age, I see myself so wholly distempered, and so estranged from them, as if I had been born and bred in the Antipodes.' The poor woman—though somebody should have told her being born and bred in the Antipodes really isn't that bad.

Charlotte Charke was another woman who struggled with her cross-dressing. Her autobiography, published in 1755, reveals that she was dressed in male clothes from infancy and was ultimately abandoned by her family as an 'Alien'. She worked as a male servant and male impersonator on the stage, a straightforward matter for her because she was 'of the Bulk and Stature of our modern Fine Gentlemen'. Some women transvestites received good-humoured recognition as 'adventurers' or 'roaring girls' but Charlotte never did. Her life was characterised by anxiety and unhappiness. 'My being in Breeches was alledged to me as a very great Error … I have throughout the whole Course of my Life, acted in Contradiction to all Points of Regularity … There is none in the world *more fit than myself to be laughed at.*'

The 1835 novel *Mademoiselle de Maupin* by Theophile Gautier is about a seventeenth-century actress who dressed as a man in order to seduce women. At first she describes herself as 'madcap', echoing the sentiments of stage heroines, but it becomes apparent that her transvestism is more than just a superficial dress-up part.

I possess hardly a womanly attribute except a bosom … It is my body but not my mind which wears a skirt. Beneath my smooth forehead and silky tresses, male and ruthless thoughts are astir … I am free from women's foolish servility, diffidence and petty-mindedness; I am free from men's wicked ways, gross lechery and brutish tastes. I belong to a third sex of its own which has not yet been given a name; higher or lower, better or worse … My imaginary ideal would have to be of each sex in turn.

The practice goes back much further than the eighteenth century, though. An early depiction of cross-dressing can be found on a fifth-century BC red-figure cup from Greece which shows both transvestite and homosexual scenes. And if there was anything gender specific about bear skins, it may well have gone on among cave dwellers even earlier than that. The Roman Caesars were fond of frocking up and Suetonius reports that Caligula, displaying perhaps one of his more benign eccentricities, was partial to wearing women's clothes. The emperor Heliogabalus is said to have come through the gates of Rome in a long silk robe in gold, sporting blackened eyebrows, rouge and a tiara, demanding to be honoured as 'empress' by the Romans.

For as long as cross-dressing has existed there have been attempts to suppress it. Its symbolic connection with anarchy meant that it was traditionally perceived as a threat to social order, with ancient Greek historian Herodotus saying of the Scythian transvestites at Kalends and Saturnalia festivals: 'Dionysos leads these people on to behave madly.'

Unsurprisingly, the church hated it too. The anarchy was

one thing but the links with paganism and libertarianism made it an intolerable threat to Christianity. The priests, though, were as into it as anyone else; at the mediaeval Feast of Fools, clergy as well as laymen would dress as women, howl in the church aisles and send up the rituals of the mass. In 1445 the Faculty of Theology at the University of Paris referred to priests 'who danced in the choir dressed as women'. There are also accounts of priests in France who cross-dressed and sang in falsetto.

Despite some members of the clergy's enthusiastic embrace of transvestism, the church's official stance was decidedly anti. Religious prohibitions took their inspiration from Deuteronomy: 'The woman shall not wear that which pertaineth unto a man, neither shall a man put on a woman's garment; for all that do so are abomination unto the Lord thy God'. So it's not surprising that it took the secularisation of the Feast of Fools in the sixteenth century to improve the documentation of transvestism. Scholar Henry Stubbes wrote that the Lord of Misrule who presided over the feast chose 'twenty or sixty or an hundred lustiguts to serve him', who were dressed in female clothing 'borrowed for the moste parte of their pretie Mopsies'. Protestant cleric Thomas Naogeorgus, writing in *The Popish Kingdome* (1570) about the Shrovetide festival, observed:

> Both men and women chaunge their weede, the men in
> maydes array,
> And wanton wenches drest as men doe trauell by the way.

There were social as well as religious attempts to suppress the practice, including imprisonment and execution, because it was considered so subversive. And until as recently as the 1970s some medical approaches to it were severe. In his book *Deviant Sexual Behaviour* (1974), John Bancroft describes the psychology behind transvestism as being due to 'completely abnormal personality developments of the severest kind, on a psychopathic basis, which are contiguous with well-known phenomena in the region of the psychoses'. Then he describes an attempt at a cure: 'At the beginning of each session an injection of apomorphine was given and the patient told to cross-dress in his usual manner. He was urged to continue the ritual and look at himself in a mirror whilst vomiting and nausea continued.' Transvestites were also asked to stand naked on a wired mat through which electric shocks were delivered.

But despite centuries of suppression attempts and persecution, transvestism has survived because, according to novelist and biographer Peter Ackroyd, it is so firmly anchored in festive celebration, from the pagan rites of antiquity to mediaeval folk ceremonies, seasonal festivals and all kinds of modern-day pageants.

When transvestism revealed its anarchic possibilities, particularly on a political level, the practice was considered more threatening than usual. Political rebels cross-dressed to demonstrate or riot; they did it against royal tax officers in Dijon in 1630, and in Wiltshire in 1631 frocked-up peasants rioted against the king for enclosing their forest lands.

But when it could be controlled—in festivals, for example —transvestism was rendered temporarily socially acceptable because it was seen as a useful outlet for otherwise dangerous tensions. And in societies short of women available for sexual purposes, transvestite prostitution has been tolerated because it performed a social function. There were instances, going back

to Babylonian times, of transvestite prostitutes offering themselves to celebrants at the shrines of Ishtar, the Asiatic Venus, as
a way of appeasing them.

Not all transvestite prostitutes were on such a sacred mission,
though. Travellers and social historians have often described
homosexual prostitutes dressing up as a way of boosting business in what was clearly an international phenomenon. In New
Mexico the Pueblo Indians kept a trained male prostitute, called
mujerado or 'man-woman', in each village. Homosexual prostitutes in India who dressed as women were known as *zunkhas*,
while male geishas in Japan were trained in feminine arts and
were known as 'sister-boys'. In Sung dynasty China (1127–
1279) transvestite prostitutes—who were known as *hsiang ku*
or 'mock women'—were organised into guilds. The Egyptian
versions, called *El-Ginkeyn*, were a high-maintenance bunch
even by transvestite standards: their bodies were completely
depilated, their fingers, lips and toes were decorated with henna,
and they wore a blossom behind each ear.

There's a piece of writing by a 'Barbara Barrie' in a 1970s
transvestite magazine which describes the ham-like feminine
act that many drag queens display when dressed.

> Barbara managed to slip lady-like into her car, adjusting
> skirts over nylon clad—dare I say it!!—shapely legs, and was
> off. Driving en femme proved to be a great thrill … It
> was nice to sit down with skirt discreetly pulled over closed
> legs, have a lady-like smoke, and sip a bitter lemon.

This reminds me of Marcia's pouting, eyelash fluttering performance when we met for a drink, and the way he swirled

the recorder around his face at the beginning of the interview. The beautiful lady boys you see around Bangkok's Khao San Road, far better groomed than most women and moving with a pronounced wiggle, are part of the same phenomenon. Real women simply don't dress like that. You'd never catch a lady boy, or Marcia for that matter, in a knee-length skirt, T-shirt and flat sandals, the ideal ensemble for strolling Khao San Road. Overtly feminine stereotypes are clearly so ingrained in the cross-dressing community as to be unavoidable. And when dressing up is driven by sex, it's all about display rather than disguise.

33
YIFF, YIFF HURRAY!

I'd almost given up finding a plushie to interview, though I'd been reading about them on the internet. I'm using the word 'plushie' as an abbreviation of plushophile, but often the stuffed toys are called plushies too. There are loads of variations among those with a thing for plush and some of it is nothing more than the fondness a five-year-old feels for a favourite teddy. There are even adults who just adore collecting and, literally, sleeping with stuffed toys, which seems to be more about not wanting to grow up than anything kinky. Others, though, find dressing in a full fur suit (or zootsuit) a turn-on, some like their sexual partners to wear one and still others like to have sex with little stuffed toys, a practice known as 'yiffing'. With this level of intimacy modifications are required: a man will cut one of Bunny's seams open to create a hole to penetrate and a woman (though apparently it's mostly men) will make a special 'appendage'. When the toy starts to get a bit icky there are plenty of tips online about how to clean and rejuvenate it, as well as instructions for serious deconstruction, washing, stuffing replacement and reassembly for those times when a damp sponge simply won't do.

Anyway, after years of trying to track down a plushie Jay Foxie, a twenty-four-year-old from western Sydney, contacted me and agreed to meet. Just when I thought we'd nailed a time he got a job in a call centre in the Philippines, so our first chat is by phone on a bad line.

Between the call dropping out, his shyness and giggling and my incomprehension about plushophilia (despite my internet swotting), we manage to establish that he's been a fur fan since he was about six. It started with fantasies about Tails the Fox from the *Sonic the Hedgehog* cartoon as well as a fleeting thing for Blinky Bill. No kidding.

'It was mainly an imagination thing. I wasn't really into the whole plushie thing when I was younger. I'm only just getting into it now. So it was imagination until I got the internet when I was fourteen and found other people,' he says.

He and his friends invent animal characters that they identify with for physical or personality reasons and they all call each other by their creature's names. Jay's character is a blue fox.

'Foxie mimics my own personality which has a very high amount of sexual tension,' he giggles. 'I'm one of the more promiscuous people in the fandom who sees sex as more of a bonding thing between friends, not so much as a big deal.'

He explains that he has friends he sleeps with, then he has his *good* friends, then his online friends who visit often and are like his extended family. Sex feels different with each of them.

'Right, I'm just a little bit confused,' I say. 'All these friends you're talking about, are they human friends or …'

'I'm talking about human friends who have that same interest and their own animal characters,' he says patiently before the line drops out again.

Later, in an email, he says he's coming home sooner than expected, is still happy to meet and will bring his friend the kitty if I want him to. I do. Meanwhile he wants to straighten a few things out.

I know you're writing a book about sexual fetishes and I won't lie, the furry thing is a fetish, but I just want to stress that it's not sexual for everyone. Some have similar beliefs to the Native Americans who believe they have a spiritual animal that represents the way they think and act. Others may just like the fandom for the people or because they were big fans of cartoons like Thundercats.'

The fandom, he says, is a very broad community including Goths, punks, preppy kids, straights, bis, gays, older people, labourers, business people and 'yes, even emos', who just want to share a common interest.

I would just like to stress this because furs have had a bad rap in the past due to people portraying them as sickos that just hunt animals down to fuck them or that we can't get aroused unless you're in a fur suit. It's like any group/fandom, there will always be people who like certain things and others that don't.

So we arrange to meet at Summer Hill station at 10.30 am and Jay agrees to bring his 'bitch' with him. Summer Hill, a fairly Anglo suburb in Sydney's multicultural inner west, is popular with young families because of the primary school and with the mentally ill because of the halfway houses. When I arrive I'm expecting to see one young man, possibly concealing said bitch inside his jacket, but the only people waiting are two blokes. I hover for a few minutes, looking around for a man on his own, then approach one of the pair and find it's Jay. We shake hands, then I ask the other man his name.

'I'm Angel,' he says softly; this is 'the bitch' and he's an eighteen-year-old Goth. A human.

Jay's tiny naked photo on the website hadn't given many clues to his appearance other than short bleached hair, which is why I didn't immediately recognise this guy with mouse-coloured hair, combed forward and plastered with product. He is wearing blue jeans, a denim jacket and an olive green T-shirt with a motif of spotted boxer shorts on the chest. I guess the biggest clue is the blue leather dog collar fastened high on his neck, as he has said he is submissive.

As the three of us walk down Lackey Street I poke my head into each café along the way to assess noise and privacy, but they're all pretty full of mothers and babies and my recorder's not going to be able to compete. Eventually we find one with a quiet courtyard out the back and I tell Jay and Angel to go and choose a table while I order a Coke for Jay and a cappuccino for Angel.

I go through to find them sitting at a small table *right* near another one where a bleary-eyed man in a crumpled white T-shirt has just ordered breakfast. Oh dear, he's going to hear everything we say, which could be a bit much for him first thing in the morning. I check if Jay and Angel are happy sitting here (there aren't really any alternatives) and they are, they're ready to roll.

These two are an odd pair but they tell me their main connection is the plush scene, which is how they met. Angel has only just left school and still lives at home with his parents, who think his Goth dress is just a phase.

'It's been going on for the best part of ten years but they're still hoping it'll pass,' he says.

It's a warm day but still he swelters under layers of black— jeans, Doc Martens, T-shirt and ankle-length coat—as well as a black leather dog collar with a neo-pagan pentagram hanging from it. His dyed black hair drains his complexion and contrasts with the pale red whiskers sprouting on his chin.

Jay says their plush group hasn't been meeting that regularly lately because of conflicting interests.

'It's the whole emo thing that's going around at the moment. People are all too wrapped up in their own self-pity. You organise something and if one person doesn't like it they'll come along and pretty much drag everyone else down.'

The gripes seem fairly petty and are usually about the activities organised. Because many of the members are underage they tend to stick to meetings in parks, where they just hang out, or they go to Galaxy World and play computer games. There is a fair overlap between plushies, computer games and fans of Japanese anime, it seems.

'It was fair enough to bitch about the last meet, though,' Jay says. 'Someone stupidly organised for us to go to the most expensive bar in Sydney, which was ridiculous because most of us are poor.'

They're looking forward to the Sydney Gay & Lesbian Mardi Gras again this year. The plush float is to have a *Planet of the Apes* theme, but they haven't organised their outfits yet.

'Because there's usually a lot of padding the outfits can cost anywhere from $1000 to $6000 for the one I want,' Jay says. 'Mine's expensive even though it has absolutely no padding. It has fur but it's stretch lycra. I don't like all the padding because it's so hot. A lot of people have small pockets built into them for ice packs to keep you cool.'

Angel says those in the full suits ride on the float because they get too hot if they have to walk the length of Oxford Street.

'But I'd rather be walking,' Jay says. 'You get to play with the crowd more.'

So, short of winning $6000 for the dream suit, what is he going to wear?

'I've just got tail and ears at the moment. I'm going to get some gloves and a head and get my tail redone because it's kind of getting a bit dodgy.'

I'm not asking how it got dodgy but at least it wouldn't be the hassle to launder that the full suits are.

'You've got to be careful,' he says. 'You can wash them on a really, really light cycle in a washing machine but otherwise dry-cleaning is best. Obviously the cleaners will give you a weird look but we've got a few friends who actually work in a drycleaners, so we have connections.' He smiles.

Angel's going as a tabby cat, which is his chosen character, and explains why Jay referred to him originally as his good friend the kitty. But why a tabby cat?

'I don't know. I've always had more of a connection to felines as opposed to any other species of animal.'

Jay adopted the fox character when he discovered, in the absence of any artistic talent, he could draw the Tails the Fox perfectly, freehand.

'And then it turned out I have the stereotypical personality of what people see as a fox. Sly. A bit slutty. Most people see the fox as submissive but you actually see quite a few dominant foxes as well.'

Who are these people that look at a fox and think, 'Yeah, now *there's* a slut'?

I ask if a person's sexual position on the dominance/submission scale would affect the animal they chose to relate to but Angel says it doesn't.

'It's personal preference over everything else.'

They say in Sydney the fur scene's closely linked to the gay community but is more heterosexual in Brisbane, something I imagine is reflected in most scenes simply because of Sydney's massive gay population. There's also a huge age range internationally and they mention a couple in the US who hold plush conventions and have a six-year-old daughter who's involved. I'm alarmed by that given the sexual side of the scene and ask how clear the boundaries are between those with a child's love of fluffy toys and those with a fetish for them. Jay and Angel aren't sure.

'There may be a sexual element with that US couple but a lot of furs do it as a security blanket, where they can just be who they want to be. Others do it more like the Native American thing, having a soul animal, and others just do it because it's fun,' Jay says.

Angel reckons being free from the constraints of society when you're in character is the main part of the appeal.

'You can be who you want to be, not who you're supposed to be. Suspension of disbelief is the best way to put it, especially online. Everyone's in their characters, you don't get random break-offs and dramas.'

'But the whole plushie thing is just like normal guys buying sex dolls. It's just something you see as an interest and you go okay, cool,' Jay said. 'When I was younger I was attracted to certain character types but as I've gotten older I've become more open-minded and relaxed a bit; it's more about the person than the character they are.'

Jay was secretive about his plush interest when he was younger but the openness he has on the internet these days has made him more relaxed about it. But it's not as though many teenagers share sexual stuff with their parents, is it?

'Especially with a father like mine! My father asked my fourteen-year-old brother a few years ago if he'd "banged any chicks yet". He's like a really tough straight guy but I happen to know a few things about his past so it's not exactly true.'

Angel doesn't have the same problems with his parents.

'I'm living with my family but when I'm at home I'm in my room on my laptop so I really don't have to withhold anything, I suppose. Last year, around Mardi Gras time, Mum found out I was part of the fandom. No biggie about it or anything, whereas most other parents would probably explode. Dad just chooses to ignore everything so, for him, it works.'

When Angel told his parents he was gay a few months

before, the reactions were similar; his mother said she'd known for years and his father just kept out of it.

Jay, who lives with a friend who's part of the fandom, feels being gay and into fur are integral to who he is and he doesn't expect to change.

'I do it at home and act the part when there's nobody else around anyway,' he says, but at twenty-four still hasn't discussed his sexuality with his parents.

'I've come out to my grandmother. My grandfather knows but chooses to ignore it. My mum I don't get to speak to too much and my dad I'd rather not speak to at all. You have to sometimes at family things. I've decided that if he asks I'll tell him but until then I won't.'

Jay's comment that some of the people in the plush scene relate to their animal like the American Indians relate to their chosen totems, without sexual thought, is interesting. And, while I believe him, I can't think of another example where the kinky and the non-kinky coexist in the same scene. There are people, such as bikies, who like wearing leather for practical and identity reasons, but they don't hang out with people who wear it because it turns them on. In fact there's something a bit worrying about the overlap in the fur world, especially in cases like the couple whose six-year-old daughter also has a plush interest. Do her parents have to quarantine her toys at parties so she doesn't find them violated the next morning?

34

SHRINKS

The level of insight among my kinksters into their proclivities has varied wildly. Martin, for example, had seen psychiatrists and studied the psychology of fetishes, probably because he'd experienced a fair bit of angst over his, and had formulated detailed theories about why he liked pain, pee and wearing ladies' knickers. But others, probably like most of us, had no idea of the origins of their turn-ons and just embraced them. So having interviewed people with quite a range of kinks, and still not being entirely clear on their origins, I'm curious to know how current psychological theories explain them. I also want to know if they ever cause problems with the law and what can be done if they do.

I speak to a clinical psychologist, Dr Mark Anns, who has worked for years as a sex therapist, and to a forensic psychiatrist, Professor Paul Mullen, who's had more to do with the criminal end of the fetish spectrum. Anns is earnest, Mullen is funny, but they share an anti-Freud position on how unusual stimuli become sexualised, neither being keen on the childhood-origin-of-kinks idea; both are more inclined to believe that most sexual tastes develop in the hypersexual years around puberty.

According to Mark Anns, the most common theory nowadays is classical conditioning.

'A boy gets spanked when he's about eleven and starting to get sexual feelings, and the two sensations get paired. Consequently he finds that getting the same stimulation *creates* sexual feelings. Then of course over time the brain adapts—and this can apply to any sensation—and the level of intensity has to increase to maintain the same pleasure.' That's when a serious hankering for pain develops, he explains.

Californian psychoanalyst Dr Robert Stoller believes all hard-core masochists had serious physical illnesses as children and had undergone regular, terrifying painful medical treatment. His view is based on having interviewed masochists at specialist sadomasochist establishments in Los Angeles; he found that their lengthy confinement in hospitals, unable to unload their rage and despair, led to their 'perversions'.

Interpreting the findings in his book *The Brain that Changes Itself* (2008), psychiatrist and psychoanalyst Norman Doidge proposes:

> As children, they consciously took their pain, their inexpressible rage and reworked it in daydreams, in altered mental states, or in masturbation fantasies so they could replay the story of the trauma with a happy ending and say to themselves, *This time I win*. And the way they won was by erotizing their agony.

Doidge's book, on the plasticity of the brain, argues that acquiring sexual tastes such as masochism require a rewiring of the brain's pleasure systems; i.e. the brain has to make pleasant that which is inherently unpleasant. He argues against the assumption that each of our sensations and emotions is either pleasurable (joy, triumph, sexual pleasure) or painful (sadness, fear, grief) with examples such as tears of happiness and the exciting fear of a rollercoaster ride.

> An emotion that we think inherently unpleasurable, such as sadness, can, if beautifully and subtly articulated in music, literature or art, feel not only poignant but sublime ... The human brain seems able to attach many of our feelings and sensations either to the pleasure system or to the pain system, and each of these links or mental associations requires a novel plastic connection in the brain.

He suggests that the people Stoller interviewed must have formed a pathway that linked the painful sensations they had endured to their sexual pleasure systems, resulting in a new composite experience, 'voluptuous pain'. The fact that they all suffered in early childhood suggests this rewiring occurred during the critical periods of sexual plasticity, Doidge says.

The Freudian, or psychodynamic, angle is that something happens in a child's psychosexual development where it projects onto an object or particular behaviour some sort of sexual feelings. This seems very like Doidge's theory minus the neuroscientific back-up. Then there's the modelling approach, which says that if you're exposed to fetishes early in your life it just becomes the way you have sex.

KINK

According to Mark Anns there are very few people for whom the 'paraphilia' or fetish is so critical to arousal that they can't get going without it. This fits with everyone I've interviewed, all of whom (with the possible exception of Baby Angelica) have been capable of vanilla sex but have preferred to do it with the added intensity their kink provides. Those who can't get aroused without it probably fit the classical-conditioning paradigm, Anns says.

'None of the models is entirely satisfactory and it comes down to how you define fetishism. You can see it as a continuum from more normative sex, where somebody might just bite their partner or scratch them lightly, through to very vicious, painful stimulation. Historically, outside of the sexual arena, people thought a certain object represented some sort of spirit and worshipped that spirit through that object. So in a sense a fetish is just that projection on to something that creates an altered state within us.'

Mullen believes many fetishes at the 'lower end' of the spectrum, as sexual enhancements, are simple to explain.

'If you go back to the generations where titillating magazines were few and far between and where the women were wearing underwear and suspender belts rather than the more gynaecological images you see today, you can understand how a man's concept of a sexually exciting woman developed and how he might link underwear to sexual desirability.' Kinks, he adds, are far more common among men than women.

Culture also influences fetish development, which is why Mark Anns talks about 'normative' rather than 'normal' sex.

'What's normal varies depending on which culture you're

in. In Muslim cultures where women are covered, ankles can become eroticised. In societies where breasts are shown openly, they're not eroticised. So what's erotic is a construct of a society at a particular time and place.'

Mullen observes that the way a female displays herself to indicate a desire to be sexually attractive is also determined by her culture. The potency of cleavage as a sexual lure comes down to what he suggests is the most common fetish among Australian males—a fixation on large breasts.

Things which have a particular feel can also become fetishistic, he notes, and wonders whether it's rubber's slipperiness that has made it such a common fetish.

'For some reason the feel of rubber has become associated with sexual excitement and it's similar with leather. Leather's easier to explain, I think, because you see its use very much in the iconography of sexuality in our society, sexual imagery which people acquire at really quite a young age.'

Sadomasochism and bondage Mullen describes as 'fetishising related to certain *kinds* of sexual activity as well as of leather, chains, handcuffs, masks etcetera. So you've got sexual arousal around largely sadomasochistic fantasy rather than practice.'

It might be fantasy for some but some of the stuff I've seen at suburban parties is pretty real.

Mark Anns says part of the appeal with bondage comes from the blindfolding and immobility.

'In essence, you're decreasing the range of sensations so the mind will focus on other sensations.'

It must have been precisely this dynamic that made Sarah's first encounter with Richard so much fun.

KINK

Psychoanalysts describe 'transitional' stimuli, where the association between the object—lacy knickers, for example—and the desired—the woman—has shifted so the knickers themselves become the turn-on.

'There's also turning *oneself* into a fetish, which is what happens with some transvestites who get sexually excited by dressing as women,' Mullen explains. 'That's the usual transitional stuff. You're fantasising whatever you want to be having sex with. Assuming it's a heterosexual transvestite, you're fantasising someone of the opposite gender, therefore you dress yourself as your fantasy object. That's pretty banal, really. Silly, but banal.'

Ah, so perhaps that's what Marcia is doing (despite claiming impotence when wearing women's clothes).

'Yes, that's where the dressing up is about actually becoming one's own sexual object of fantasy.'

'So he's pretty straightforward then.'

'Yes. Daft but straightforward.'

I ask if getting turned on by fluffy toys is something that originates in childhood.

'We're all stuck in the dying embers of the psychodynamic ideology and this notion that anything peculiar about you somehow must have its origins in childhood. It's pretty shonky really but it's just something we've got so used to thinking we assume it must be true. But when you actually try to demonstrate any of these propositions it becomes a very difficult matter indeed.'

Mullen concedes there are a few anomalies of 'interpersonal sexual behaviour' which do present very young, but generally the kinks emerge in the five to ten years after the onset of puberty.

'It's in that period when people can make connections between sexual excitation and a whole range of things which are not actually other human beings.'

So even the nappy-wearing fetish is unlikely to have its roots in childhood, Mullen believes.

'*Maybe* it's infantile but what do young boys wank on when they're in bed at night? A handkerchief? A rubber mat? Or a *towel*? Then you've got the connection between the feeling of towelling and masturbation. I have no idea whether you could actually trace it that way but you can see a whole lot of plausible connections.'

There are broader fantasies about being a child that don't involve nappies but do involve submission and are about being the object of attention, being washed, cuddled and petted. Surely that has its origins in early childhood?

'Not necessarily. It may very well have its origins, much more plausibly, in early sexual fantasies by sexually mature but still childlike individuals who conceive physical and/or sexual contact with females as an extension of the caring and being looked after role.'

The popularity of fetishes about medical procedures is also simple to explain, he says.

'You can see yourself as the passive recipient of intimate contact, having things done to you. Again, I don't think you need any complicated early-experience type models, just what would come to mind to a hypersexual boy trying to think of situations in which women might actually grab them by the bollocks. There aren't that many if you're an inexperienced little boy. Maybe one of them is doctors and nurses. The whole role of doctors and nurses in traditional iconography of adolescent and childhood sexuality is all about "You show me yours and I'll show you mine". So there's all of those possibilities which occur around the time of early sexual development in that peri-pubertal period which can feed into developing a model of sexuality.'

I ask Mark Anns about the sexualisation of shit.

'Here's one scenario—oh no, this is going to sound Freudian: basically it's something in the toilet training of the child where it learned to overly focus on either holding in or expelling and then, when they became sexualised while learning to masturbate, because they had that fascination, it somehow got paired together. So the learning theory would probably be the most appropriate.'

There might just be an obsession with bodily fluids, a curiosity that wasn't extinguished which is independent of anything interpersonal, like a child who gets fixated on a certain toy or a particular colour.

'Then there are people who develop this as adults where there isn't a history. Then you might be asking, "What does shit represent?" Is it the act of somebody shitting on them? Is it power? It's the interaction where shit happens to be present. It just becomes a representation of some power dynamic—"I am not worthy. I am only worthy to eat or play with your shit."'

Even when it's not the dynamic but the stuff itself, a more classical fetish association, it's about what the person is projecting onto it.

'Is it that they're identifying with shit and in their mind it has some powerful status? Or is it that shit, in their minds, represents something like unworthiness. If I had a client with this fetish I'd be asking is it the substance itself, or the dynamic that goes with the substance?'

He says for many context is crucial, and that if they saw shit outside of sexual play there'd be no response whatsoever because it's the dynamic that creates the eroticism.

When I describe Jason to him, the man I met in Hyde Park who couldn't find a partner for his longed-for scat play, Anns isn't surprised.

'It's much more difficult when a person's heterosexual. There's no rationale to this number but they say that there are ten times more men than women into fetishes. So if you happen to be a gay male you're more likely to find a partner than if you're a heterosexual one.'

With Jason the shit was likely to be linked with a desire for humiliation and submission, something he said he craved as an otherwise assertive character.

'Yes. It's the other aspect of his personality, because in his day-to-day life there isn't that balance,' Anns says. 'Just think of it as an extension of the other polarity—I'm totally in control and I want to surrender control to someone else.'

The other dimension to scat play is described by Godfrey and Regina as reaching an extreme of intimacy.

'Yes, that's a very common thing, much commoner in the sadomasochism world than in the fetishistic world,' Paul Mullen says. 'Most fetishists recognise that what they're doing is abstracting their sexuality from the other human being but what many practitioners of sadomasochism will tell you is that it is the ultimate intimacy.'

He explains that when young people explore the limits of their sexuality with someone they're attracted to they're often seeing how far they can push the limits.

'People often feel that by going beyond what they have been brought up to believe is normal then they have reached a greater level of intimacy. Of course for most of them they're indulging in things ninety-nine per cent of their fellow citizens are also indulging in, but they don't know it. But for some it's really pushing the envelope in very strange ways.'

Scat, like extreme pain, can also have a role in 'edge play', according to Mark Anns.

'If you think about sexual arousal as being an altered state, many couples have intercourse as their main way of sexual expression and the focus is on achieving orgasm. Once you move away from that and you put the focus on maintaining pleasure, and increasing the amount of time when you're close to orgasm but don't reach it—the tantric-sex type thing. While in that state there's heightened arousal and heightened bio-chemical changes in the brain.

'If you combine that with pain, which after a while will make the body produce endorphins, it can all get tied together. In that peak period where endorphins are flowing and there's high arousal, the introduction of another stimulation can easily get conditioned.'

So if shit (or blood or urine) is introduced the person is confronted with an 'edge' where at one level there's disgust, and at another level there's the sexual excitement.

'Now, if the disgust is too high the sexual arousal will go down, the person will just cut out and say they can't handle it. But if it's gauged right, the disgust feeling contributes to the arousal state—it becomes the edge that people play with.

'It doesn't have to be disgust, it could be pain. It's where you're getting two different stimulations and it's that point where they're starting to be conditioned but haven't been yet. You're holding the person there until the brain adapts.'

Mullen's slant on this was similar.

'One of God's great errors, as George Bernard Shaw said, was to confuse the organs of generation with those of excretion. And given that these two sets of organs so obviously overlap it would be quite extraordinary if you didn't get occasional people who got them mixed up.'

He says one of the problems of beginning sexual activity is often overcoming the disgust at the connection between urine, faeces and sexual activity.

'So it's transcending the learnt disgust at the products of excretion as part of becoming comfortable with sexuality. You can see how if that process goes too far you could substitute one for the other.'

Mullen describes a third type of fetish—when the object becomes everything.

'At this stage, the fetish becomes the sexual encounter itself so everything else becomes unnecessary and it substitutes itself for any form of interpersonal or relational sexual activity.' Fetishes like this he describes as 'the weird stuff'.

'I mean, how in the world could you get sexually excited by safety pins or pedigree prams?' he asks.

KINK

Mullen has had patients into both these things and, while he doesn't detail pram man's case, he says pin man was one of those whose fetish was critical to arousal—he couldn't get it up unless he was in the presence of a safety pin. What follows is me getting my head around this particular bit of 'weird stuff' as Professor Mullen's desert-dry humour emerges.

'He only used one at a time. Never reused them,' Mullen says.

'What did he do with them?' I ask.

'He saved them. He was a sentimental man. You never throw away a lover.'

'But what did he do with them in the first place?'

'Oh, he just looked at them!'

'While he masturbated?'

'Yes! He didn't do anything revolting like stick himself with them or anything like that.'

'So he just looked at one safety pin while he masturbated then popped it away somewhere safe.'

'Well, he had a special drawer for them.'

'Right, then he'd get a fresh one for next time.'

'Yes.'

But pin man was seeing Professor Mullen not to get his fetish sorted out—that didn't worry him at all—but because he had epilepsy. In fact fetishes are rarely the reason anyone presents at a psychiatrist's rooms, Mullen tells me.

'The only time we ever see them is when it leads them to break the law. So the panty-pinchers who are not satisfied buying their panties at Woolies and have to have them off the washing line or, worse still, have to have them before they reach

279

the washing machine, and that can lead to theft. By and large most fetishes don't bring people into problems.'

If a panty-pincher gets a thrill out of stealing then they can be harder to treat, Mullen says, and occasionally the ones whose fetishes are ruining their lives do receive medication to reduce their libidinal drives.

'But that's very, very rare, and only when they're really begging you to do something about it.'

Medication works by giving doctors a window of opportunity to fix the problem but the side effects, such as loss of bone density, limit how long anyone can take it. In the past medication was prescribed more enthusiastically, but again, only when the fetish was linked to criminal activity.

'When you look at serious sex offenders they're often people who have a whole range of unusual sexual activities and practices. So for a while there was anxiety that fetishism might be a predictor of violent and deviant activities, but I think that was just getting things the wrong way around. If you've got a grossly disturbed individual they're going to have a whole range of grossly disturbed sexual activities, whereas most fetishists are not grossly disturbed. I think the fear that fetishism might predict serious offending has long since disappeared.'

Today a 'wait and see' approach is often considered appropriate, because as the sexual drive diminishes with age fetishes generally become easier to control.

'But they're not a major medical problem. Among our sex offenders, people with fetishes would be a very small group. That said, among serious sexual offenders fetishism is relatively common, but they're not in jail because they're fetishists, they're there because they're rapists or child molesters and the fact that they also have fetishistic behaviours is not really a big issue,' Mullen says.

It's not even necessarily a big issue if you can't find a compliant partner to accommodate your particular fetish, because there are increasing numbers of brothels that will cater for almost anything.

'And of course a lot of fetishistic activity can be worked into more mundane sexual relationships. I remember seeing one couple where the wife was really pissed off because her husband couldn't ever seem to get an erection without putting on a pair of very high heels. I think her main irritation was there was no room in the wardrobe for her shoes because it was full of *his* bloody high heels. Clearly it was a marital problem but it didn't take much to sort it out.'

'What did it take?'

'A new wardrobe.'

Sometimes, though, fetishes can have a catastrophic effect on a relationship.

'I saw one couple who had a very happy relationship until one day when she casually said she wanted to cut her hair and he became panic-stricken. It became very clear that her hair was what he found sexually exciting about her. She was appalled by this and immediately cut all her hair off, which destroyed the marriage. That was because she said she wanted to be loved for herself. An extraordinary notion! I think we're usually loved for what we're not, thank God, which is why we're so much better people for being loved. She just didn't understand that her hair was part of her for him, and without it there was nothing left.'

There was a similar case in *Psychopathia Sexualis*, though it had a happier ending. On his wedding night the groom contented himself with kissing his wife and running his fingers through her long hair. In fact, that was so good that's all he did the second night as well. Then on the third night he produced a huge wig with extremely long hair and begged his wife to wear it, which she did because she loved him. As soon as it was on, her husband 'richly compensated her for his neglected marital duties'. Problem was, as soon as she took it off, his libido dived. Weirdly, the wig only worked for two or three weeks, after which a new one was required. Krafft-Ebing sums the relationship up thus: 'The result of this marriage was, after five years, two children, and a collection of seventy-two wigs.'

As a group, people with fetishes tend to be less on doctors' radars than those of relationship counsellors, Paul Mullen says, because fetishes can be difficult to hide in the long term. Mark Anns agrees.

'Often they're not coming to see me about a fetish, they just happen to have a fetish but they're coming to me about relationship issues. It's more about co-dependency, boundary issues, and sex is maybe one area where it manifests itself. Only occasionally will someone come to me and say, "I've got a fetish and I don't want it."'

He'd be concerned, as a psychologist, if the fantasy life and symbolic play was very violent and was linked to any child-hood or teenage psychopathology, such as killing animals. Using amphetamines or psychostimulants might also ring alarm bells for Anns because of their potential to cause a psychotic reaction.

'If [a patient] had violent fantasies and they'd just started to use psychostimulants and the fantasy seemed to be getting more extreme, I'd be concerned that they might take those fantasies into real life. So it's about their boundaries. If they said they had violent fantasies that they shared with their partner and it was contained and there didn't seem to be any psychosis involved, then I wouldn't be that concerned. I would be if there was a history of psychopathology, drug and alcohol use and of actual violence.'

If it was obvious that the fetish was interfering with a patient's ability to form a relationship, then he'd see a problem.

'But my approach wouldn't be to help them eliminate the fetish. It would be to help them expand their other sexual turn-ons so then hopefully the fetish became just one of them.

'I had a guy come in here who was into being whipped. He'd done years of psychotherapy, he had loads of insights into this, he'd read all the literature, he could write essays on it. Fairly classical; his nanny had spanked him when he was growing up. So he'd go to a sex worker once a month and get beaten, essentially. He'd spent thirty years of his life doing this and he'd go into a profoundly altered state. Endorphin rush. I think the reality of him giving that up would be zilch but he wanted a relationship.'

The idea was to cut back dramatically on the brothel beatings and try to expand his sexual repertoire, beyond the thrashing zone, to improve his chances of forming a relationship. Anns asked his patient to consider what other forms of stimulation might work for him—something he'd never thought about until then—and to try them out with sex workers. Over time it worked. He ended up with a nice little collection of things he liked and, in time, found love.

So, other than getting someone to expand their repertoire, cognitive behaviour therapy (CBT) often works.

'Control is what we tend to teach,' Dr Anns says. 'You need to look at how long the person can go without acting on their fetish and then look at the cues that activate the pattern. What do they look at, what do they think that starts the cycle? Or, when you get those cues, what are the thoughts that are going on? Fairly classical CBT; you're teaching the person to control their own thinking. You're teaching them that when they have these thoughts, they can replace them with other thoughts. So they recognise that "Yes, I find this arousing but, no, I'm not going to do this at the moment". Or that they can find other things arousing. You're teaching them a different way of responding to those internal thoughts.'

The difficulty is that if they're too far into the cycle and arousal's already too high, controlling the thoughts might be difficult.

'So the trick is to try and teach them *early on* to recognise the thoughts and disrupt the arousal cycle *early on*.'

Another strategy is to get them to trigger the arousal and then, when they're there, get them to stop and do something else to break the state.

'And once you've got them to stop you get them to think about other things, to tie in other ideas that could potentially become arousing. You could get them to use more normative pornography, masturbate to it and imagine they're that character, so you're conditioning them to more normative sexual behaviours. It will take a fair number of repetitions and the person needs to want to do it.'

One patient took about ten months to kick his fetish and find the new stimuli exciting but, having always struggled to find a relationship, he was motivated.

Anns says managing fetishes or particular sexual tastes can be difficult once a relationship is established and gave the hypothetical example of a man wanting anal sex with his wife but never having told her.

'At what point does he bring it up? And when he does, what if she goes "No way!"? He either has to foreclose on it, many people do, or try and get her to do it—"if you loved me you would" sort of thing—or decide that once a year he'll go outside the relationship and see a sex worker and get this out of his system. They're the three major ways of dealing with it. Not easy.'

Assuming anal sex was important to the man for his sexual satisfaction, not getting it might emerge as a lack of interest in sex altogether and sabotage the sexual relationship.

'Or the man will start going more and more into his head to get the sexual satisfaction by fantasising and disconnecting from his partner, who after a while will pick up on that so the sexual relationship will decline over time. Often the solution is the person's got to be brutally honest about what they enjoy sexually. But the difficulty is, many women, more so than men, have a lower tolerance of going outside more normative sex.'

And therein lies the problem: some people desperately want to share their secret kinky desires with their partners but fear rejection, a fear that's apparently well founded.

'At one level fetishes can be very destructive to relationships, particularly if one person feels coerced. Then it becomes a question of boundaries when that person doesn't feel able to say no. It might not be physical coercion, just emotional coercion. If there is physical coercion, I just say, "Get out of the relationship."

'Where one person has a kink and the other doesn't it is very difficult because you can encourage honesty but honesty will sometimes destroy a relationship. The person with the sexual kink may fear being rejected and that fear could be real, it could easily happen. But if they don't express their sexual desires, it can impact on the relationship in the long term because there's sexual dissatisfaction.'

This all paints a rather grim picture, but Professor Mullen says in reality fetishes don't usually cause major problems in relationships or anywhere else.

'What you must have found by talking to these people is they're not stressed by it. If they're stressed by it they don't do it. Simple as that. Sometimes people get irritating habits where they really can't get excited without some particular aspect of the intimate interaction being just so and they find this limiting, but they can usually get their head around that and change. But for most of them it's fine. I mean, you've really got to envy them, haven't you? It's really rather wonderful to be able to turn one's sexual excitement on and off with such a simple trigger. Some of them aren't so simple, I suppose, but so many of them are gobsmackingly simple. Far from treating it, sometimes I think we should *bottle* it!'

EPILOGUE

When I started this research nearly four years ago I thought a kink would be a curse, something to wrestle with in private and broach only tentatively in a relationship, if it ever let you get that far. Now I know it's hardly ever that bad. Most people manage to enjoy vanilla sex and their fetish just gives things a pleasant, though not entirely crucial, boost.

I had no idea what a massive role the internet would play in helping people find mates with similar—or at least complementary—tastes. It might not be as simple as writing an accurate profile on a website because, even when all the right boxes are ticked, sometimes the chemistry won't be there. But narrowing the field like this is a big advance on taking your chances in a vanilla world.

I've become intrigued by the dynamics of dominance and submission, not in any corsets-and-costumes kind of way, but in trying to work out the rules. And the thing is, there don't seem to be any. Sometimes it's about the sexual submissive being otherwise assertive and needing to find some balance, and other times it's the athletic, alpha male futures trader who craves dominance in the bedroom as much as he does everywhere else. Then again, complexities invariably arise when you scratch the surface; I met one dom who ran the show at work, at the gym and in the bedroom, but it turned out he was just out of a marriage in which his wife had been the boss in family matters, including overruling his reluctance to have third and fourth children. Divorcing her was his opportunity to take back control and he was determined to hang on to it in every aspect of his life thereafter.

I did end up reading *Venus in Furs* after Pierre urged me to and, while I wouldn't say it was a must-read, it did provide a clear portrait of the most extreme form of submission, that fuelled by physical cruelty. It was also interesting to see how closely Pierre had modelled himself on the main character, Severin. This irritating personality spent the entire book begging his wife Wanda to whip him, insult him and humiliate him by taking a lover, then threatened to kill her when she ended up falling for the other man, Alexis. It ends with Severin having his kink beaten out of him by Alexis, an outcome possibly reflecting the mores of the nineteenth century.

I had thought scene parties might be edgy, thrilling, perhaps even slightly spooky, but I was way off the mark. The catering— burnt sausages and warm lemonade—pretty much reflects the excitement level of these suburban get-togethers. That probably says more about the way I'm wired though, because these parties remain popular among the kinky—and I do have a tendency to heap scorn on any event with lousy catering.

KINK

I've been surprised at the conformity among people in 'the scene' and still wonder why they need platform boots to display their dominance, or to crawl around on the end of a leash to display the reverse, when others just take a quiet, psychological approach. This has led me to privately ponder where on the spectrum friends and colleagues might sit as I analyse the dynamics of their relationships, and to think long and hard about the forces behind my own.

The frankness of my subjects has astounded me. What is it about being questioned by a journalist that makes people reveal such intimate details of their lives? I know I wouldn't do it, not for anyone. Admittedly my sample was skewed by the fact that most people had *chosen* to contact me and there would have been hundreds more who wouldn't, so obviously they were keen to share their stories. One exception, of course, was the tight-lipped Regina, dragged along to a Rozelle café by her husband Godfrey because *he* wanted to talk (and he thought there might be a shag involved if he did).

But Martin was another thing entirely. Not only did he share details about his entire sex life, from childhood to the present, he involved me in some of it. That was undoubtedly the biggest surprise of all and, while it was useful, I'm glad it didn't last. I had become far too central, albeit as an observer, to Martin's activities and it was starting to get creepy.

Having a kink your partner doesn't share or is only prepared to tolerate rather than embrace requires similar negotiation and compromise strategies to those you'd need with any other kind of interest which requires a partner. Think salsa classes (I'm speaking from experience here). There's often a degree of coercion to get them involved and, if that fails, another partner might be sought. It's only the consequences of taking another mate that differ; my husband is delighted if I dance with other men but might react differently if I was stripping them, putting them in stocks and whipping them.

I discovered that practical considerations are real and that you can be a coprophiliac and still not want to make a mess on the shag pile. Leaking nappies are still a hassle for an eighty-kilo man, and overcoming the problem requires phenomenal diaper-design feats.

And who was I kidding when I thought I was unshock-able? I still don't blush readily but seeing Amanda, a sex worker, suck Martin's dick without a condom and having Kellie tell me she'd sucked her dog's dick *at all* both cleared up that particular question.

But there's only so much kinky sex a straight girl can take. Enough already. I've got restaurants to review and I've fallen way behind in my cake baking. I've also found a new recipe I'm desperate to try. It's a banana cake with the usual stuff—flour, butter, sugar, eggs—but it has an extra ingredient which I think will transform it. Vanilla.

BIBILOGRAPHY

Ackroyd, Peter, *Dressing Up: Transvestism and drag: The history of an obsession*, London, Thames and Hudson, 1979

Aelian, *On the Characteristics of Animals*, (trans. A.F. Schofield), Harvard University Press Loeb Classical Library, 1959

Allen, Clifford, *Textbook of psycho-sexual disorders*, London, Oxford University Press, 1962

Ashbee, Henry S. [Pisanus Fraxi, pseud.], *Index librorum prohibitorium* (1877), London, Skilton, 1960

Bancroft, John, *Deviant Sexual Behaviour: Modification and assessment*, Oxford, Clarendon Press, 1974

Barbusse, Henri, *L'Enfer*, (1908) (trans. John Rodker), London, Joiner and Steele, 1932

Bird, John, *Percy Grainger*, London, Elek Books Ltd, 1976

Blake, William, *Visions of the Daughters of Albion* (1793), London, Dent, 1932

Bland, John (trans.), *Song of Solomon*, London, J. Wren, 1750

Bloch, Ivan, *Sexual Life in England Past and Present*, Berkeley, University of California Press, 1938

Bloch, Ivan, *Anthropological Studies in the Strange Sexual Practices of All Races in All Ages, Ancient and Modern, Oriental, Primitive and Civilized*, New York, AMS Press, 1974

Bradford, William, *Of Plymouth Plantation, 1620–1647*, New York, Alfred A. Knopf, 1970

Charke, Charlotte, *A Narrative of the Life of Mrs. Charlotte Charke* / by Charlotte Charke, edited with introduction and notes by Robert Rehder, London, Pickering & Chatto, 1999

Cleland, John, *Memoirs of a Woman of Pleasure*, 1749, Hammondworth, UK, Penguin Books, 1985

Creager, A. & Jordan, W. (eds), *The Animal/Human Boundary: Historical perspectives*, New York, University of Rochester Press, 2002

Doidge, Norman, *The Brain that Changes Itself*, Melbourne, Scribe Publications, 2008

Ellis, Havelock, *Studies in the Psychology of Sex*, vol. 3, Analysis of the Sexual impulse, Love and Pain and the Sexual Impulse in Women, BiblioBazaar, LLC, 2007

Ellman, Richard, (ed.), *Selected Letters of James Joyce*, London, Faber & Faber, 1975

Gosselin, C. & Wilson, G., *Sexual Variations*, London, Faber & Faber, 1980

Kern, Ernest, 'Cultural-Historical Aspects of Pain', in 'Pain: A medical and anthropological challenge', J. Brihaye, F. Loew & H.W. Pia (eds) in *Acta Neurochirurgica* (a medical journal), 1987

Krafft-Ebing, Richard von, *Psychopathia Sexualis* (1886), London, Staples Press, 1965

Marlowe, Christopher, *The Works of Christopher Marlowe*, London, George Routledge and Sons, 1826

Masoc, Leopold von Sacha, *Venus in Furs,* London, Luxor Press, 1870

Money, J., *Gay, Straight and In-between: The sexology of erotic orientation*, New York, Oxford University Press, 1988

Murray, T. & Murrell, T., *The language of Sadmasochism: A glossary and linguistic analysis*, New York, Greenwood Press, 1989

Noyes, J., *The Mastery of Submission: Inventions of masochism*, Cornell University Press, Ithaca and London, 1997

Ostrow, R., *Burning Urges: Australia's sexual fantasies*, Sydney, Pan, 1997

Payer, Pierre J., *Sex and the Penitentials*, Toronto, University of Toronto Press, 1984

Reik, Theodor, *Masochism in Modern Man*, (trans. Margaret H. Beigel and Gertrude M, Kurth), New York, Farrar, Straus and Co, 1949

Ruggiero, Guido, *Boundaries of Eros*, Oxford and New York, Oxford University Press, 1985

Salisbury, Joyce E. (ed.), *Sex in the Middle Ages: A book of essays*, New York, Garland Publishing, 1991

Tannahill, Reay, *Sex in History*, New York, Stein and Day, 1982

Trimmer, Dr E.J. (ed.), *The Visual Dictionary of Sex*, London, Macmillan London Limited, 1978

Vernet, J., 'Los Medicos Andaluces', *Libro de las Generaciones de Medicos de Ibn Yulyul*, Annuario de Estudios Medievales, vol. 5, 1968

Welldon, Estela V., *Ideas in Psychoanalysis: Sadomasochism*, Cambridge, Icon (United States), Totem, 2002

Wilson, Colin, *The Misfits*, London, Grafton Books, 1988

Wright, Thomas, (ed.), Giraldus Cambrensis, *Historical Works*, London (1863), New York, AMS Press, 1968

NOTES

p. 7	'My breasts … amus'd her hands …', Cleland, quoted in Wilson, p. 82
p. 34	'When an erotic motif …', quoted in Noyes, p. 100
p. 35	'Oh! Were I made her porter …', quoted in Ellis (1927) p. 155
p. 51	'What had just fallen …', Barbusse, p. 33
p. 51	'No, again no! …', Barbusse, p. 34
p. 85	'The masochist seeks …', Noyes, p.4
p. 91	Krafft-Ebing, p. 102
p. 92	'He bared the upper portion …', Krafft-Ebing, p. 103
p. 94	'What Drudgery's here! …', quoted in Noyes, p. 83
p. 94	'For his lust sleeps …', quoted in Noyes, p. 83
p. 95	'Seizing now …', Cleland, quoted in Noyes, p. 80
p. 95	'But what yet increased …', Cleland, quoted in Noyes, p. 82
p. 97	'She had a dozen tapering whip thongs …', quoted in Noyes, p. 12
p. 97	Bloch, quoted in Noyes, p. 14
p. 98	'It burned my behind like fire …', Hirschfeld, quoted in Noyes, pp. 13–14
pp. 98–101	Excerpts from the letters of Percy Grainger quoted in Wilson, pp. 202–207 and reproduced here with the permission of Stewart Manville, Percy Grainger Library, White Plains, New York
pp. 102–3	Allen, p. 181
p. 103	Sade, quoted in Wilson, p. 71
p. 106	Sade, quoted in Wilson, p. 62
p. 106	Wilson, p. 63
p. 117	'A man who had made love …', quoted in Wilson, p. 72
p. 118	'It was revealed …', Wilson, pp. 72–3
pp. 118–19	'It was striking …', Wilson, p. 17

Stephanie Clifford-Smith

p. 119	'The martyrs of early Christianity …', Reik, quoted in Noyes, p. 100
p. 119	Bloch, p. 82
p. 121	Krafft-Ebing, quoted in Wilson, p. 75
p. 121	'This then seems to provide …', Wilson, p. 75
pp. 121–2	Wilson, pp. 75–6
p. 122	'The moment of desire! …', Blake, quoted in Wilson, p. 137
p. 123	'producing new and strange varieties …', Wilson, p. 75
p. 133	Aelian, quoted in Salisbury, p. 173
p. 133	'I am told that a dog fell in love …', Aelian, quoted in Salisbury, p. 174
pp. 133–4	Leviticus 18:23, 19:19
p. 135	'The peasant told the physician ….', quoted in Salisbury, p. 180
p. 136	Bradford, p. 320
pp. 136–7	'A. was convicted …', Krafft-Ebing, p. 464
p. 164	'The joints of thy thighs …', Song of Solomon 7:1
p. 165	'Either I stand before …', Krafft-Ebing, p. 161
pp. 171–5	Excerpts from the letters of James Joyce quoted in Elman, pp. 181–5
pp. 252–3	Frith, quoted in Ackroyd, p. 72
p. 253	Clarke, quoted in Ackroyd, pp. 76–7
p. 254	'I possess hardly a womanly attribute …', Gautier, quoted Ackroyd, p. 144
p. 254	Herodotus, quoted in Ackroyd, pp. 51–2
p. 255	Faculty of Theology, University of Paris, quoted in Ackroyd, p. 52
p. 255	Deuteronomy 22:15
p. 255	Stubbes, quoted in Ackroyd, p. 52
p. 255	'Both men and women …', Naogeorgus, quoted in Ackroyd, pp. 52, 54
p. 256	Bancroft, quoted in Ackroyd, p. 31
p. 257	'Barbara managed to slip …', Barrie, quoted in Ackroyd, p. 23
p. 269	'As children …', Doidge, p. 125
p. 270	'An emotion …', Doidge, p. 126

ACKNOWLEDGEMENTS

I'd like to thank all those trusting souls who agreed to tell me their very intimate, personal stories. Thanks also to Jane Palfreyman for her enthusiastic support of the book in a conservative publishing environment and to my brilliant editors Ali Lavau and Ann Lennox. But my most heartfelt thanks must go to my husband who, while clearly not a fan of this project, helped lug essential reference books to and from libraries for me and valiantly continues to put up with a very wilful wife.